To the Morgan family

with much love

Alec

March 2013

New City

CONTEMPORARY ARCHITECTURE IN THE CITY OF LONDON

Alec Forshaw

Photography by
Alan Ainsworth

MERRELL
LONDON · NEW YORK

INTRODUCTION   6

1 AROUND ST PAUL'S   28

2 GUILDHALL AND CHEAPSIDE   50

3 BANK AND MANSION HOUSE   68

4 THE CLUSTER OF TOWERS   84

5 FENCHURCH STREET AND MONUMENT   100

6 CHANCERY LANE AND FLEET STREET   114

7 SMITHFIELD AND NEWGATE   130

8 BARBICAN AND MOORGATE   146

9 BROADGATE   162

10 SPITALFIELDS AND HOUNDSDITCH   174

11 ALDGATE AND THE EAST   188

12 THE RIVERSIDE   202

FURTHER READING   220

INDEX   220

THE CITY OF LONDON SINCE 1986: AN ARCHITECTURAL OVERVIEW

THE CITY REBUILT

The City of London has reinvented and rebuilt itself many times in its long history. There is probably no equivalent in the world of real estate with so many layers of successive development, not even the nine cities of Troy. The first settlement, Roman Londinium, was rebuilt in the aftermath of its sacking in AD 60 by Boudicca's Iceni hordes and again in 120 after a catastrophic fire, leaving thin layers of ash for archaeologists to find centuries later. King Alfred resettled the abandoned Roman London in the ninth century, reusing the surviving materials but establishing a new, more organic street plan. During the Middle Ages timber structures came and went, while more prestigious buildings, such as churches and guildhalls, used local brick or expensive imported stone.

After the Great Fire of 1666, when two-thirds of the City's area and nine-tenths of the buildings within the original perimeter walls were destroyed, reconstruction was remarkably quick. Pressure from landowners, displaced residents and businesses did not allow Christopher Wren's ambitious plans for a reordered street layout to have any realistic chance of adoption. The City was rebuilt almost entirely on its medieval street plan, plot by plot, although new building regulations required better fireproofing, with brick, tile and stone replacing external timber, lath and thatch. The 13,000 houses destroyed by the fire were replaced by only 4000 within the City boundaries, marking a significant shift towards predominantly commercial buildings.

In the following centuries the City continued to renew and replace its built fabric. During the eighteenth century, when British naval and military power supported a colossal increase in colonial trade, fostering and sustaining London's growth as the largest city and commercial port in the world, most of the City's post-Fire buildings were replaced. Similarly, during the self-confident period of Queen Victoria's reign, new offices, banks, warehouses, markets and exchanges were needed, together with larger and more luxurious premises for the livery companies. All these, coupled with such ambitious infrastructure projects as over- and underground railways, new sewers and road widening for trams and to ease traffic congestion, resulted in the destruction of most of the Georgian City. Between 1850 and 1900, some 80% of the buildings were replaced. A consequence of the boom in commercial activity combined with better public transport was that the City's once sizeable resident population was substantially reduced, from 150,000 in 1851 to 25,000 in 1901. The brokers, bankers and clerks in the counting houses and ledger halls now lived in burgeoning London suburbs and commuted every day by train or tram, or on foot.

In the golden age of Edwardian opulence and during the recovery after the First World War, the City was the financial capital of a British empire that covered a quarter of the globe. Many Victorian buildings were replaced by palatial, splendid new headquarters, usually faced with Portland stone, fitted with ornate interiors and panelled boardrooms, and designed by the leading architects of the day: Edwin Lutyens, Ernest George, Aston Webb, Edwin Cooper and Herbert Baker. This period fostered and entrenched the hierarchical, person-to-person, 'my word is my bond' work practices for which the City became renowned. By 1939 the residential population had shrunk to a few thousand, mainly publicans and caretakers.

During the Second World War one-third of the City was destroyed by incendiary and high-explosive bombs, and areas around St Paul's, Holborn, the Barbican and the riverside were almost totally devastated. After 1945 there was little debate over the necessity and urgency of renewing the fabric. Any idea that the City, the ancient core of London, might somehow be set aside, preserved and rebuilt in replica as a monument to London's medieval past, was barely considered. On the contrary, the bomb sites were seen as an opportunity to create a new forward-looking City, a 'brave new' post-war world. Many damaged (and indeed undamaged) buildings that might in today's conservation-minded climate have been kept and repaired were demolished to produce larger or easier sites for redevelopment. As for the City's medieval past, it seemed that hardly enough was left from before the war to justify rebuilding along the lines of such war-torn Continental cities as Warsaw or Nuremberg. Only the damaged Wren churches, the Guildhall and the livery halls were prioritized for repair.

The post-war plans for the City were bold indeed: a ring of dual-carriageway motorways (London Wall to the north and Upper and Lower Thames streets to the south), a raised platform deck across the whole of the City to segregate pedestrians from vehicles below, clusters of Corbusian office slabs and podium blocks arranged rationally and methodically, and a new residential quarter at the Barbican. These schemes, including offices at Paternoster Square and Bucklersbury, were conceived and built with the intention of extending the format throughout the Square Mile. Medieval lanes, courts and alleys were extinguished where they were in the way. It would be a City fit for the second half of the twentieth century, or so it was thought; with post-war budget constraints, the results were often bland and nondescript.

From the late 1980s the buildings of this post-war redevelopment became increasingly unfit for purpose. The comprehensive and radical reconstruction of the City that has taken place since then therefore comes as no surprise, but is nevertheless remarkable because it has happened so fast, and (IRA bombs excepted) has not been caused by any major conflagration. Nowhere else in Britain has the pace of change been so manifest. More than three-quarters of the City has been rebuilt in that time, and an even higher percentage of the actual floor space. Furthermore, some districts have seen almost complete renewal even since the turn of the millennium.

For people who used to know the City but have not been back for a while, it can be an unrecognizable place. For better or worse (usually better), most of the 1950s, 1960s and 1970s buildings have gone. Only a few of the original blocks remain along London Wall in the ordered echelon formation so admired by Nikolaus Pevsner in the original edition of *The Buildings of England* (1957). Now buildings from the 1980s, notably at Broadgate and Bishopsgate and in Monument Street, are being replaced. Twentieth-century sections of the 1997 edition of *The Buildings of England* are alarmingly out of date. The new Ropemaker Place, completed in 2007, is the third development on its site since the war; this will give future archaeologists something to unravel. That is the enduring and endearing dichotomy of the City: it is the oldest part of London – where Roman masonry, medieval streets, livery halls and baroque churches survive – and simultaneously boasts a spectacular palimpsest of new buildings.

A section of Roman and medieval wall is preserved in Noble Street in front of Alder Castle House **029**, with One London Wall **030** behind.

FINANCIAL DEREGULATION AND THE ECONOMIC ROLLER COASTER

The deregulation of the financial markets that officially took effect on 27 October 1986 – the so-called Big Bang – was almost as explosive an event in stimulating change as the Great Fire or the Second World War in terms of its impact on the City of London. Instigated as part of a programme of reform by Margaret Thatcher's government, deregulation was intended to introduce free-market practices that would allow more competition and encourage meritocracy. On the Stock Exchange the distinction between jobbers and brokers (agents and traders) was abolished, fixed charges and standard commissions were removed, and the ancient tradition of open outcry (oral and visual transactions on the trading floor) was replaced by electronic screen-based trading. Before these changes, physical proximity had been vital; stockbrokers needed to be near the jobbers at the Stock Exchange to conduct business and because bargains in government securities were settled the same day by hand-delivered cheques. The insurance sector in the east of the City, originally huddled around Lloyd's, had similarly depended on such local links and paper transactions.

While deregulation was a sensible response to new technology, it also set out to change the elitist, clubby old-boy network, with its strict codes of behaviour, that had long dominated the City and which in the spirit of Thatcher's doctrine was seen as holding the City back. More significantly, the rules that had barred foreign companies from operating in the City were scrapped. The switch from face-to-face to screen-based trading saw the value of transactions rocket, with a threefold increase in three years. The floodgates had been opened.

The influx of foreign banks and the sudden growth in financial markets, greatly assisted by London's geographical position halfway between New York and Tokyo, resulted in a seemingly insatiable demand for large-floor-plate offices that existing stock could not satisfy. Moreover, electronic dealing meant that these new financial 'supermarkets' no longer needed to be very close to the Bank of England or the Stock Exchange. Property developers were quick to react, notably Stuart Lipton and Godfrey Bradman with Rosehaugh Stanhope Developments at Broadgate, where British Rail land was lying idle. In the west of the City, the abandonment of Fleet Street by printers and newspapers, another aspect of the Thatcher revolution, conveniently provided development opportunities. In the building frenzy of the late 1980s dozens of new schemes were realized, generally using fast steel-frame construction and clad in a variety of exotic stones in the latest postmodern styles. By the end of 1993, half the office stock in the City had been replaced.

Perhaps inevitably, the boom was followed by a crash, symbolized by 'Black Wednesday' (16 September 1992, when Britain's membership of the European Exchange Rate Mechanism was suspended), and a downturn in the property market. A five-year lull was followed by another surge in 1997 when the new Chancellor of the Exchequer, Gordon Brown, provided a further stimulus to growth in the financial sector. His policies, which gave operational independence to the Bank of England – including the power to set interest rates – and transferred responsibility for banking supervision to the Financial Services Authority (FSA), brought confidence and optimism. The FSA, under the strong leadership of Howard Davies (1997–2003), supported expansion, merger and foreign institutions, and did little to inhibit growth. The role of the City as a major contributor to Britain's balance of payments was greatly encouraged. Today the Square Mile accounts for 2.5% of GDP for the entire United Kingdom.

A wave of new architecture responded to bullish pressure for larger and more prestigious headquarters, providing a cascade of 'statement', 'landmark' and 'gateway' buildings, and a new cluster of towers. During the late 1990s and 2000s, more than 100 new buildings were commissioned, half the total office floor space in the City. Despite the financial crash in 2008 and a continuing climate of recession and uncertainty, this wave is still rolling in, carrying plenty of surfers with it.

A forest of construction cranes is not always an indicator of good times; indeed, there may be an unhealthy correlation between architectural hubris and economic fallout. The delay between first concept, design, planning application/permission, construction and completion can be many years, and with the uncertainties and complications of site acquisition and lease-expiry, obtaining financial backing and signing pre-let commitments and contractual agreements, it is not surprising that the balance of supply and demand in the property world is not always perfect. A competitive but sometimes ostrich-like property market, fuelled by optimism, striving to be in the vanguard but also 'keeping up with the Joneses', does not make for a steady ship in the stormy sea of a volatile economy. Some commentators, such as Richard Bronk in his book *The Romantic Economist* (2009), suggest that decisions are not always the result of pure logic and clinical analytical thought. Company bosses and their advisers, like anybody else, have hunches, ambitions, a sense of destiny and a tendency to jump on bandwagons.

Nonetheless, the ship continues to sail. Much, it seems, depends on that elusive factor, confidence, particularly when it comes to borrowing money to fund construction. Confidence has sustained the enormous programme of renewal over the past decade and, despite current wobbles, that will continue as long as the rewards are seen to outweigh the risks.

THE CITY OF LONDON CORPORATION

Alongside the private property-development sector, the City of London Corporation has been a crucial influence. Its very existence and survival are mysterious or anachronistic to some outsiders, a semi-fairy tale in which a Lord Mayor with a golden coach lives in a Palladian Mansion House and aldermen nominated by livery companies meet in a medieval Guildhall; autonomous and anomalous in modern terms, still with a town clerk, a sheriff, a chamberlain, a comptroller and a remembrancer. Many politicians have suggested abolishing the City (and distributing its territory and wealth among adjoining boroughs), but most have quickly backed down.

In reality, the Corporation has played a huge role in the regeneration of the City,

acting both as the local planning authority, implementing policies and dealing with planning applications, and as a major landowner and property developer in its own right. A number of councillors, notably Michael Cassidy and Judith Mayhew (successive chairs of the Policy and Resources Committee 1992–97 and 1998–2003), have been crucial in promoting and supporting a new vision for the City. Within the planning department, a number of long-serving officers have managed and shaped the enormous rebuilding programme with great skill and commitment. Peter Rees, City Planning Officer, joined in 1985 and has unashamedly indulged his passion for high-quality modern architecture, and his belief that the City should attract the world's best designers. Annie Hampson, Planning Services and Development Director since 1989, ensures that individual schemes are honed

As seen in this view from Bankside in October 2012, new landmark towers are emerging to change the City skyline. On the left, the Leadenhall Building **101** rises in front of 30 St Mary Axe **106**, while 20 Fenchurch Street **132** makes a powerful statement near the river. The Millennium Bridge **316** is in the foreground.

to comply with detailed policies for the conservation of energy, disabled access, bicycle parking, contributions to the public realm and a host of increasingly onerous requirements for new buildings, and her team has handled developments worth many tens of billions of pounds. Paul Beckett has been Planning Policy Manager since the early 1990s, ensuring continuity and consistency. Following a restructuring in 2011, Philip Everett became Director of the Department of the Built Environment, combining planning, transport and street works in a joined-up service; released from his managerial duties, Rees is now freer than ever to pursue his interests.

The Corporation does much else to guarantee the smooth operation of the City, including coordinating the closing or digging up of roads by contractors, public utility companies and other statutory undertakers. It even has its own police force. The Corporation manages and maintains the public realm, including issuing licences (some 1500 in 2010) for filming on the City streets. It is remarkable how many advertisements feature City buildings in the background: image is everything.

Equally important is the Corporation's role as developer. It owns a quarter of the City itself, and huge tracts of land elsewhere in London (much of Tottenham Court Road, chunks of Oxford Street and swathes of north Islington). On many of its freehold development sites, such as London Wall and Smithfield, the Corporation operates joint-venture partnerships. The City Surveyor, Peter Bennett, not only looks after the Corporation's own portfolio but also supports and facilitates private development where there are difficulties. The investment bank Nomura's headquarters at Waterside Place, west of London Bridge, for example, required electric cables to cross the river via Southwark Bridge, which is owned by the Corporation. When rights-of-lights disputes between neighbours threatened the proposed 'Walkie-talkie' scheme at 20 Fenchurch Street, the Corporation used its powers to make sure that reasonable compensation was paid, and that the developer, Land Securities, was not held to ransom. (Rights-of-lights disputes arise when a proposed development is felt by

neighbours to be likely to affect the natural light in their property.) The City Property Advisory Team was set up specifically to resolve such problems, to provide day-to-day contact for managers of estates, facilities and property, and to help businesses find and retain premises in the Square Mile most suitable for their needs.

Combining the role of poacher and gamekeeper can be uncomfortable and controversial. The Corporation rarely takes kindly to external meddling, be it by the Mayor of London and the Greater London Authority, English Heritage or central government, but prefers to sort out its own affairs. Politically, the City is committed to growth and opposed to immigration controls, supports more airport runways and hates the idea of a tax on financial transactions. The proposed constituency boundary review, whereby the tiny residential electorate of the City of London stands to be combined with south Islington, rather than with Westminster, has not found favour among the City fathers. The prospect of a Labour MP representing the City might ruffle some feathers.

HANDLING THE COMPETITION

While deregulation of the markets and the removal of restrictive practices paved the way for growth and a building boom for the financial sector in the City, they opened competing doors elsewhere. Other European cities, such as Paris and Frankfurt, which share London's advantageous time-zone position, also sought to benefit. Frankfurt, with its new financial district, high standard of living and easy commuting, was seen as a particular threat, a largely hollow one as it has turned out, despite Foster + Partners' flagship fifty-three-storey headquarters for Commerzbank. At present, London's position with New York and Tokyo as one of the three main financial centres in the world looks reassuringly secure, while the prospect of Paris becoming a global centre for derivatives trading recedes. Opportunities for development in central Paris are severely restricted, and major new office developments are directed

towards the suburb of La Défense. The higher taxation rates introduced in France in 2012 also threaten to inhibit investment in the capital. Not for nothing does Goldman Sachs keep 6000 of its 7000 European staff in London. Many Parisians now live in London.

That, of course, is not solely down to the success of the Square Mile. The reasons so many foreign investors choose to locate in London are manifold. With its heritage, arts, culture and sport, social tolerance and liberal politics, London is unrivalled as a world city, a halfway house between the United States and Asia, and a gateway to Europe. Of the $3.98 trillion traded daily across the world (estimated in 2009), London accounted for 36.7%, a position of extraordinary dominance and one that is growing. The overseas market has been hugely influential in the City since the early 1990s. Most recently the Arab Spring and the eurozone crisis have attracted money from those wanting a safe haven for their assets, but there is always the potential for more. The task of promoting the City carries on, through working with its competitors. The Corporation has delegations in China and India, and keeps a close eye on Europe from its office in Brussels, ever wary of proposals that seek to rein in the City.

Equally serious for the Corporation has been competition within London, although there has not been much elsewhere in Britain. Alongside Thatcher's deregulation came the Enterprise Zones set up by the Conservative government, whereby industry in depressed areas was given tax breaks. One of the first and biggest was London Docklands, designated in 1981 and raring to go in 1986. Exemptions from property taxes, together with simplified planning regulations and capital allowance, resulted in the development of Canary Wharf as a massive rival to the City, a new financial centre of gravity for London. Cesar Pelli's tower for the Reichmann brothers' development at One Canada Square, completed in 1991, was an obvious visual and economic challenge to the City. The lack of good public transport to Docklands (not resolved until the opening of the Jubilee Underground line), coupled with the recession of 1992, when Paul Reichmann's Olympia & York Canary Wharf Limited filed for bankruptcy, provided the breathing space that enabled the City to

make sure it would benefit from the next boom, in the late 1990s.

Emerging concentrations of office development in other parts of London are also rivals to the pre-eminence of the City. Paddington Basin, Victoria, Bankside/London Bridge and King's Cross all have their own attractions, not least good public transport to airports. With Argent's development of the King's Cross railway lands it is no surprise that the French bank BNP Paribas is looking into relocating its London headquarters close to the Eurostar terminus at St Pancras International. The so-called Mid-Town of Holborn, St Giles and Covent Garden is much hyped for its convenience, civility and proximity to the West End. While top-end rents of about £60 per square foot have been achieved in the City at 20 Fenchurch Street and the Leadenhall Building, rents in Mayfair are much higher.

Immediately across the river from the City, the Shard at London Bridge is an inescapably towering and aggressive competitor to the City's own skyline.

Despite such competition the City has remained resilient, and it is still the prime location for the financial and legal sectors. Canary Wharf may now claim to employ more bankers than the City, but its 1.5 million square metres of offices and 90,000 workers compare with 8 million square metres and 300,000 workers in the City. Docklands may offer opportunities for giant buildings and mega-banks, but it seems likely that the future will favour medium-sized specialists, which the City is well suited to accommodate. It is also better placed for those who want to live in fashionable Islington and Camden, from where they can walk or cycle to work. The development of secondary or back-office areas in Southwark and the 'tech-city' at

Sunrise over Canary Wharf; the view east from 30 St Mary Axe **106**, with Aldgate and the blue hoops of St Botolph's House **291** in the foreground.

11

Silicon (Old Street) Roundabout in the fringes of Shoreditch and Clerkenwell also supports the City, and is not regarded as a threat.

Despite the financial hiccups of 2008, the construction of top-quality (Grade A) offices in the City has continued apace, and many are due to be completed in 2014. These schemes total nearly 3.5 million square metres, of which one-third is refitting existing buildings, but – more significantly – they make up 65% of everything in the office pipeline for the whole of London. The City has very successfully kept its nose in front, and aims to continue to take the lead.

POLICIES AND PLANNING FOR CHANGE

The Corporation responded swiftly to the sudden demand, after the Big Bang, for more offices. In 1989 it raised its plot ratio planning policy (which sets a limit on the ratio of total floor area to that of site) to 5:1, to allow more intensive development, although it remained a crude formulaic tool best suited to regulating the monolithic post-war vision of podium and slab blocks. In 1994 the new City Development Plan abandoned plot ratios altogether and introduced building control and design policies that enabled a more sensitive and sophisticated approach, maximizing the potential for individual sites. That, at least, is the official line. Cynics describe it as a blatant response to the threat of Canary Wharf. To compete, the City had to be able to build high, to sixty storeys if necessary, rather than six. Mercifully, the twin disciplines of urban design and conservation have emerged since the late 1980s to ensure a balanced approach, and to make sure that past mistakes are not repeated and are put right where possible.

The policy that protects the setting of St Paul's Cathedral, operated since the 1930s (see p. 30), has been incorporated into new London-wide rules for preserving views of the dome. Additional policies have been introduced to protect views of the Monument and the setting of the Tower of London. In areas not constrained by such height limits, the Corporation has encouraged developers to exploit opportunities for large structures, even next to historic buildings. The concept of 'interesting contrast' has become a convenient way of justifying great discrepancies of scale.

Traditionally the Corporation has not sought planning gain (payment towards community benefits in return for planning permission) from developers; the development itself has been seen as sufficient investment in the City. Following the establishment of the Greater London Authority in 2000 and of new powers for the London Mayor, planning obligations (known as Section 106 Agreements) have been required for larger schemes. Ken Livingstone (Mayor 2000–2008) was particularly keen on affordable housing, public access, improvements to public transport, the creation of training opportunities and sustainability, and the Corporation, at first reluctant, now does what it can. Funds for affordable housing have been spent extending or improving the Corporation's own residential estates in seven other London boroughs, such as Southwark and Islington. Meanwhile the Corporation has responded to the government's Community Infrastructure Levy of 2012 (a supposedly fairer and more consistent way of obtaining planning gain, including contributions to London-wide projects, such as Crossrail) by commissioning the planning and property firm Gerald Eve as its consultant.

The Corporation has continued resolutely to favour offices, believing that nothing should inhibit commerce as the primary function and source of wealth, and it still believes that housing will sterilize and freeze the City. Protests from articulate residents about noise, light pollution and loss of sunlight reinforce this policy. Just as some town-dwellers dislike farmyard smells, church bells and cockerels when they move to the country, so, it seems, a few inner-city settlers object to a vibrant 24/7 economy. Since 1990 very little housing has been added to the post-war residential enclaves of Golden Lane and the Barbican, or the Middlesex Street and Guinness Trust estates in the east. Bridgewater Square (1997) was little more than a consolidation next to Golden Lane, and the Heron at Silk Street/Moor Lane (to be completed in 2013) is similarly an adjunct to the Barbican. Three Quays, beside the Tower of London (due to be finished in the same year), is more of an exception, and may be an indication of pressure from developers for further lucrative riverside flats, where returns might far outstrip those of offices. The Corporation successfully lobbied against government proposals that empty offices might change to residential use without needing planning permission, and a carefully worded clause in Paragraph 51 of the National Planning Policy Framework of 2012 protects its position.

Instead, the Corporation has welcomed new residential schemes close to its borders in Islington, Tower Hamlets and across the river in Southwark. Within the City the Corporation has preferred hotels or serviced flats as a compromise where short-stay and non-domiciled visitors are less likely to complain about local government (and, more importantly, have no vote). The boom in construction of hotels since 2000 has been staggering, particularly in the east of the City near the Tower. In 1986 the only hotel in the City was the seedy Great Eastern at Liverpool Street, now the five-star Andaz.

Shops have been actively encouraged, particularly along Cheapside, where the aim has been to create a high street for the City. (Cheapside and Poultry was the location of the medieval marketplace.) After years of resistance by developers and investors, mixed use is now widely accepted, particularly in the form of shops and restaurants on the ground floor, office above and bars and gyms in the basement. The units let readily, pay good rent and are liked by the public. At last the City has caught up with what has been done elsewhere for years. Now there are even nightclubs, although not of the raunchier variety; those the Corporation prefers to be located beyond its jurisdiction (like the medieval 'stews' or brothels in Southwark).

The conservation of historic buildings has enjoyed fluctuating fortune and varying support in the Corporation since 1986. At times the 600 statutorily listed buildings and twenty-six conservation areas have been regarded as a hindrance to growth and prosperity, and City planners have been accused of 'stopping things happening'. Conservationists tread a delicate path. The

Victorian buildings next to the Viaduct Tavern on the north side of Newgate Street were kept after a struggle; those at Number One Poultry were lost. There was a clutch of additions to the statutory list in the late 1980s (part of a re-survey led by Michael Heseltine, then Secretary of State for the Environment), but very little has been added in the twenty-first century.

Recent debate has focused on post-war buildings, not so much the listed residential Barbican and Golden Lane estates (where little change is envisaged), but rather the commercial sector. Bracken House near St Paul's, listed in 1987, was a one-off, and the Grade I listing of Lloyd's in December 2011 might have raised a few eyebrows, but a ferocious and very public row had blown up earlier in that year over proposals to demolish 4 and 6 Broadgate, built in the late 1980s (see chapter 9). The recommendation by English Heritage (the government's adviser on historic buildings) to list came after planning permission had been granted for redevelopment. The Secretary of State for Culture, Jeremy Hunt, heavily lobbied by the Corporation and the developer British Land, ruled that Arup's buildings were not of sufficient interest to list. In a much-reported spat, Peter Rees accused Simon Thurley's English Heritage of being 'heritage Taliban'. Thurley retorted that Rees's comments 'beggared belief', and suggested that the City's attitude to architecture was two-faced, praising new buildings when it wanted them to go up, only to condemn them a few decades later when it wanted them replaced. The economic imperative at Broadgate was that UBS wished to consolidate its staff in new premises that were not sitting above the Circle line, which was perceived to be vulnerable to terrorist attack. Make architects' new no. 5 is twice as big as the former nos 4 and 6. It remains to be seen how the Corporation will react if and when there is pressure to list other post-war offices,

Views of St Paul's Cathedral have been carefully protected; 25 Cannon Street 020 is in the foreground here.

such as Finsbury Avenue, Exchange House and, eventually, Number One Poultry and 30 St Mary Axe (the 'Gherkin'). Mischievous commentators have even suggested that the design of new buildings might be 'dumbed down' to avoid any chance of future listing.

Set against such individual cases is the happily more widespread acceptance that the City's heritage is one of its greatest assets, setting it apart from Canary Wharf and from Frankfurt, Tokyo and Shanghai. Problems can become opportunities: the tricky issue of what to do with redundant banking halls was resolved by allowing their conversion to bars and restaurants, rather than insisting that they remain as offices. The retention of the City's labyrinth of lanes, alleys and courts is now regarded as crucial. The redevelopment of Paternoster Square, Plantation House and One New Change has put back medieval alleys that twentieth-century slabs had obliterated; Walbrook Square will reinstate the eastern arm of Watling Street. The Double Tree (formerly Mint) hotel and even the vertiginous Heron Tower reinstate historic building lines, avoiding the temptation of wider pavements.

Archaeology has also been handled well by the Corporation, which expects developers to provide time and funding for investigations and recording to be done properly. Since 1990 great discoveries have been made, and techniques for the recovery of evidence have improved enormously. While the Museum of London contains many of the artefacts, there are also fascinating *in situ* remains at Spitalfields, the Temple of Mithras, Tower Hill and below the Guildhall Gallery.

GROUNDSCRAPERS AND SKYSCRAPERS

In the aftermath of deregulation in 1986 large dealing floors were largely provided by low-rise, big-footprint buildings, typified by the first phase of Broadgate (around the Arena and Finsbury Avenue Square) and by such gigantic blocks as Terry Farrell's Alban Gate on London Wall, Goldman Sachs's extensive headquarters on Fleet Street, and J.P. Morgan's fortress-like premises at 60 Victoria Embankment. The City also spread beyond its strict boundaries, at Finsbury Square, Aldgate and Spitalfields, where neighbouring boroughs saw the potential for regeneration. The Big Bang did not spark proposals for high buildings, since deep, unobstructed floors with atriums do not fit into slim towers. RHWL Architects' Beaufort House and 1 America Square, GMW Architects' Minster Court and Fitzroy Robinson's Little Britain, all completed in 1991, are assertive in scale, rising to twenty storeys, but are not skyscrapers by any stretch of the imagination.

There is no doubt that Canary Wharf, and One Canada Square in particular, rang alarm bells in the City. Barclays Bank, which might have been tempted to move to Docklands, was given strong encouragement to redevelop 54 Lombard Street in the middle of the City, and GMW Architects' 103-metre-high tower, completed in 1994, was regarded at the time as a positive statement. With the demand for dealing floors now met by the proliferation of broad groundscrapers, attention moved skywards.

The Greater London Development Plan of 1969 had identified the north and east of the City as areas (among others, such as Croydon) where clusters of tall buildings might be appropriate. This was largely a reaction to the seemingly random location of such isolated towers as Centre Point, Millbank, Euston and the Hilton Hotel on Park Lane, which threatened to ruin London's skyline. Even though nobody was proposing towers at the time, the Strategic Planning Guidance for London (1989) repeated the cluster idea, and introduced protected strategic views of St Paul's. In the City the eastern cluster was focused on the existing group of the Stock Exchange (1969), Commercial Union (Aviva),

Richard Seifert's Drapers' Gardens and, most noticeably, Seifert's tower for the National Westminster Bank (1981). The IRA bomb at the Baltic Exchange in 1992 created a site in St Mary Axe where a new tower could reinforce this cluster. Norman Foster's proposal in 1996 for a Millennium Tower, which later became the Swiss Re Tower or 'Gherkin', marked a radical change in direction. When the NatWest Bank moved out of its tower, some doubted that the modest floor-plates would easily re-let, but its revamp as Tower 42 in 1998 and rapid reoccupation by small offices boosted confidence.

A wave of proposals for tall buildings followed, and a plethora of planning publications: the Commission for Architecture and the Built Environment (now Design Council CABE) and English Heritage's *Guidance on Tall Buildings* (2007), the Mayor Boris Johnson's *London Views Management Framework* (2010) and the City Corporation's own *Tall Buildings Evidence Paper* (2010). Some schemes – notably the Heron Tower and 20 Fenchurch Street – won approval following objections from English Heritage and lengthy public inquiries. Ken Livingstone, who was consulted on anything over 150 metres tall, was supportive – 'high buildings should be assessed on what they add to the skyline, rather than what they take away' (quoted by Kenneth Powell in *Architects' Journal*, 20 January 2011) – and Johnson is like-minded.

Outside the cluster, tall buildings have not had an easy passage. Santiago Calatrava's proposal almost to double the height of Britannic Tower (City Point) in Ropemaker Street did not proceed. The Corporation has been meticulous about requiring absolute adherence to St Paul's Heights, negotiating numerous schemes to preserve or improve backdrop views of the cathedral dome; it has also sought to protect the setting of the Tower of London. The raked profile of the tapering Leadenhall Building, or 'Cheesegrater', is a result of the planners' requirement to preserve the silhouette of the cathedral dome from Fleet Street. After such efforts, the ostentation of the Shard has been felt in the City like a kick in the teeth.

David Wootton, Lord Mayor in 2011–12, suggested that the Shard was 'out of tune with the times. Every downturn sees this kind of thing. The property industry goes slightly too far, because of the time lag. But developers are sensitive to public mood and build buildings that fit the spirit of our times, which rightly would be more in favour of sharing and connection, trying to lessen the differences rather than heighten them' (*Newsforum*, London Forum of Amenity and Civic Societies, Spring 2012). That might be diplomatic wishful thinking.

Peter Rees thinks the skyscraper boom may be coming to an end. Despite research by Stuart Lipton to find ways of building skyscrapers more cheaply, Rees has seen a growth in planning applications for the refurbishment of existing office blocks. Commenting in *Building.co.uk*'s newsletter in 2012, Rees said: 'If a client has a particular requirement and they want to build tall I'm open to that. There's maybe room for a couple more towers in the cluster, but we've probably built enough for the foreseeable future. My prognosis is there will be fewer towers and that's no bad thing. There are a lot of late-eighties buildings we shouldn't be throwing away.' It is possible that buoyancy in the insurance sector and its beloved EC3 postal district may sustain a few more towers alongside the 'Cheesegrater', such as the so-called 'Scalpel' next to Lloyd's in Lime Street. Time will tell.

The towers have certainly served their purpose in providing a massive injection of new floor-space, often with spectacular views. The eastern cluster, when complete, is

↗ Aiming skywards in Ropemaker Street, where CityPoint **233** and Ropemaker Place **232** jostle for space.

→ New Street Square **151** shows that high-density, top-quality offices with excellent public realm can be achieved without building towers.

likely to contain nearly 70% of all the offices in the City, and 10% of the shops. The towers' visual and environmental effectiveness is harder to judge. Rees believes that towers alone, however well designed, do not make or mend a place, and he cites the Strata residential building at Elephant and Castle as an example of a new, highly conspicuous tower that has done little to revive the fortunes of its locality. It could be argued that, before the current spate of building, Tower 42 provided a clear focus for a cluster now muddled by the Gherkin and the Heron Tower. The Pinnacle, if completed, would be significantly higher and might create a new central culmination to a more coherent cluster. Already the distinctive shape of the Gherkin has been lost from many longer views, blocked from the north, for example, by the Bishopsgate Tower. From afar the individual forms may merge into an amorphous whole.

The towers' local impact gets little mention anywhere. Time will tell whether individual iconic towers can provide really attractive green space at their base; the collegiate campuses of New Street Square, Paternoster Square and Angel Waterside may prove more successful. As Paul Finch (deputy chairman of the Design Council) has often said, 'You don't have to build tall to be dense.' Unlike in Dubai, the sun is never overhead in London, where towers cast long shadows. Few people choose to eat a picnic at the foot of a tall building (although there is now al-fresco dining outside the Gherkin). Those who have had their umbrellas blown inside out might note the brief sentence in the Corporation's ninety-seven-page *Evidence Paper* that says: 'The impact of wind on surrounding streets and spaces will need to be assessed.' It might be a bit late for that.

QUANTITY AND QUALITY, ARCHITECTS AND STARCHITECTS

The main part of this book examines in detail the hundreds of individual schemes that have rebuilt the City in recent years. The combined effect has been one of startling transformation. Before the 1980s the City was scarcely a showcase for good modern commercial architecture; the finest British œuvres of the 1960s or 1970s are found in universities, arts complexes and social housing (including Golden Lane and the Barbican). Staid office architecture in the City before and after the Second World War remained safely in the hands of a relatively small number of large firms, including Richard Seifert, Fitzroy Robinson, Trehearne and Norman, Roger Preston & Partners and T.P. Bennett.

Richard Rogers's building for Lloyd's of London (1986) represented an extraordinary break with tradition. It astonished some of the more conservative aldermen on the Corporation (including one who thought the window-cleaning cranes on the towers meant that it was unfinished). For many years it was an almost freakish one-off for the City, and, with its dramatic scale and visual dazzle, it remains one of the key buildings of the modern epoch.

The upsurge of development following deregulation in 1986 saw the arrival of a clutch of new architectural practices on the scene, notably Arup with Broadgate, GMW Architects and RHWL Architects. Terry Farrell's postmodern style became popular, and a trio of giant American firms, SOM, Swanke Hayden Connell Architects and KPF – all able to complete big schemes efficiently – opened offices in London. A vast amount of floor space was built very quickly, not all of it of the highest quality. In his capacity as chairman of the Corporation's Planning Committee, Michael Cassidy founded the City Architectural Forum in 1991 in response to criticism voiced by Prince Charles. The idea was to improve standards of design and construction in time for the next generation of commercial buildings in the Square Mile.

The recession in the first half of the 1990s provided the breathing space for

an architectural change of tack. Chunky, muscular postmodern designs clad in polished granite and marble became unfashionable. Number One Poultry was already passé when it was completed in 1997. The building boom that emerged in the economic resurgence of Tony Blair's Labour government brought a fresh international style, dominated by steel and glass, and a craving for 'signature' and high-tech buildings. Arguably the shift was heralded by adventurous projects on the fringe of the City, such as the Helicon Building on Finsbury Pavement and Insignia House on Mansell Street, but the modernist baton was resolutely carried forward by Foster + Partners, Richard Rogers Partnership (now Rogers Stirk Harbour + Partners), Foggo Associates (started by Peter Foggo of Arup), Sheppard Robson and KPF. There was a danger of another clique. Foster + Partners alone has completed a dozen schemes in the City since 2000.

Alongside these 'usual suspects', smaller firms have also made a significant mark. David Walker, who arrived as design principal in Swanke Hayden Connell Architects' London office in 1989, set up on his own in 2002. His tiny practice has designed and completed an impressive collection of schemes, at 1 Coleman Street, Bow Bells House, Riverbank House and the Heron, buying in outside professional help when needed. Woods Bagot, John Robertson Architects and Fletcher Priest Architects are also modestly sized offices that have made important contributions to the City. Rab Bennetts, who founded Bennetts Associates with his wife, Denise, in 1987, believes passionately that medium-sized firms have a major role to play, as they retain the ability to pick and choose projects. Bennetts Associates' City portfolio is proof enough of that.

In the late 1990s and early 2000s architects and their clients embraced the spirit of the times. The newsworthy 'millennium projects' (wheels, bridges, domes and towers) were matched by a craze for fashionable big-name architects. Eric Parry, Nicholas Grimshaw, John McAslan, Michael Hopkins, Richard Rogers and Norman Foster fitted the bill, but the desire for prestige also attracted foreign superstars, notably Jean Nouvel at One New Change, Rem Koolhaas with New Court and Rafael Viñoly at 20 Fenchurch Street. Ken Shuttleworth, who designed the Gherkin for Foster + Partners, broke away to set up his own practice, Make. Lee Polisano similarly left KPF to found PLP Architecture. Larger London-based firms, such as Allies and Morrison and Sidell Gibson, have acted as executive architects on several projects, as well as designing their own City schemes. Office developments can be traded in the same way as any other commodity, and each transaction, with its lawyers and consultants, brings pressure to redesign, cheapen, expand or contract. It is common for one architect to obtain planning permission, another to supervise construction and a third to implement the tenant fit-out. It can be complicated to attribute the provenance of a building.

The media loves icons. 'Exciting' projects with novel nicknames fill column inches, but they are only part of the story. Adherence to St Paul's Heights and Protected Views constraints has meant that low-rise groundscrapers have continued to be built, but more sensitively and stylishly than most of the crop immediately after the Big Bang. Swanke Hayden Connell Architects' sinuous block for Deutsche Bank at Winchester House and its scheme for Merrill Lynch at Newgate are outstanding. At Tower Place and Bishops Square, Foster + Partners has demonstrated that big buildings can be accommodated almost unnoticeably, with the focus instead on public space. David Walker's Riverbank House and Fletcher Priest's Watermark Place have a more complex visual balance between the architectural form and colour of the buildings and the public realm.

Not every new building can or should be iconic. To be an urbane and humane place, the City also needs good background buildings. Some architects have tried too hard. Fashions become outdated, and too restricted a specification leads to inflexibility. Ken Shuttleworth is convinced that the days of 'crazy shapes and silly profiles' are numbered. Critical of his own design (with

Richard Rogers's trademark colours and wall-climbing lifts feature at Lloyd's Register, 71 Fenchurch Street **119**.

Foster) for the Gherkin, he believes that the latest towers are already obsolete in terms of energy use. Although triple glazing and other technical advances have improved performance greatly, the orgy of glass may be over, with a return to simpler, more solid forms. The City Corporation has sustained Edwardian traditions of Portland stone by encouraging crisply detailed limestone cladding on many recent projects, as has Islington Council in Finsbury Square. Nor does every client want a controversial or showy statement: Bloomberg has commissioned a very plain building for its new European headquarters at Walbrook Square.

The fashion of dedicating large ground-floor areas to public access with a mix of restaurants, bars and shops (called 'malls' in America) has found increasing favour, much encouraged by the planners' desire for permeability. New streets run through Merrill Lynch's headquarters at Newgate, and through City Point, St Botolph's House and Plantation Place. Nobody wants to visit or work in a fortress any longer. Several recent schemes contain generous and opulent foyers, sprinkled with artworks, comfortable seating and stylish enquiry desks. Their size and transparency, even the quality of the self-opening doors, become a status symbol, but also make places to do business outside the confines of the office. Technological advances in swipe cards, face-recognition cameras and minimalist personnel barriers have revolutionized security. Discreet staff, smartly besuited to look like partners rather than servants, deal with any undesirables.

While one would not advocate the lurid Legoland of Renzo Piano's development Central St Giles in Holborn, there is a welcome trend of introducing colour to relieve the monotones of steel, glass and Portland stone. Some firms have their house style (such as Rogers's ventilation ducts), but other English architects have found it hard to break away from habitual greyness. Without the respective splash of yellow and the blue strip, Riverbank House and St Botolph's House might be dull buildings.

Much credit must go to Rees for encouraging excellence and ambition. He admits to having 'a low boredom threshold', and dislikes lazy architects churning out 'repeat' schemes. Rees is very much in charge of design discussions with developers and their architects. Although the City has an Architecture Forum (chaired by Richard Saxon, formerly chairman of the architectural practice Building Design Partnership), it does not get involved in negotiations with applicants or their architects, and is not a design panel. Apart from the Barbican Association, there are no local amenity societies to make comments. The Corporation's Planning Committee acts more as a board of trustees, expecting officers to do the hard work. Rees was therefore able to direct the Corporation away from pressure to create sites for megalithic and faceless Canary Wharf-style buildings. It is a strategy that has worked well. The fine grain has been kept, yet the City has been transformed. The concentration of high-quality new schemes, cheek by jowl on a medieval street plan, is staggering, and without equal in Europe even including the monumental rebuilding and renewal of Berlin after reunification. The City has deservedly become a Mecca for architectural tourists.

A SUSTAINABLE CITY

Concentration of activity in the City arguably creates a highly sustainable environment. There are no derelict or abandoned sites (the long-empty site at 21 Lime Street is a rare exception), and most historic buildings are kept in very good repair. In terms of transport, most people who work in the City travel by train, Underground and bus, or increasingly by bicycle. Commuting by car is heavily discouraged (the Corporation, unlike other bodies, did not object to the congestion charge). New development provides parking only for the disabled and servicing, and many older basements that formerly housed car parks have become fitness centres, bars, bicycle stores or service accommodation. Distances within the City are short enough to encourage walking, although there are still too many taxis on the streets, particularly empty ones. The Corporation has remorselessly promoted improvement to infrastructure, lobbying for Underground station upgrades, especially at Bank, and reputedly contributing £200 million to Crossrail. The new Thameslink stations in the City handle 78,000 passengers each weekday.

The provision of services and power is a greater challenge, not least accommodating the spaghetti below ground. Demand for electricity is forecast to grow by 10% between 2012 and 2020. Cabling and Wi-Fi are essential to the City, and supply has to be resilient and flexible, with no scope for blackouts or blinking lights. The energy requirement for just one new building can be the equivalent to that of a small town, and, despite the inclusion of solar panels on some recent projects, on-site generation has proved difficult to connect to the grid. Since land for new substations is limited within the City (although one is included in Limeburner Lane), there is increasing reliance on locations outside its borders, at Bankside, Brick Lane and Pimlico. It is not just because of the threat of terrorism that many City businesses have wasteful duplicate emergency back-up offices and server centres elsewhere.

The Corporation has endeavoured to ensure that new buildings and refurbishments are as energy efficient as possible, and it now insists that all new buildings attain Building Research Establishment Environmental Assessment Method (BREEAM) Excellence, the top rating. The Corporation's laudable programme of installing fifty new drinking-water fountains and hundreds of gum/butt receptacles across the City will reduce the mountain of plastic bottles and unsightly rubbish, and architects who are genuinely committed to sustainable energy, such as Justin Bere of Bere:Architects, have been commissioned for public-realm schemes.

Green and brown roofs, reuse of grey water, thermal glass and ground-water cooling can do their bit, but far too many big new commercial buildings are air-conditioned, artificially lit and lavish in their use of resources. According to the Corporation's report *Tall Buildings and Sustainability* (2002), lifts account for 10% and lights 20% of the total energy use in a tall building. Ways need to be found of harnessing and reusing the colossal amounts of heat emitted by existing buildings. Disappointingly, the combined heat and power plant in Smithfield runs mainly on oil. Perhaps

The spacious entrance and ticket office for the new Blackfriars station **313** were opened in 2012.

No. 20 Cannon Street **019** was reclad and refitted in 2012. Part of 25 Cannon Street **020** can be seen to the left.

hydrogen fuel cells and such new superconductors as graphene will be the miracle solutions of the future.

Meanwhile Prince Charles, in a lecture to the Institute of Civil Engineers in 2012, criticized modern buildings as 'energy-guzzling glass boxes', 'ripe for demolition' within thirty years. In a speech to the New London Architecture conference in November 2011, Ken Shuttleworth claimed that 'glass is dead', and Make's schemes at Broadgate and London Wall do indeed use far less glass than has been normal. Using less glass, however, does not on its own answer questions about whole-life costs of buildings, embodied energy (that used in construction and lost during demolition) and how long they are designed to last.

The reuse and refurbishment of tired buildings ('retro-fit', in the jargon) is a big subject, in theory cheaper, quicker and less wasteful than demolition and rebuilding. Advances in fibre optics and satellite communications mean that large floor-to-floor heights allowing for service ducts are no longer required. There are good examples, such as 125 Old Broad Street and 20 Cannon Street, where the result looks and feels like a new building. With some schemes, however, little original fabric is kept and environmental credentials are dubious. Those at 10 South Place and 8–10 Moorgate have done little more than retain part of the facades, and even the celebrated saving and refurbishment of Bracken House was mainly new construction.

The greatest challenge now for refitting deep-plan offices is to devise ways of naturally ventilating and lighting them, to reduce energy consumption. Such buildings do not convert easily to other uses, either. Nevertheless, some experts believe that retro-fit is the way forward. With many twenty-five-year leases due to close before 2020 (representing some 1.5 million square metres, according to the property firm Savills), and an over-supply of new office buildings, it is time for ingenuity, and – with groundscrapers – literally lateral thinking. Some clients, however, will still want the cachet of a new building and big-name architect, while for developers the possibility of getting something far bigger than the original is ever tempting.

AN INCLUSIVE CITY

Since the Big Bang of 1986, the City has successfully shed its old-fashioned image of bowler hats, furled umbrellas and public-school dinners. The downside of the Thatcher revolution may have been the 'loadsamoney' yuppie, but fundamental changes in working practices have made the City look and feel very different from the way it did in the late 1980s. The influx of foreign banks means that the City is as cosmopolitan as the rest of London.

Women have played a big part, with increased numbers working in banking, accountancy and law, and such key players as Judith Mayhew and Annie Hampson in the Corporation. The retail boom in the City, strongly promoted by land-use policies, is a direct response to changes in society, since it is no longer the case that 'the wife in Godalming' does the shopping. It may be true that most women, and men, would rather work in the West End, close to Selfridges or John Lewis, but the opportunity for retail therapy in the City is improving. Women and men also have different expectations of what constitutes a civilized working and recreational environment: while there are still a few traditional chophouses serving bubble-and-squeak and spotted dick (and some that rebrand apple crumble and custard as 'tarte tatin avec crème anglaise'), the City now offers ambience and cuisine from every corner of the world. Coffee shops, health-food shops and juice bars are everywhere.

The inclusion of walk-through malls and atriums, publicly accessible foyers and high-level viewing galleries in larger schemes has also helped to open up the City, with security generally handled more subtly than before. The Corporation has been exemplary in requiring disabled access throughout the City, not just into and within buildings but also in streets and open spaces. London as a whole now ranks highly in those league tables, beloved by the popular press, of 'the world's most liveable capitals'.

Peter Rees believes passionately that the City's lifeblood is young cosmopolitan workers, intellectually and socially active, 'seeking nightlife and a job to pay for it'. While he regards luxury shopping, as at

One New Change **023** offers shops and restaurants on three levels, and has greatly enhanced the role of Cheapside as the City's high street.

One New Change, to be a 'key piece in the jigsaw', it is the City's intimacy, the network of alleyways, the possibilities for chance contact and gossip, that make the area what it is (he is quoted in the *Architects' Journal*, 20 January 2011). Architecture can help, but it is nothing without people. If anything, it is now trying to break down the closed doors of the exclusive institutions and return to the eighteenth century, when deals were done in coffee houses and taverns.

There is still a way to go. While part-time and flexible hours, home working and better maternity conditions recognize the importance of women in the labour force and vitality of the City (although workplace crèches never really happened), many 'glass ceilings' remain. Only 6% of executive board positions in financial services companies are held by women (according to a *City A.M.* poll in 2012). Male-dominated institutions usually resist the imposition of quotas. Even in the architectural profession, where lots of women work on the shop floor, few (Zaha Hadid, Patty Hopkins, Amanda Levete) become household names. The City still has plenty of exclusive clubs, in its livery companies, and old-boy networks, which are now made up of those born in the 1950s rather than the 1930s.

Roger Gifford, merchant banker and Lord Mayor of London from November 2012, believes that the City needs to explain better to the outside world what it does, its role in society and its attitude to philanthropy, and that making money should not be seen as an end in itself. When newly elected as chairman of the Corporation's Policy and Resources Committee, in May 2012, Mark Boleat suggested that the City's future prosperity rests on its role in the wider community. He stressed its duty to educate and train young and disadvantaged people, encouraging programmes of corporate social responsibility and maintaining recreational and cultural services for all to enjoy. The Corporation's own charity, the City Bridge Trust, annually dispenses grants worth £15 million to charity projects across London. The Corporation does a huge amount of good work, often outside the City itself. Within its boundaries, as it strives to retain its status as the world's pre-eminent global financial centre, there are, perhaps, inevitable limits to its inclusivity.

PUBLIC REALM

Terrorist attacks by the IRA in 1992 and 1993 had a great impact on the City, not only because of the immediate damage and disruption. As an emergency response to stop any further lorry bombs, the Corporation instigated a series of road closures and police checkpoints, the 'ring of steel'. The consequent 40% reduction in traffic showed what the City could be like. The air quality improved overnight, and the Corporation considered how to put the spare capacity to better use. The Street Scene Challenge was launched in 2002 with the aim of transforming the City's streets by closing roads, widening pavements and creating a more pedestrian-friendly environment, a 'walkable City'. Ken Livingstone's congestion charge further reduced traffic from 2003 onwards. Under the guidance of the Street Scene Manager, Victor Callister, and inspired by European exemplars, such as Barcelona and Amsterdam, various schemes have been integrated with developments on private land and have revolutionized the public realm.

Established traditions have been continued, such as 75-millimetre-thick York stone slabs for pavements, and the Corporation's stipulation that street lights be fixed to buildings to avoid the need for lamp posts (long the envy of other boroughs). The adoption of a simple palette of natural materials, with York stone and large granite slabs for pavements and roads, copied good practice by others in Regent Street, the Strand and Kensington High Street, but its consistency and high quality are laudable. Cheapside is the most impressive scheme to have been completed so far: its carriageway is reduced to two narrow lanes and the traffic calmed to bicycle pace. It now feels like a civilized shopping street, free of clutter. The biggest project, not yet complete, is the Riverside Walk (see chapter 12). The medieval alleys of Carter Lane, Bow Lane and Lovat Lane have been pedestrianized. There are ambitious plans for Holborn Circus, King Street (following on from Queen Street to the south), Fleet Street, Fenchurch Street and Ludgate Hill, and even the ghastly roundabouts at Aldgate and the west end of London Wall. Meanwhile a host of existing public spaces, churchyards and squares have been revamped, and some

small new ones created, employing a series of talented young landscape architects, but with the Corporation retaining strict control. Specialist gangs of masons and paviours are retained to work only in the City. Callister has resisted suggestions that cheaper materials – such as imported Chinese stone, unsustainably quarried – be used. Traditional Corporation bollards, embellished with coats of arms, and heavy bronze (rather than timber) planters may be expensive, but they last longer and are less easily stolen. Attractive and comfortable wooden armchairs supplement utilitarian benches.

Funding for such improvements has come from many sources. At Aldermanbury Square, Sun Court and Devonshire Square money came largely from the developers, but elsewhere planning obligation funds, grants from the City Bridge Trust and the Corporation's substantial parking revenue surplus (at risk in 2003–2004 of confiscation by the Greater London Authority) were used. Some £25 million of Section 106 money (half the pot; see p. 12) has been spent on environmental work since 2002, with a further £10 million allocated. The Corporation wisely avoided offers of sponsorship for the excellent new Wayfinder maps, which are helpfully located throughout the City.

In 2012, after a decade of endeavour, the individual projects (seventy completed and forty in the pipeline) were joining up, infusing environmental improvement through the City and beyond its boundaries in Whitecross Street and Smithfield. Challenges remain, however. Paranoia over security and the fear of terrorist attack are rife, hence the obstructive bollards facing the new Blackfriars and Cannon Street stations and the substantial planters outside Deutsche Bank's offices in London Wall. Anti-capitalist protesters are not made welcome, as was seen when the Occupy London camp was evicted from outside St Paul's Cathedral in February 2012 and from Finsbury Square five months later. Some 'public' realm remains private, gated and undemocratic.

The massive increase in cycling (all City streets are now two-way for bikes) following the Underground and bus bombings in July 2005 and the introduction of the popular 'Boris Bike' rental scheme in July 2010 has required extra bike parking on and off the

Rothschild's New Court
074 in St Swithin's Lane
adjoins the churchyard
of St Stephen Walbrook,
re-landscaped in 2012.

street. Given the scale and density of some new developments, shared space, courtesy crossings and time restrictions for on-street servicing will be increasingly important in managing the public realm. In a poll carried out in June 2012 during the City Corporation and New London Architecture's exhibition *The Developing City* (June–September 2012), 75% of respondents chose more open space as their highest priority, rather than more shops or tall buildings, or even reduced traffic.

Public art has blossomed in recent years. During the 1980s and 1990s it was largely left to private enterprise and enthusiasm (provided generously at Broadgate and Fleet Place), and such patronage has continued, particularly in the semi-public foyers and malls of prestigious developments. Spitalfields now has one of the most eclectic collections of twenty-first-century sculpture in London. Having commissioned various pieces in the 1950s and 1960s, the Corporation, after forty fallow years, adopted the City Arts Initiative in July 2011 and established an advisory panel for its own programme for new art. Such superstars as Antony Gormley and Thomas Heatherwick have made permanent contributions to the street scene. In addition, the American idea of temporary installations has taken root in the Great St Helen's Sculpture Space, St Helen's Square, a joint venture begun in 2011 involving local businesses (including the insurance firm Aon and the developer British Land) and key members of the Corporation, such as Michael Cassidy and Martin Farr (chairmen respectively of the Planning and the Planning & Transportation committees). In 2012 the show featured eight international artists, including Julian Opie, Tracey Emin, Dan Graham and Yayoi Kusama.

Michael Bear, Lord Mayor in 2010–11, summarized the intention of the project in a Corporation press release: 'These sculptures reflect the City's commitment to developing an evolving public space that fits with the changing architectural landscape in the Square Mile.' It is to be hoped that some of these temporary exhibits will find a permanent home in the City, while the panel also tackles the thorny problem of decommissioning older 'sacrosanct' public art that no one much likes. The continuous and devoted support given by the Corporation to the Barbican Arts Centre, the Guildhall School of Music and Drama and the annual City of London Festival, with its street pianos and multifarious events, also plays its part in animating the business environment with world-class arts.

LOOKING AHEAD

In June 2012 the curator of the exhibition *The Developing City*, Peter Murray, asked three teams – Woods Bagot, Gensler and John Robertson Architects/Arup – to display their vision of the City in 2050. The result was some controversial and far-fetched thinking, and squeaky-clean variations on Fritz Lang's dystopian film *Metropolis* (1927). In reality, such grand plans are unlikely to be carried out. More probably, some of the less successful post-war 'visions', such as London Wall and Upper Thames Street, will be unstitched through incremental change.

Meanwhile, many property and financial analysts gaze into an opaque crystal ball. There are optimists and doom merchants aplenty, and those who hedge their bets. Pessimists point to economic turmoil and recession. Some observers, such as Jonathan Guthrie of the *Financial Times*, consider the deregulation of 1986 to have been a colossal mistake, leading to insuperable conflicts of interest, malpractice, greed and calamity.

Employment in the City has fallen from a pre-credit crunch peak of 350,000 in 2007 to 270,000 in 2012, and is likely to drop further. Estimates made by the City Corporation in 2009 that it might recover and rise to 400,000 by 2016 now appear to be a long way off the mark. After the spectacular company collapses of 2008, shrinkage has become piecemeal, as the whole financial sector is squeezed, but the cumulative effect is worrying. The considered view of Simon Davies, formerly chief executive and chairman of Threadneedle Investments, is that there is negligible scope for employment growth in investment banking and management, and even that significant retrenchment of up to 25% is possible. That would still leave more people working in the sector than was the case in the 1990s, however; it is easy to forget the extent to which capacity was

↗ One New Change **023** and 25 Cannon Street **020** are viewed from St Paul's. The right-hand tower beyond is the core of 20 Fenchurch Street **132**, under construction in 2012.

→ Barclays Bank **091** partly obscures the view of Tower 42 **095** from Monument; to the right, the Heron Tower **110** is the most distant but the tallest structure in 2012.

increased through new and expanding firms in the boom years.

While lack of new floor space has been a problem in the past, an over-supply is now self-evident, with fewer developers able to pre-let and several big construction sites 'capped' and put on hold. As a result, many City rents are almost unchanged (£30–£35 per square foot) from 2002 levels. Some property investors are now expressly avoiding the City altogether.

Canary Wharf remains a threat, with its New York-style towers, grid of boulevards, efficient, unconstrained space, competitive rents, new Crossrail station and proximity to London City Airport, and more big banks may move there. Clifford Chance, one of the 'magic circle' legal giants, has already relocated. It remains to be seen whether the Olympic legacy and the Thames Gateway project, which seeks to attract development to both sides of the Thames from inner east London to the estuary, will benefit Docklands more than the City.

The alternative, upbeat outlook is that the City is well positioned against its competitors, even in a period of austerity. Owing to a shortage of supply, West End rents have spiralled (£100 per square foot) and are nearly double top-end City rents. The glut of accommodation in the City will make it a cheaper option, particularly for small private banks and hedge-fund managers that are feeling the pinch in the West End. The City could probably house most of them in just one of its new supertowers. Centrality and transport infrastructure are ever crucial, and the City is well placed and well supplied, with the Thameslink complete, and Crossrail and improvements to the Northern line under way. Financial squeezing results in mergers, and the City has large buildings that can accommodate such amalgamations under one roof. The demand for smaller offices remains buoyant, and there are even rumours that some newspapers want to move back to the City. The digital and high-tech hub on the City fringe, at Old Street Roundabout, is booming; technology, media and telecoms companies there doubled in number and size between 2010 and 2011.

Sceptics may label them lemmings or lunatics, but there will always be risk-takers and opportunists who want to invest in property, even in the worst times. The intimate face-to-face environment of the City can become its strongest asset. Peter Rees is convinced that places attract people. Connectivity, both virtual and physical, in an interactive environment stimulates collaboration, creativity and the spill-over of knowledge. Physical agglomeration, social interaction and gossip remain powerful factors, as in a village. It is significant that Bloomberg, despite being a digital company, has chosen to be in the heart of the City: according to Rees, 'to be close to its customers'. The City's essential function, as an exchange, remains strong.

It is widely agreed that the days of speculative and iconic architectural design are over. New buildings need to be 'future-proofed' by being flexible and efficient, preferably with a good address and attractive public realm. They have to be designed for the occupier, not the architect's ego, and performance will be more important than appearance. Working patterns and technology are changing fast. The architect Frank Duffy points to a future where work and play merge, where a young, agile workforce does business on the move, where offices have a cafe culture and campus atmosphere (as well as stylish conference rooms for confidential meetings) rather than battery-hen conditions of tedious lines of desks. The current fashions for hot-desking and smart working will become more sophisticated, perhaps with lower densities and healthier working conditions. In a mobile, fluid workplace, Wi-Fi, the 'Cloud' and 'Bleisure' (the practice of combining business and leisure travel) are changing everything. Will the City be resilient and light enough on its feet to move with the times?

There remains a less rosy view. The army of bowler hats trudging across London Bridge on the daily commute may have gone, but the City remains smug and insular, still sucking on its inherited silver spoon. Should it rethink its policies? Is the remorseless concentration of offices the best approach, or has the cluster of towers of the insurance sector in the east of the City resulted in a soulless, uninspiring environment, ultimately uncompetitive, with too many eggs in an unattractive basket? Diversity may be the answer. The Corporation might look carefully at the multi-let Shard and the smaller-scale mixed-use districts of Clerkenwell and Holborn, where residents rich and poor live happily above and among offices, shops, galleries and restaurants. Rather than aiming for an additional 1000 residents in the City by 2020, why not an extra 25,000? Its 30,000 citizens would probably work near by (or not at all – why not retire to a City flat?), and would constitute a substantial electorate. There, of course, lies the rub. Too small to sustain residential services, the City would be susceptible to encroachment by larger neighbouring boroughs. Rees is convinced that it would be the death of the City, which can justify its survival, and retain its world domination, only by being an exclusive, protective and protected business district. That raises the question whether a concentrated financial district is needed in the first place; perhaps it would be better if it were spread more evenly across London.

Introducing a conference on the City of London in November 2011, Peter Murray (as Chairman of New London Architecture) noted succinctly that 'the future is hard to see'. Uncertainty continues to be one thing of which we can be sure.

NAMES AND NUMBERS

A word of warning: the names of buildings can be confusing. Given the history of the City, it is no surprise to find plenty of 'Exchanges', but the recent spate, or scattered flock, of 'Herons' surely gives scope for muddle. The changing signage of occupying companies sometimes disagrees with the name or address of the building, since developers want catchy names and occupiers individualistic addresses. Numbering is inconsistent: sometimes odd numbers are on one side of a street and evens on the other; sometimes numbers run consecutively up one side and down the other. There are gaps in the numbering, where large new buildings cover a footprint once occupied by many smaller premises, and numbers are sometimes obscurely displayed, etched into glass or inscribed in stone. Where a new building comprises a whole block, perhaps facing four streets, it is not always clear which frontage is the official address – there may be several. The rookie postal worker or courier is to be pitied.

To its credit, the Corporation has doggedly retained the extraordinary and singular medieval street names, and all are clearly and consistently displayed. The story goes that when a particular firm, which was moving to premises in Gutter Lane, asked the Corporation to change the street name to something more salubrious, the reply was 'No, but we have no objection to you calling yourselves Gutter Brothers.'

One suggestion: Victorian and Edwardian commercial buildings often display a date, a popular custom from times when the year of construction was something to be celebrated. The practice has regrettably fallen out of favour. Were it to be a requirement of the Planning Committee when approving detailed elevations, it would make the life of future architectural historians a good deal easier.

New Wayfinder maps and information boards, as well as consistent design of traditional street signs, are an important part of the public realm throughout the City of London.

1

AROUND ST PAUL'S

001 Paternoster Square **002** Warwick Court **003** *Angel's Wings* **004** Temple Bar **005** Procession House, 55 Ludgate Hill/110 New Bridge Street **006** 11 Pilgrim Street **007** 100 New Bridge Street **008** 160 Queen Victoria Street **009** 1–3 Ludgate Square **010** 69 Carter Lane **011** Grange St Paul's Hotel **012** City of London Information Centre **013** Firefighters' War Memorial **014** 101 Queen Victoria Street **015** 95 and 99 Queen Victoria Street **016** Senator House, 85 Queen Victoria Street **017** Old Change House, 128 Queen Victoria Street **018** Bracken House, 10 Cannon Street **019** 20 Cannon Street **020** 25 Cannon Street **021** Watling House, 33 Cannon Street **022** Festival Gardens **023** One New Change **024** Bow Bells House **025** 1 Bow Churchyard **026** 150 Cheapside **027** St Paul's Cathedral Alignment Pavement

In Panyer Alley, close to the Newgate Street exit of St Paul's Underground station, an ancient stone inscription is set into the wall of a new building. It reads: 'When you have sought the City round yet still this is the highest ground, August the 27, 1688'. Here, in the shadow of St Paul's Cathedral, is a good place to start this detailed survey of the recent architecture of the City of London, on the topographical, if not the moral, high ground (although part of Cornhill may in fact be a few centimetres higher). The cathedral and the approaches to the Millennium Bridge attract more tourists than any other part of the City, although, as with many such honeypots, it is remarkably easy to escape the crowds by taking the side streets.

St Paul's Cathedral has long been dominant in the planning and development of the western half of the City, as well as being its ecclesiastic heart. Even before the Second World War there were concerns about the setting of the cathedral. The construction in Queen Victoria Street of Faraday House telephone exchange (1932) by the Ministry of Works breached the long-standing London Buildings Act code of a maximum height of 100 feet (30.5 m) for new buildings. The architect Walter Godfrey Allan, then Surveyor to the Fabric of St Paul's Cathedral, was appalled by its impact on the skyline, and coordinated an effective campaign to protect the surviving views of the cathedral. The so-called 'St Paul's Heights' constraints, a fine-grained grid showing maximum building heights above Ordnance Datum, were introduced by the City of London Corporation in 1936, covering large swathes of the City and beyond.

The area around St Paul's was one of the most badly bombed in the City during the Blitz, particularly the former booksellers' and publishers' precinct around Paternoster Row with its historic labyrinth of alleys and courts. Eventually, following the adoption of a plan by the architect and town planner William Holford, the cleared sites were replaced with a brave new world of 1960s office slabs and elevated walkways, most designed by the firm Trehearne and Norman. The new buildings severely breached the St Paul's Heights rules and (particularly the ghastly Sudbury House) blighted views of the dome from the north. Within only two decades, Paternoster Square **001** had become a symbol of unsympathetic post-war development, described in retrospect by the Lord Mayor, Robert Finch, as 'ghastly, monolithic constructions without definition or character' (*The Guardian*, 24 May 2004).

A competition was launched in 1986 to produce something better. This, too, became a saga, and a focus for the debate between modernist and traditionalist architecture. Arup's competition-winning scheme was challenged in a high-profile speech by Prince Charles at a Mansion House dinner in December 1987, promoting an alternative neoclassical proposal by John Simpson. Arup's scheme was dutifully dropped, and Simpson's ideas were worked up with Terry Farrell. After much procrastination, a masterplan by William Whitfield of Whitfield

Paternoster Square **001**
is seen from the dome of
St Paul's Cathedral. The
London Stock Exchange
moved into the arcaded
building on the right in
2004. William Whitfield's
column forms the
centrepiece of the square,
with Temple Bar **004** to
the bottom left.

Partners was adopted and built, albeit incorporating many of Simpson's ideas. The new Paternoster Square was opened in 2003; the client was the Japanese corporation Mitsubishi Estate. Part of the delay involved the unravelling of the layers of ownership and the underground car parks and services, with considerable help from the City Surveyor and the City Property Advisory Team.

The new scheme removed the elevated pedestrian concourse and reinstated a true ground-level environment. To achieve architectural variety, a consortium of firms – Allies and Morrison, Eric Parry Architects, MacCormac Jamieson Prichard (now MJP Architects), Sheppard Robson, Sidell Gibson and Whitfield Partners – worked to a code of building heights, footprints and materials. The result is a compromise, harmonious or banal depending on the point of view, and described by Kenneth Powell in the *Architects' Journal* as 'polite modernism' (20 January 2011, p. 32). The pedestrian environment is good and affords some wonderful views of St Paul's, particularly from the narrow passage running south from Newgate Street beside St Martin's Court. Permeability is a vital part of the concept, although the 'public' realm was quickly qualified in the Occupy London anti-capitalist demonstration in October 2011, when the London Stock Exchange (relocated to Paternoster Square in Parry's building of 2004) became an obvious target. An injunction and security staff rapidly denied public access.

In the middle of the central square stands the 23-metre-high Paternoster Square column of Portland stone, designed by Whitfield and illuminated at night, capped with a flaming urn of gold leaf, sometimes called 'the pineapple'. It makes reference to the more famous Monument by Christopher Wren and Robert Hooke, built to commemorate the Great Fire of 1666; Whitfield's column honours the 6 million books that were destroyed in the firestorm of 29 December 1940. More prosaically, it serves as a ventilation shaft for services below.

Warwick Court **002** by MJP Architects, fronting Warwick Lane to the north-west of the site, is one of the more eye-catching buildings of the scheme, in white stone relieved with small decorative areas of orange terracotta. Further south, where Warwick Lane becomes Ave Maria Lane, in the passage leading back into Paternoster Square is an even more striking piece of sculpture, *Angel's Wings* (2002) **003** by Thomas Heatherwick (well known now for his design of the updated London double-decker bus and the Olympic cauldron, both in 2012). This pair of silver metal spirals also disguises a cooling vent for electricity transformers below.

The southern exit from the central space is underneath the arch of Temple Bar **004**, re-erected here in 2004 rather incongruously in terms of both its location and its orientation. Temple Bar originally bestrode Fleet Street, marking the western boundary of the City; it was removed as a traffic nuisance in 1878 to Theobalds Park in Hertfordshire, and rather forgotten about. One can applaud the quality of the restoration, financed by the City Corporation and several livery

Thomas Heatherwick's
Angel's Wings (2002) **003**,
between Ave Maria Lane
and Paternoster Square.

Orange terracotta panels
contrast with white
limestone on Warwick Court
002 fronting Warwick Lane.

Procession House 005, at the corner of Ludgate Hill and Pageantmaster Court. The brick, terracotta and stone cladding panels stand proud of the main structure.

companies, which deservedly received a Stone Federation Award for craftsmanship. Its historic stone is more convincing than the pastiche Corinthian columns and faux Classicism on the adjoining curving building frontage to Ludgate Hill.

It is hard to believe today that Ludgate Hill, the westerly approach to St Paul's, was once marred by a railway bridge, the Ludgate Viaduct, which carried the tracks of the London, Chatham & Dover Railway into Holborn Viaduct station. The reopening of the Snow Hill tunnel (which was closed in the late 1960s) and the construction of a new low-level connection to Blackfriars Bridge beneath Ludgate Hill, as part of the Thameslink railway project (1986–89), provided a string of redevelopment sites above (see chapter 7 for the north side up to Holborn).

On the south-east corner of Ludgate Circus, on top of the entrance to the new City Thameslink station, Procession House (55 Ludgate Hill and 110 New Bridge Street **005**) was developed jointly by Goldman Sachs and the City Corporation in 1999. The design by RHWL Architects employed an unusual form of off-site construction, using prefabricated steel plates carrying panels of handmade bricks, terracotta and Portland stone to create a curtain wall or rainscreen of traditional materials standing 30 centimetres proud of the main structure. The effect is curious and slightly flimsy, worth a close inspection from Pageantmaster Court or Pilgrim Street to see how the jigsaw works. Behind it, 11 Pilgrim Street **006**, redeveloped in 1999 by GMW Architects (originally Gollins Melvin Ward Architects), received a makeover in 2010 by TTSP. A duller effort by RHWL (1992) at 100 New Bridge Street **007** is enlivened by Brian Clark's canopy faced with stained glass and mosaic. The rear of this building, found via the narrow alleys of Waithman Street and Black Friars Lane, more surprisingly also displays decorative tiling on the walls and footbridge over the railway.

Brian Clark's colourful entrance to 100 New Bridge Street **007** is particularly impressive at night.

Black Friars Lane and its entrance into Playhouse Yard offer the best approach to one of the largest redevelopments in the area, 160 Queen Victoria Street **008**. This site, originally known as Printing House Square, was vacated by Times Newspapers when it moved to Gray's Inn Road in 1974, and was finally redeveloped in 2003. Now known as the Bank of New York Mellon Centre, it is one of SOM's more conservative designs (constrained no doubt by the St Paul's Heights limits), but the use of narrow red bricks and strips of stone, coupled with pale-grey window frames and grilles, gives a very horizontal and sedate feel, particularly in Playhouse Yard. This charming and intimate space has been immaculately re-cobbled and forms the main VIP entrance and taxi drop-off point. Down on Queen Victoria Street, a whole storey lower because of the falling land, the effect is less appealing as the full extent of the footprint is revealed along a massive flat frontage.

St Andrew's Hill and Friar Lane run back up to Carter Lane in one of the City's conservation areas, where among the network of tight streets and alleyways new architecture is hard to spot. A listed building at 1–3 Ludgate Square **009** was sensitively rebuilt, warehouse-style, in 2000 by PKS Architects as a five-storey residential block, following a disastrous fire. Squire and Partners' 69 Carter Lane **010**, constructed in 1991 with patterned brick, chamfered corners and a triangular projection, is tactfully contextual. Carter Lane itself has been excellently repaved by the City Corporation; the profusion of bollards is presumably to protect the buildings and shopfronts from the glancing blows of delivery vans.

The Grange St Paul's Hotel **011** is the largest recent insertion here, with a bold new frontage to Godliman Street and a spectacular 25-metre atrium with public bars and restaurants sunk into a three-storey basement formed from the bunkers of a wartime communications citadel. The hotel, designed by Buchanan

From the dome of St Paul's, the huge footprint of 160 Queen Victoria Street **008** is readily apparent, contrasting with small-scale buildings in the Carter Lane Conservation Area in the foreground.

The main entrance to the Grange St Paul's Hotel **011** in Godliman Street leads into a large public atrium, also accessible from New Bell Yard at the rear.

The entrance to the Bank of New York Mellon Centre **008** is on an impressive yet human scale. Playhouse Yard has been attractively resurfaced.

Architects and opened in 2010, is actually in two parts, separated by the public alleyway of New Bell Yard; the annex facing Addle Hill is in pale brick punctured by cheap-looking sash windows. On Addle Hill, the ornate Victorian railings and fancy portico of the previous building were kept, although they appear rather 'glued on' to the new frontage.

As one emerges from the east end of Carter Lane, the reward is a remarkable panorama of the south side of St Paul's and, in the foreground, Make's anvil-like Information Centre for the City of London **012**, opened in 2007. The folded triangular structure – origami in stainless steel – was cleverly engineered by Arup, and it is worth walking around and going inside. The roof collects rainwater for recycling and the interior is kept cool by water from boreholes, ticking most of the boxes for energy efficiency. The double-sided map of the whole City on the pavement outside is an excellent help for visitors; near by is John W. Mills's war memorial **013** of 1991 to the firefighters of the Blitz, Winston Churchill's 'heroes with grimy faces'.

The pedestrian route from St Paul's to the river, Millennium Bridge and South Bank is probably the most popular and populated improvement made to the City in recent decades. On a sunny day Sermon Lane and Peter's Hill throng with people, enjoying the views and watching where they tread on the complicated layout of ramps and chamfered steps (to be redone by the Corporation as part of the Millennium Bridge Approach scheme). The path crosses a narrowed Queen Victoria Street, where traffic-control signals and the volume of pedestrians help to calm the traffic. At the south-east corner of this junction stands the elegant new headquarters building of the Salvation Army, 101 Queen Victoria Street **014** (2004), its transparency encouraging people to look inside, as though it were a huge shop window for the organization's good works. Architect Sheppard Robson designed more than a simple glass box, and the steel structure is clearly expressed to give the building shape and rhythm. It is encouraging that the charity sector can still find a place in the City in the twenty-first century.

Adjacent, at 95 and 99 Queen Victoria Street **015**, Sheppard Robson completed more commercial offices in 2003 for developer Stanhope, predominantly of glass and rising to a curved prow at the north-east corner, now labelled as 95 QVS. It is a complete contrast, and a good example of changing fashion, with the polished pink stone of Senator House next door at 85 Queen Victoria Street **016**, designed by Chapman Taylor in 1991 and oddly set back, as if for road widening. This is one of a clutch of late 1980s blocks running up to the junction with Cannon Street, a group that receives little praise from Nikolaus Pevsner and Simon Bradley in *The Buildings of England*; no. 63, which incorporates Mansion House station, 'anthologizes the worst clichés of stone-clad Postmodern offices' (p. 586). Thankfully, Cleary Garden on the south side of Queen Victoria Street makes good use of the slope and SLOAP (space left over

The City of London Information Centre **012** to the south of St Paul's Cathedral makes a striking and playful contrast with the neighbouring buildings.

The headquarters of the Salvation Army at 101 Queen Victoria Street **014** provides a lively frontage to the Millennium Bridge Approach, which links St Paul's with Tate Modern and Bankside.

View from St Paul's
Cathedral of 95 Queen
Victoria Street **015**, with
the tower of St Nicholas
Cole Abbey and the
southern entrance to
Old Change Court in the
foreground. To the left of
no. 95 is part of Senator
House **016**, and in the
distance buildings line
Upper Thames Street.

after planning) next to Senator House, and its bed of Japanese tree peonies, presented by the island of Daikonjima in 2006, is a seasonal marvel. No. 71 Queen Victoria Street is due to be overhauled by SPPARC Architecture, including a new glazed street facade and replacement of the ugly roof plant with a new top floor.

On the north side, the elegant 128 Queen Victoria Street or Old Change House **017** by Rolfe Judd (1997) is pleasantly brick-clad. Old Change Court, south-east of St Paul's, had been flattened and rebuilt after the war in a similar manner to Paternoster Square, and its reinvention by Rolfe Judd was a welcome improvement. The imaginative landscaping by Charles Funke Associates was completed in 2000 and preserves views of the tower of the church of St Nicholas Cole Abbey. In the centre, beside the steps, is a sculptural two-storey pavilion restaurant/bar, a curious mix of futuristic Soviet-style revisionism and Art Deco. It is a shame that few visitors stray into Old Change Court, magnetized instead by the signposted route from Tate Modern to St Paul's.

East of the cathedral, the reconstruction after the wartime devastation resulted in several notable buildings. One of these is Bracken House, 10 Cannon Street **018**, built by Albert Richardson between 1955 and 1959 for the *Financial Times* (Bernard Bracken was its chairman at the time), and soon recognized by architectural critics as a masterpiece. When it was threatened with demolition in 1987 it became the first post-war building in England to be listed. Michael Hopkins, who that year had completed the new Mound Stand at Lord's cricket ground, was commissioned to adapt the original building for the developer Obayashi, which his practice did extremely skilfully. The central printing hall of the original H-plan was replaced by new dealing floors, bulging out like a doughnut from between two retained blocks containing the newspaper offices. The new bays fronting Distaff Lane and Friday Street (which now provides the main entrance) are distinguished by four-storey projecting windows delicately

Old Change Court is a steeply sloping site imaginatively re-landscaped.

Bracken House **018** incorporates new fabric between 1950s brick wings. The main entrance is on Friday Street.

encased in dark green–grey metal. These sit on a base of red sandstone to match that of Richardson's building. Hopkins Architects' contribution, completed in 1992, is now also regarded as masterly, and helped to catapult the firm to international acclaim.

Bracken House is an early example of what is now called 'retro-fit', although it was brought about by the heritage lobby rather than being done for environmental, sustainability or economic reasons. Across Friday Street, the carcass of 20 Cannon Street **019**, originally an unremarkable 1960s block, has been remodelled and refaced for a second time, having been vacated by the law firm Herbert Smith in 2008. In 2012 the slick black 1980s high-tech cladding by the Whinney Mackay-Lewis Partnership was stripped away from the concrete skeleton and replaced by a more energy-efficient panelled curtain wall, with copper-mesh solar screens to the south face. The Australian firm Denton Corker Marshall also cut away the ground floor of the north-west corner, to create a new entrance facing St Paul's. It effectively looks like a new building, but one achieved in half the time and at half the cost. Advances in fibre-optic cabling and service provision mean that such buildings as this, with low floor-to-floor heights, can be refitted to modern standards; previously 4 metres was deemed to be the minimum height.

The opportunity to maximize the prospect of St Paul's was taken even more enthusiastically at 25 Cannon Street **020**, which – despite its address – is strongly orientated to face New Change and to enjoy spectacular views of the east end of the cathedral and its precinct. Set on an island site and incorporating a foreground of beautifully maintained public gardens designed by Elizabeth Banks Associates (now Robert Myers Associates) in 2000, this is the most strictly classical building to have been erected in the City in the twenty-first century, showing great deference to its setting. The chairman of the client

25 Cannon Street **020**, the headquarters of Fidelity Worldwide Investment, is strikingly classical in style. Bracken House **018** is to the right, One New Change **023** to the left.

and developer, Fidelity Worldwide Investment, cares passionately about design. Edward (Ned) C. Johnson III is a thoroughbred Bostonian, imbued with traditional New England style, and he strongly encouraged the architect, RHWL, in that direction. The result is a dignified and well-proportioned composition, providing about 11,000 square metres of high-quality floor space, with a colonnaded and pedimented western front, cornices and dentil courses all round, and a vaulted entrance hall.

The height of Watling House, 33 Cannon Street **021**, immediately to the east, was strictly limited by its proximity to St Paul's. Arup's design, completed in 1999, also displays a classical language with a clear bottom, middle and top, but with a more modern interpretation and use of materials than no. 25. The gardens in front of the latter are complemented by the Festival Gardens **022** opposite, which were given fresh green lawns, espaliered limes and a water feature by the City Corporation for the Queen's Diamond Jubilee in 2012, and a striking bust of the poet John Donne by the sculptor Nigel Boonham.

The newest addition, One New Change **023** immediately to the north, is extraordinarily different from anything else – indeed, one of the most talked-about and controversial new buildings in the whole of the capital – but is already a seemingly established part of the City and on its way to becoming an icon. The initial debate centred on the loss of Victor Heal's New Change Buildings, a vast curve of staid neo-Georgian red brick and stone built for the Bank of England in the 1950s, compared favourably with Bracken House by some critics, who promoted its retention. Later debate concerned the suitability of the proposed replacement by the renowned French architect Jean Nouvel, whose initial sketches were likened in the popular press to a stealth bomber. The canted and chamfered metal cladding did not appeal greatly to Prince Charles, either; but the City Corporation was strongly supportive.

The £540 million scheme was worked up in detail in partnership with Sidell Gibson, with the developer Land Securities as client, retaining the complex shapes and angles of Nouvel's original concept. Even more significant than the design, perhaps, is what the development provides: more than 20,000 square metres of luxury shopping and dining on three levels, with 32,000 square metres of offices above, on four floors. The scheme was at the heart of the City Corporation's vision of re-establishing Cheapside as a retail and leisure destination, and of reinstating old alleys and streets that Heal's monolith had obliterated.

The new building, completed in 2010, achieves this sense of openness very successfully, and even if one has no intention initially of visiting the boutiques and restaurants it provides attractive and convenient walkways through the site. The medieval street pattern has been re-created north–south and east–west. The building has also been a commercial success, not only because of its celebrity-chef restaurants (Gordon Ramsay's cavernous Bread Street Kitchen and Jamie Oliver's Barbecoa), which will come and go, but also because half the retail spend is at the weekend. It has proved to be a new attraction for tourists and visiting shoppers, who enjoy the easy unrestricted parking on Saturdays and Sundays. To get sensational views, and to appreciate how cleverly and stealthily the fritted glass has been sculpted to lie within the protected views of St Paul's, catch the lift to the sixth floor and the City's first genuinely public roof terrace, which is adorned with Charles Wheeler's statues from Heal's building.

The pedestrian network of One New Change continues east of Bread Street, where John Milton Passage runs parallel to Cheapside through Bow Bells House **024**, an eight-storey office scheme with ground-floor shops completed in 2008 for Stanhope and Mitsubishi Estate. David Walker Architects redesigned an earlier scheme by HOK, moving the core to a better position and achieving BREEAM Excellence (see p. 18). With Hamilton Associates' offices on the south

No. 33 Cannon Street **021**, with its main entrance on the corner with Bread Street, is a modern interpretation of classical form and proportion.

side at 1 Bow Churchyard (1997) **025**, it provides a crisp new setting for the churchyard of St Mary-le-Bow and its grand steeple.

The transformation and enhancement of the public realm in Cheapside has been a big project for the City Corporation in recent years, aiming to create a coherent and attractive environment for pedestrians to complement the increased shopping and leisure opportunities. The vehicle carriageway has been reduced to two lanes, greatly widening the pavements, all of which have been resurfaced in natural materials – York stone slabs and granite blocks – and reducing the clutter of posts, bollards and traffic signs.

At the western end of Cheapside, on the north side opposite One New Change, 150 Cheapside **026** provides a dynamic treatment of the corner with St Martin's Le-Grand and an impressive entrance to Cheapside. Completed in 2009 by Michael Aukett Architects and set behind a generous pavement, this is a sweeping eight-storey curve of glass with shops on the ground floor and offices above, and with a touch of colour in the brise-soleil projections to the side in Foster Lane. The design is a grand gesture to the spacious setting of St Paul's, but also gives the occupants of the building wonderful views towards the cathedral. Only the octagonal oddity of 5 Cheapside remains of the post-war Paternoster Square development (except for Elisabeth Frink's charming sculpture *Shepherd and Sheep*, which survives in the new concourse). Planning permission was granted in 2009 for a replacement building and new tube station exit designed by John McAslan + Partners, but problems of building above the Underground mean that refurbishment is the more likely option.

Although this book is mainly about new architecture in the City, it would be churlish in this chapter, which has circumnavigated St Paul's, not to mention the extraordinary work of restoration and repair that has been carried out on the cathedral since 1990. Under the astute and inspiring guidance of Martin

Festival Gardens **022**, south-east of St Paul's Cathedral, was refreshed with new paving, planting and sculpture in 2012.

One New Change 023
incorporates pedestrian
routes and a spectacular
roof terrace with free
public access. Inside there
are three levels of shops
and restaurants.

No. 150 Cheapside 026
marks the entrance from
St Martin's Le-Grand into
Cheapside, and provides
a colourful setting for the
church of St Vedast on
Foster Lane.

Stancliffe, seventeenth Surveyor to the Fabric (who retired in 2011, after twenty-one years of admirable service), the stonework has been cleaned inside and out to achieve a homogeneity not seen since the time of Wren. The great flight of steps at the west end has been taken up and relaid, and the churchyard railings, which sat for years in a builder's yard in Kent, were tracked down and reinstated. On the south-west side, disabled access has been created by an ingenious new ramp, which incorporates a new artwork by Richard Kindersley. Made of Purbeck marble and Welsh slate and set into the ground, the St Paul's Cathedral Alignment Pavement **027** is a plan of the modern cathedral superimposed on that of its great medieval predecessor. The garden marks the footings of the Chapter House.

The dome of St Paul's offers a wonderful bird's-eye view of the western half of the City, and we must be thankful that it is no longer hemmed in by the tall slabs of the 1960s. There are continuing concerns and debates about the obstruction and diminution of views of the dome from such places as Primrose Hill and Waterloo Bridge, by London's growing collection of high buildings, but the immediate setting of St Paul's is probably better today than it has been since the war. If only Faraday House could be replaced with something lower.

2

GUILDHALL
AND CHEAPSIDE

028 2 Gresham Street **029** Alder Castle House, 4–6 Aldersgate Street **030** One London Wall **031** 25 Gresham Street **032** Shelley House, 3 Noble Street **033** 100 Wood Street **034** 31 Gresham Street **035** 88 Wood Street **036** 5 Aldermanbury Square **037** 1 Aldermanbury Square **038** 1 Love Lane **039** 10 Aldermanbury **040** 51–57 Gresham Street **041** Guildhall Art Gallery **042** City Place House, 55 and 60 Basinghall Street **043** City Tower, 40 Basinghall Street **044** 1 Basinghall Avenue **045** Woolgate Exchange, 25 Basinghall Street **046** 4 Coleman Street **047** 1 Coleman Street **048** 97–99 Gresham Street/36–40 Coleman Street **049** 54–60 Gresham Street **050** 52 Gresham Street **051** 2 Bank Buildings **052** 30 Gresham Street **053** 107 Cheapside **054** 100 Cheapside **055** 20 Gresham Street **056** 1 Wood Street **057** Dresdner Bank House, 125 Wood Street **058** Abacus House, 33 Gutter Lane **059** 10 Gresham Street **060** 6 Gutter Lane

If St Paul's Cathedral is the ecclesiastical heart of the City, then the Guildhall is its secular administrative centre, and in its own way just as remarkable a bastion of power and tradition. The complex of buildings that comprises the Guildhall sits in the network of streets that, of anywhere in the City, most resembles a grid plan. This area, bounded by London Wall to the north, Cheapside in the south, Coleman Street in the east and St Martin's Le-Grand and Aldersgate Street in the west, has seen an extraordinary amount of rebuilding, street block by street block, much since 1997 – more reconstruction, indeed, than almost any other part of the City. It was also very badly damaged in the Second World War, including several Wren and pre-Great Fire churches, and was generally reconstructed with unremarkable 1950s and 1960s office buildings. The height of new development has been constrained by protected views of the cathedral, particularly on both sides of Gresham Street and southwards to Cheapside. To the north, however, the scale increases to meet and match the height of the 1960s slabs that were built when London Wall was laid out in a bold piece of post-war planning.

Gresham Street forms a straight, largely west–east spine across this area, and an axis for exploring either side. At its junction with St Martin's Le-Grand and designed by Gensler in 1998 is the low-rise 2 Gresham Street **028**, six storeys to parapet, mainly in stone, with double-height columns respectful of the former Post Office buildings opposite. Its entrance foyer on Gresham Street is enlivened by statuesque zebras, symbolizing the South African origin of the occupier, the specialist bank Investec. The rear, to Foster Lane, is much less satisfactory, set back with a crude curved recess to create a car park directly opposite the grand entrance to Goldsmiths' Hall. The developer, St Martin's, also commissioned nearby 150 Cheapside, completed in 2009 (**026**; see chapter 1). The development of design expectations over the decade between them is telling.

The north-western approach to Gresham Street is dominated by Alder Castle House, 4–6 Aldersgate Street **029**, completed in 1999, just a year after 2 Gresham Street. Sidell Gibson's frontage is symmetrical and determinedly postmodern, with round turrets at the corners, but the character changes completely at the side and rear. Skirting behind the gardens and low red brick of St Anne's church, the elevations to Noble Street are in a more austere warehouse-style yellow brick. Archaeology played a crucial part in the shaping of the building, given the requirement to preserve and display a substantial section of Roman fort and medieval city wall. Arup designed the foundations so that the main entrance at 10 Noble Street bridges the 'moat' of wild flowers and ancient fabric below.

The drama of Alder Castle House has since been overshadowed by its neighbours. Abutting to the north is Foster + Partners' One London Wall **030**, a project that was begun in 1992 but underwent radical change during a protracted design process and was not completed until 2005. Its dominant use

No. 2 Gresham Street **028** at its junction with Foster Lane is classically proportioned, with double-height entrance and base, a three-storey middle, and a single-storey top. Additional floors are set back behind the cornice, to be inconspicuous from the street.

One London Wall 030 forms a prow on the corner with Noble Street. The footbridge across London Wall leads to the raised Barbican walkway and the Museum of London.

The rear (west) elevation to Oat Lane of 100 Wood Street **033** is an amphitheatre of glass enclosing the site of St Mary Staining. In the background is the rear of 88 Wood Street **035**.

of glass, Art Deco curves and stepped, set-back upper floors is in strong contrast to the brick piers of 10 Noble Street. It presents its most elegant face to the north, where footbridges span London Wall to connect with the raised Barbican walkway and the entrance to the Museum of London. The spiral staircase from the pavement on the corner with Noble Street is somewhat ungenerous, but the escalators on the Aldersgate roundabout are more inviting.

Back at the east corner of Noble Street and Gresham Street, Grimshaw's 25 Gresham Street **031** for the Lloyds Banking Group looks as radical today as when it was completed in 2002. Cantilevered over and canted back from the consecrated gardens of the destroyed church of St John Zachary (re-landscaped by the Goldsmiths' Company in 1995) to lessen the impact of its ten storeys on Gresham Street, the building has a metallic, high-tech character, with echoes of the practice's Waterloo train shed and even Sainsbury's supermarket in Camden Town. It is very clearly a 'Grimshaw' building. The details are worthy of close inspection, particularly the metal spider fixings for the Broughton Moor slate panels, expressed as stitches of steel, and the delicate cut-outs in the projecting metal ribs. To the north, on the other side of Oat Lane, Shelley House, 3 Noble Street **032**, by Sheppard Robson (1999) is extraordinarily bland in comparison, equally metallic but with simple flat silver–grey panels that make no concession to ornament.

Oat Lane, at its junction with Staining Lane, is the best place to experience the spectacular rear of 100 Wood Street **033**, another Foster + Partners scheme, completed in 2000. A sloping amphitheatre of nearly sheer glazing forms a dramatic setting, both sheltering and reflecting the mighty plane tree in the garden on the site of St Mary Staining. The pedestrian route through and under the building via St Alban's Court to Wood Street is well done, inviting close contact with the building. Few buildings anywhere can have such contrasting elevations front and back, and Wood Street reveals the other side of Foster's coin, a plain chequerboard of glass and stone panels. The diamond-pattern curved roof is scarcely visible from street level. The invention of the building seems even greater set against the pastiche facades of 31 Gresham Street **034**, which lies immediately south, fronting Wood Street, Staining Lane and Gresham Street. This development (1998) by Stanhope and Legal & General for the asset manager Schroders stipulated a conservative brief to the architect, SOM, resulting in a very safe design, its stone blocks expressed traditionally, with recessed joints.

Foster's 100 Wood Street, however, appears subdued against the assertiveness of Richard Rogers Partnership's 88 Wood Street **035** immediately to the north (1999). This began in 1988 as a commission from a Japanese bank, Daiwa, and it was Rogers's first job in the City since the completion in 1986 of his famous Lloyd's building (see chapter 4; his practice is now called Rogers Stirk

No. 25 Gresham Street **031** is set back behind the gardens of St John Zachary at the junction with Noble Street.

Harbour + Partners). Rather like One London Wall, 88 Wood Street went through a complete redesign following the withdrawal of the original client and the decision to build speculative offices. The design challenge was how to 'square up' to the enormous hulk of Terry Farrell's Alban Gate, a true monster of the late 1980s, described in detail in chapter 8. Rogers's eight-storey elevation to Wood Street is surprisingly plain, but the fun is in the entrance and in the north elevation, where towers rise to eighteen storeys and the wall-climber lifts are fully expressed. Here we see obvious references to the Pompidou Centre in Paris with the brightly coloured nautical ventilators (blue: in; red: out) and the splashes of brilliant yellow, but a remarkable sense of lightness and transparency is achieved by the use of crystal-clear triple-skin glass. Unlike Foster at One London Wall, Rogers does not attempt to solve the problem of integrating with the raised walkways to the north. That problem is left to Alban Gate.

On the east side of Wood Street is another vibrant addition to the ensemble of twenty-first-century commercial architecture. Eric Parry Architects' 5 Aldermanbury Square **036**, completed in 2007, was designed to fit around the listed Wood Street Police Station, and Parry's choice of stainless-steel cladding was a conscious exercise in contrast. In common with 88 Wood Street, the building rises to eighteen storeys (replacing the even bulkier 1960s Royex House), but in a very different form, with two inward-leaning blocks enclosing a central atrium. The entasis (convexity) is less pronounced than at Grimshaw's 25 Gresham Street, but it is a noticeable feature, intended to decrease its impact. The floors are also grouped in pairs to improve the proportions. For the pedestrian, the best feature is the creation of an open street through the building, a wide and lofty connection through to Aldermanbury Square, decorated with black and white stones, shuttered concrete (reminiscent of

The curved roof of 100 Wood Street **033** is glimpsed from Love Lane above the chimneys of Wood Street Police Station and the pinnacles of the solitary tower of St Alban.

No. 88 Wood Street **035** rises in spectacular fashion from London Wall.

5 Aldermanbury Square
036 strongly terminates
the view westwards along
Basinghall Avenue (above),
while on Wood Street
(right) the elevation has a
noticeable convex curve.

the Southbank Centre and already becoming stained) and ornamental water features. The foyers to BNP Paribas are pleasantly transparent, although the overall effect is perhaps rather grey in winter, and views back to Wood Street are brightened by Rogers's yellow columns. The scheme was on the Pulitzer and Stirling prize shortlists in 2009, and won a Royal Institute of British Architects award in the London category in that year.

Significant improvements have been made to Aldermanbury Square itself, with new trees and paving. On the south side, 1 Aldermanbury Square **037**, designed in 1989 by Amos Broome Associates and occupied by the Standard Chartered bank, now seems very dated, drably multicoloured with pointed gables. Attached to its south side, 1 Love Lane **038** is more dignified, a 'pretty stone-faced building' (*The Buildings of England*, p. 414) of 1991 by Rolfe Judd. Surprisingly, it includes a health clinic on the ground floor, overlooking the gardens and remains of the church of St Mary Aldermanbury (after war damage, most of the masonry was sent to and re-erected in the United States).

Between Love Lane and Gresham Street, Sheppard Robson's 10 Aldermanbury **039** of 2000 (previously known as Barrington House or 59–67 Gresham Street) is from a similar mould to SOM's 31 Gresham Street. Sensible, solid elevations of Portland stone provide 42,000 square metres, pre-let to Flemings, now part of the financial services firm J.P. Morgan. It wraps around the side and back of GMW Architects' atrium block of 1991, 51–57 Gresham Street **040**, which, like 1 Aldermanbury Square, now appears as an outdated exercise in postmodernism compared to its slicker neighbours. The sobriety of 10 Aldermanbury, subtly enriched by Alan Evans's artistic metalwork, provides a good foil to the western wing of the Guildhall compound on the opposite side of the street. Aldermanbury itself has been much softened through landscaping by Burns + Nice, particularly the beautifully planted pond (2004) outside the church of St Lawrence Jewry.

The Guildhall itself is a varied group of buildings, some extremely venerable – restored and rebuilt after fires and bombs – others less so. When Richard Gilbert Scott (son of Giles) was commissioned with D.Y. Davies Associates to create new premises for the Guildhall Art Gallery **041** on the east side of Guildhall Yard to house the Corporation's worthy collection, it was quite a challenge, particularly as Scott had already built the west side in 1975. The discovery and excavation in 1988–95 of the remains of Londinium's Roman amphitheatre at basement level, and the desire to retain and expose them and make them publicly accessible, enormously complicated the brief, and bloated the budget. It was remarkable that the new building was completed by 1999, given the complexity of the subterranean works. The result is worth a visit, if only to put the present-day world into historical perspective. What you see is impressive, but not without some contrivance: the archaeology had to be jacked

No. 1 Love Lane **038** faces the delightful churchyard garden of St Mary Aldermanbury.

Guildhall Yard with
Guildhall Art Gallery **041** at
its eastern end. The curved
dark paving marks the
perimeter of the Roman
amphitheatre.

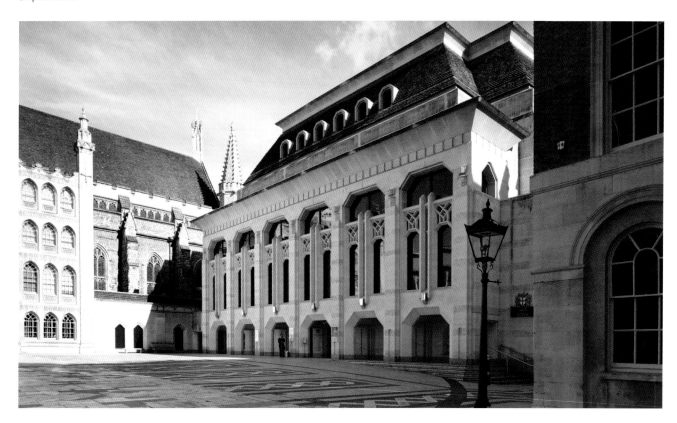

up to make room for the underground car park below. Scott's elevations with splayed arches, vaguely Egyptian Art Deco styling and well-crafted stonework present a better companion to the Gothic Guildhall than does the 1970s block, and the yard is repaved in a striking pattern that marks out the amphitheatre.

The north wing of the Guildhall was refurbished and given a contemporary foyer by T.P. Bennett in 2008 (and an additional glazed top floor for the headquarters of the City Planning Officer). The external space was also refreshed, in a more constrained way than the open treatment of Aldermanbury Square. Tall walls of black slate, formal hornbeam hedges and a lack of comfortable benches do not make this a place to linger. The series of passenger lifts deals with the level changes in the manner of a flight of locks on a canal.

The north side of Basinghall Street is dominated by two large blocks of contrasting styles. City Place House, 55 and 60 Basinghall Street **042**, is a brash American-influenced block designed by the American firm Swanke Hayden Connell Architects and completed in 1992. Immediately to the east is the sleek and simple City Tower, 40 Basinghall Street **043**, one of the original 1960s slabs built to line the new dual carriageway of London Wall. It was clad in blue glass by GMW Architects in 1985 and given a smart, crisply detailed street-level entrance by ORMS in 2002, abandoning the original entrance from the upper-level pedestrian walkway.

The corner of Basinghall Street and Basinghall Avenue is now occupied by the global headquarters of Standard Chartered bank, 1 Basinghall Avenue **044**. Completed in 2007, this 27,600-square-metre office development for Pillar Property and Stanhope was designed by Bennetts Associates, and its consistent eight-storey height succeeds in unifying the disparate scales of the immediate area. The west-facing elevation is well articulated, with a freestanding screen of stone fins. The north elevation, not requiring solar protection, is disappointingly

↗ The new street-level entrance of 40 Basinghall Street **043**. City Place House **042** is on the left.

→ The western elevation of 1 Basinghall Avenue **044** faces Basinghall Street. The reflection of 5 Aldermanbury Square **036** can be seen in the windows.

dark, flat and plain, perhaps the result of 'value engineering' (the polite expression for cost-cutting). Immediately to the south, running right through from Basinghall Street to Coleman Street, is Woolgate Exchange, 25 Basinghall Street **045**, yet again an extraordinary contrast of style with its neighbour. It is hard to believe that this huge building of 35,000 square metres, replete with quasi-classical columns in moulded white concrete, was completed only in 2000, designed initially by SOM and executed by Sidell Gibson. It is a remarkable exercise in pomposity, relieved somewhat by the generous set-back and green space on Basinghall Street.

Equally curious is 4 Coleman Street **046**, on the corner with Basinghall Avenue, designed in 1996 by T.P. Bennett. With its bays and bow windows, clad in stone, it has the feel of a pre-First World War Viennese apartment block, with a domesticity that sits strangely in its setting. At the northern end of the street, 1 Coleman Street **047** is eye-catching in its angularity and fluidity. This oval-plan building was completed in 2007 to replace Austral House, another of the rectangular 1960s office slabs that had faced London Wall. The designer, David Walker Architects, set out to break away from orthogonal convention, but was told early on by the client, British Land, that curved glass was too expensive. In response, Walker set the fenestration at alternating angles to the floor plate, giving tangential views from the building. With their slim, eyeliner-like edging, the windows resemble rows of flat-screen televisions arranged in a complex frame of canted and angled white panels, creating an arresting impression of instability. The scheme also enabled the creation of a new public space to improve the setting of the 'doll's house' of Girdlers' Hall in front. The view from the east side of Coleman Street west into Basinghall Avenue is now remarkable, displaying in one sweep the startling variety of contemporary City architecture, cheek by jowl.

View from Coleman Street into Basinghall Avenue: 4 Coleman Street **046** and 1 Basinghall Avenue **044** are on the left and 1 Coleman Street **047** to the right, with 5 Aldermanbury Square **036** in the far distance.

The London Wall facade of 1 Coleman Street **047**, with Moor House **222** on the left and the Heron Tower **110** in the distance. The complex geometry of the windows produces kaleidoscopic reflections.

The southern end of Coleman Street is unremarkable. Nos 36–40 comprise the long side elevation of 97–99 Gresham Street **048** by Sidell Gibson (1997), contextual Edwardian pastiche on the corner and main street elevation but simplified with plain, unmoulded window surrounds further along Coleman Street. Next door, 95 Gresham Street was redeveloped behind a retained facade by Rolfe Judd for Standard Life Investments in 2010.

The planners' requirement for facades of Portland stone has been rigorously applied in Gresham Street. Nos 54–60 **049** on the south side by Eric Parry Architects and Gibberd (2004), replacing the former headquarters of the City of London Police and incorporating some of its historic internal features, is almost blandly solid. Six storeys high, it has an additional three tiered levels and makes a top-heavy corner with Old Jewry. Stanley Peach & Partners' 52 Gresham Street **050**, on the junction with Ironmonger Lane, is better proportioned, a stone-clad piece of postmodernism with a round corner turret (1991). Far more stylish than either is the refurbishment from 2012 of Victor Heal's 2 Bank Buildings **051** of 1962, at the junction with Lothbury, where Fletcher Priest Architects' neat reworking for the Bank of China includes an inconspicuous glass roof extension.

The rest of the south side of Gresham Street has been comprehensively redeveloped since 2000. Sidell Gibson's 30 Gresham Street **052** of 2006 involved the amalgamation of various sites to create a new groundscraper providing floor plates of 4450 square metres each for Commerzbank. It occupies a whole street block, bounded by Milk Street, Russia Row and Lawrence Lane, even flying over the latter towards King Street. Opposite the church of St Lawrence Jewry and the southern approach to Guildhall Yard, the architectural style is dutifully contextual. Curved corners are an important feature, picked up in the extension and redevelopment of the rear of 107 Cheapside **053** by John Robertson Architects (2009), on the south side of Russia Row and Milk Street. This scheme

No. 52 Gresham Street **050** at the junction with Ironmonger Lane; to the left is 54–60 Gresham Street **049**, with its tiered upper floors.

retained the flat 1950s frontage to Cheapside, not much improved by the metal reveals and transoms to the windows, but achieved an extra 3500 square metres at the back. The new sundial on the corner with Milk Street is a welcome addition. After long delays, demolition and construction commenced in September 2012 on the redevelopment of 100 Cheapside **054**, where a ten-storey design by Michael Aukett Architects on the corner with King Street, approved in 2009, was challenged by objections to potential light infringements. The site, said to be worth £25 million, is owned by the City Corporation, and it is rumoured that the developer Quadrant Estates is in negotiations to provide the City's first Apple store.

Curved corners and a curvaceous roof are even more pronounced features of 20 Gresham Street **055**, designed by KPF and completed in 2008. Unimpeded dealing space was a key part of the brief, and there are 18-metre clear spans and an atrium positioned behind the central core. The use of stone is minimal, and the finish more metallic, but this is compensated for by the building's southerly neighbour, 1 Wood Street **056** by Fletcher Priest Architects, constructed at the same time and finished just a few months earlier. The stone elevation to Cheapside and Wood Street has been admirably described as well-mannered civility, and it certainly provides a good foil to the magnificent protected and preserved plane tree opposite. But there is more to it than that. The inclusion of shops on the ground floor and the incorporation of Compter Passage as a through route for pedestrians are intelligent and humanizing elements. Halfway along Wood Street the frontage sets back generously to make an elegant junction with 20 Gresham Street and to create a new public space, which traps the afternoon sun. Charmingly inscribed on a slab is William Wordsworth's poem 'The Reverie of Poor Susan'. The building was a pre-let to the law firm Eversheds, which has a building to be proud of.

↙ No. 30 Gresham Street **052** forms a curving frontage to the south side of the street, opposite the church of St Lawrence Jewry.

↓ The rear elevations of 107 Cheapside **053** and, on the left, 30 Gresham Street **052** both have rounded corners at the junction of Milk Street and Russia Row, providing a sense of space in otherwise narrow streets.

No. 1 Wood Street 056 is set back at its junction with the rear of 20 Gresham Street 055 to create a new public space.

Dresdner Bank House, 125 Wood Street **057**, is a relic of the late 1980s, designed by Lister Drew & Associates in 1988. With its coarse red brick it sits like an odd apple among all the twenty-first-century glass, grey metal and white stone. Rather like Abacus House near by at 33 Gutter Lane (**058**; designed by Richard Seifert in 1990 for Schroders), it has the look of a fortress, with an aggressive 'Keep Out' feel typical of its time. No building illustrates the change in attitude, design and image since the 1980s more strikingly than 10 Gresham Street **059**, which many believe to be one of Foster + Partners' best twenty-first-century office buildings. Completed in 2003 for the fund manager Standard Life Investments, its rectangular plan occupies a whole island site bordered by Gresham Street, Wood Street, Goldsmith Street and Gutter Lane. Instead of having rounded edges, each corner is marked by a stone tower containing services; even the emergency doors are immaculately faced in stone. In between, curtain walling with full-height glazing and gunmetal framing provides an elegant and modest scale of six storeys, with two more set back at roof level. Internally, the column-free 18-metre spans provide premier flexible (and multi-occupied) office space. The main entrance, on Gresham Street, is dramatic and permeable. A sweeping curve of glass and sleek sliding doors invites the public into a spacious foyer, which contains a regularly changing exhibition of artworks for sale.

Discreetly sited behind the Wax Chandlers' Hall next door is another surprise. Manicomio restaurant at 6 Gutter Lane **060** is a jewel-box sequel to the 10 Gresham Street scheme, also designed by Foster + Partners, and opened in 2008. This classy, self-contained three-storey structure has white stone flanks with slit windows and a monochrome interior. The entrance on the glassy south side faces a black monolithic wall of water, which conveniently hides the vehicle ramp of the office block. In an area of large offices covering whole street blocks, this is an ingenious and subtle piece of design on a tight site.

↗ The curvaceous recessed glass entrance to 10 Gresham Street **059** reflects more solid buildings on the north side of the street.

→ The petite scale of 6 Gutter Lane **060** with its outdoor dining tables and silver birches sits elegantly beside the larger mass of 10 Gresham Street **059** behind.

3

BANK AND
MANSION HOUSE

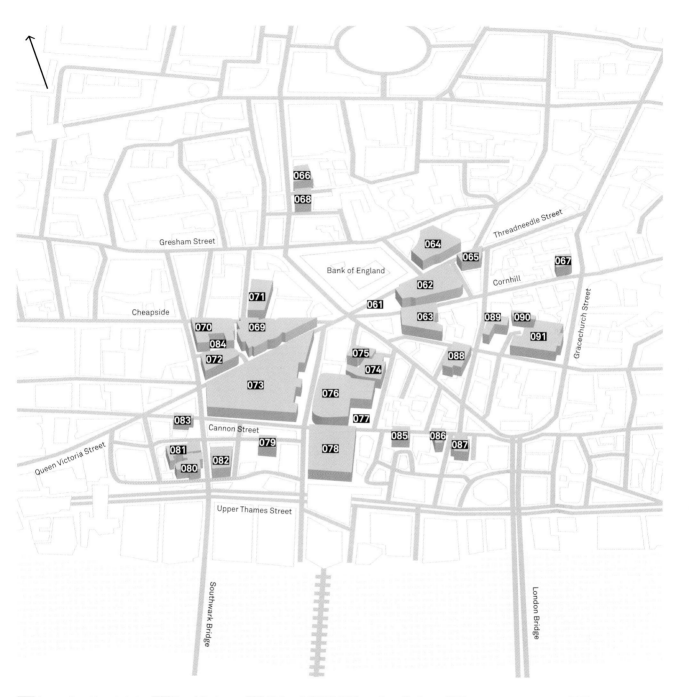

061 James Greathead statue **062** Royal Exchange **063** 14 Cornhill **064** 60 Threadneedle Street **065** 1 Threadneedle Street **066** 12–18 Moorgate **067** 62–64 Cornhill **068** 8–10 Moorgate **069** Number One Poultry **070** 80 Cheapside **071** 1 Old Jewry **072** 60 Queen Victoria Street **073** Walbrook Square **074** New Court, St Swithin's Lane **075** 8–10 Mansion House Place **076** The Walbrook **077** St Swithin's Church garden **078** Cannon Place **079** Pellipar House, 9 Cloak Lane **080** 36 Queen Street **081** 33 Queen Street **082** 62–64 Queen Street **083** 50 Cannon Street **084** St Pancras Church garden **085** 90–96 Cannon Street **086** 108 Cannon Street **087** 110 Cannon Street **088** 21 Lombard Street **089** 20 Birchin Lane **090** St Michael's House, 1 George Yard **091** Barclays Bank, 2 George Yard

The statue of James Greathead **061** stands at the western end of Cornhill, with no. 14 **063** and the entrance to Pope's Head Alley behind.

The Bank of England and the Lord Mayor's residence, the Mansion House, are close to the geographical centre of the City. They and their surrounding streets were less badly bombed in the war than many other parts of the City, and thus suffered less redevelopment in the 1950s and 1960s. The Bank Conservation Area is the largest by far in the City, and the piazza in front of the Royal Exchange is perhaps its least changed public space. Even the statue **061** of the railway engineer James Greathead (1994) is in the sculptor James Butler's most naturalistic style, and its narrow oval plinth in the middle of Cornhill is very much in the mould of the nearby equestrian statue of Wellington, erected exactly 150 years earlier, in the year Greathead was born.

After a brief period in the 1980s as the trading room for the London International Financial Futures Exchange, the Royal Exchange **062** was reconstructed internally in 1991 by Fitzroy Robinson, which unobtrusively added another Corinthian stage to the central courtyard to create extra floor space for Guardian Royal Exchange Insurance. The ground-floor shops were remodelled in 2001 by Michael Aukett Architects, with new projecting glass shopfronts. In a similar manner, 14 Cornhill **063**, the old Grade II*-listed Lloyds Bank, was completely refitted in 2008 by DLG Architects, adding two new floors hung from trusses and supported by six giant columns. The elevations to both sides of Pope's Head Alley were refaced. The capacious ground floor and basement bars in nearby premises have made this a new Mecca for late-night and weekend drinkers and clubbers.

Adjacent to the Bank of England, 60 Threadneedle Street **064** is the most striking recent addition to the area. Completed by Eric Parry Architects in 2009 for the developer Hammerson, it succeeds in breaking away from the City's conventional Portland stone, using a dark metallic finish, while also deferring to the historic curved building line and a nine-storey limit to the parapet. Strong projecting floor slabs are balanced by the double-height ground floor. Inside the

subtly coloured entrance, the foyer is huge and magnificent, its walls adorned with abstract art. This, together with its excellent environmental credentials, perhaps explains why the 20,000 square metres were quick to let. Across the street, occupying a wedge site, a major refit and facade reconfiguration by Woods Bagot of 1 Threadneedle Street **065** was completed in 2012. It respects the original Fitzroy Robinson building of 1991, much praised by Simon Bradley in *The Buildings of England* (p. 604) for its 'good, humane design'.

Many other redevelopments near the Bank have been equally contextual. Frederick Gibberd Coombes & Partners' 12–18 Moorgate **066** for Abbey National/Santander in 1998 and 62–64 Cornhill **067** by Rolfe Judd in 1990 for the Halifax Building Society are both stolidly clad in stone. At 8–10 Moorgate **068**, which is due to be completed in 2013, Allies and Morrison has retained the existing facades, adding traditional mansards and constructing a new, higher glass core, set back to minimize the building's impact on the surrounding streets.

South of the Bank, and more directly affecting the setting of the Georgian Mansion House, lies greater design controversy, and – in terms of its long planning history and public profile – none is greater than Number One Poultry **069**. This mighty saga began with the acquisition by the property developer Peter Palumbo of a collection of Victorian buildings at the junction of Poultry/Cheapside and Queen Victoria Street. His ambitious scheme, originally known as Mansion House Square, was to construct an eighteen-storey tower and plaza in the style of Ludwig Mies van der Rohe, but this was rejected after a celebrated public inquiry in 1985. In 1986 James Stirling was commissioned to design a less destructive alternative, but this was delayed by a further campaign and inquiry over the loss of the existing listed buildings.

In 1989 the Planning Inspector overruled the policy of retaining historic buildings on the premise that the new building 'might turn out to be a

The main street elevation of 60 Threadneedle Street **064**. No. 125 Old Broad Street **092** and Tower 42 **095** are visible behind.

71

Number One Poultry  forms the corner of Queen Victoria Street and Poultry. A pedestrian route connects the two streets through the building.

masterpiece'. Stirling died in 1992, and the scheme was carried on by his business partner, Michael Wilford. With its heavy masonry and coloured stripes, it looked dated when it was completed in 1997, long after the heyday of postmodernism, and seems even more so today. After so much trouble, the result is fussy and gimmicky. The best feature is the pedestrian route through the colourful central rotunda, its blues and reds echoed in the corner clock face. Its symmetry is striking when viewed from Cornhill, but perhaps Prince Charles was right when he said that it looks like a pre-war wireless.

Immediately next to Stirling's masterpiece, 80 Cheapside **070** is almost exactly contemporary, designed and completed in 1996 by Fitzroy Robinson, yet with a far cooler palette. Across the road Sheppard Robson and Pringle Brandon's 1 Old Jewry **071**, finished in 2008 as a pre-let to the software and services firm Fidessa Group, demonstrates the crisp, stone-clad, well-mannered design now favoured in the Bank Conservation Area. The combination of Portland stone and French limestone is part pre-cast panels, part hand-fixed, and neatly done.

The most stimulating neighbour to Number One Poultry is on its south side: 60 Queen Victoria Street **072** of 2000, which also has a triangular plan. Any similarity ends there, however. Foggo Associates' elevations are clad in pre-patinated bronze, almost a verdigris colour, with a subtle combination of delicacy and solidity, and capped by a perforated projecting brise-soleil. With its intriguing and mysterious hints of Islamic, Gothic and Piranesian influence, it makes a distinctive and distinguished addition to the street. It may be overwhelmed, however, by construction on the 1.2-hectare plot opposite – one of the largest development sites in the centre of the City – on the south side of Queen Victoria Street stretching down to Cannon Street.

Walbrook Square **073** has demolished the wilful and woeful post-war blocks of Bucklersbury House, once the headquarters of Legal & General, and offers the

No. 1 Old Jewry **071** occupies the north side of Poultry, opposite Number One Poultry **069**.

The metallic finish of 60 Queen Victoria Street **072**, seen here at the junction with Queen Street, makes a striking contrast with the stone buildings near by.

The open loggia of New Court **074** on St Swithin's Lane provides the entrance to the offices above and a way through to the churchyard of St Stephen Walbrook.

opportunity to reinstate the medieval pattern of lanes and reassemble the Temple of Mithras in its proper position, decades after its clumsy excavation and reconstruction at street level in the 1960s. An initial scheme was granted planning permission in 2007, designed by Atelier Foster Nouvel (the 'starchitect' group set up by Norman Foster and Jean Nouvel). This comprised four new blocks, the tallest with a domed skyline rising to 104 metres, with a futuristic chamfered organic quality reminiscent of Nouvel's One New Change (**023**; see chapter 1) but on a giant scale. It was nicknamed 'The Cloud' or 'Darth Vader's Helmet'. The original developer, the Spanish property company Metrovacesa, was replaced by Bloomberg, which discarded Jean Nouvel. Foster + Partners, left in sole charge (with Lord Foster taking a strong personal interest), has designed something rather quieter to meet its new client's more anonymous requirements. The project will contain two triangular volumes, a 50,000-square-metre headquarters for Bloomberg and a 23,000-square-metre speculative office block, due to be finished at the end of 2015. Bloomberg's existing London office in Finsbury Square (**235**; see chapter 8) is unaffectionately known by staff as 'the Death Star', and some people fear the name will transfer to the new building.

Walbrook Square, the Mansion House and the exquisite church of St Stephen Walbrook by Christopher Wren are overlooked by two more very recent developments. Praise from all quarters has already been heaped on Rothschild's New Court, St Swithin's Lane **074**. With its important landscaping and street works finally finished in early 2012, it is a remarkable building, the first permanent structure in London for Rem Koolhaas's OMA (Office for Metropolitan Architecture). Unlike at Walbrook Square, Koolhaas and executive architect Allies and Morrison have had to work with the very tight and restricted site occupied by Rothschild bank for more than 200 years in a succession of premises, the last a building by Fitzroy Robinson of 1965. Now 13,000 square

Viewed across the
construction site of
Walbrook Square **073**, the
'Sky Pavilion' of New Court
074 rises dramatically
above the curved roof
of The Walbrook **076**.
The distinctive shape of
30 St Mary Axe **106** appears
behind the Aviva Tower
104 and the spire of
St Stephen Walbrook.

The south-west corner of The Walbrook **076** forms the junction of Cannon Street and Walbrook.

THE WALBROOK BUILDING

metres of new offices have cleverly been fitted in, accommodating all Rothschild's staff in one place, with the added trick of persuading the City Corporation's planners to breach their height restrictions around the Bank. This allowed Koolhaas's extravagant Cubist four-storey 'Sky Pavilion', which accommodates executive dining, boardrooms and a Panorama Room. More inclusive is the public access at ground level. Whereas recent infill schemes near by, such as Hamilton Associates' 8–10 Mansion House Place **075**, provide impenetrable walls of beige glazed bricks, the generosity and permeability of the Rothschild entrance is fabulous. A new open concourse connects directly to the churchyard gardens, beautifully refurbished by Charles Funke Associates. The transparent foyer is palatial, completely minimalist except for a decorative pile of historic black Rothschild will-boxes beside the reception desk. As Kieran Long wrote in the *Evening Standard*, 'in this mix of bottom-heavy buildings working hard on flashy, over-engineered facades, Rothschild is a relief' (7 September 2011). The judges of the Royal Institute of British Architects awards in 2012, in which the building was a London category winner, praised its 'underlying, understated elegance'.

There is no such delight to be found in The Walbrook **076**, the enormous, plump, black-ribbed structure immediately to the south, designed by Foster + Partners for developer Minerva (2010). A few architectural critics have defended the billowing curves of this bulbous, armadillo-like groundscraper (with 38,000 square metres of offices and 3250 square metres of shops), and applauded the innovative use of the fibre-reinforced polymer cladding, a material used in making cars and boats. The fact that it has proved very hard to let perhaps tells a different story about how this radiator-grille architecture is perceived. Not even the pretty raised churchyard garden of St Swithin **077** off Salters' Hall Court, re-landscaped in 2010 by Charles Funke Associates, provides much relief from Foster's relentless horizontality, despite the conical camellias and the pointed, poignant memorial to Catrin Glyndŵr (daughter of the Welsh rebel Owain Glyndŵr), who died in 1413 and is buried there.

Opposite The Walbrook, on the south side of Cannon Street, Cannon Place **078** provides dramatic and gigantic counterpoint in a very different idiom. While The Walbrook is inscrutable and impenetrable, Foggo Associates' Cannon Place has its structure proudly on display, with massive mechanistic cross-bracing, similar to the Forth rail bridge, along its side elevation. At the end of Dowgate Hill a new stone entrance is included for Cannon Bridge House, which spans Upper Thames Street. Cannon Place's highly expressed struts and diagonals pay homage to the stainless-steel lattice and exoskeleton of Arup's adjoining building at 80 Cannon Street. Cannon Place's structural statistics are impressive, with 21-metre cantilevers and a span of 67.5 metres to support the offices above the railway. At street level the scheme provides a spectacular new

The churchyard garden of St Swithin **077**, Salters' Hall Court, with its camellia trees, is enclosed by The Walbrook **076**.

↓ → The structural framework of Cannon Place **078** is clearly evident at the junction with Dowgate Hill. Beneath the offices the scheme provides a spacious entrance to Cannon Street station and the Underground.

entrance to Cannon Street station with, for the first time, views of the platforms and trains from the street either side of a glass-box entrance to the offices above. A changing light-show backdrop is a welcome splash of colour to cheer passing commuters. It is regrettable that the fear of vehicle bombs has resulted in a forest of bollards outside.

West of Cannon Place, the scale is smaller in a network of older lanes and alleys, but containing some surprising contrasts with the megastructures described above. Tucked away behind Tallow Chandlers' Hall, Pellipar House at 9 Cloak Lane **079** is a witty, well-crafted gem, an extraordinary piece of contextual design sitting between the blank, panelled facade of the livery hall and an Edwardian block to its west. Jeremy Sampson Lloyd's scheme of 1991 for the Skinners' Company is full of fancy frills, the four-storey-high projecting bays ornamented with columns and twisted colonettes. The motifs of sixes and sevens refer to the ancient dispute between the Merchant Tailors and the Skinners over their order in the 'league' of livery companies.

On the pedestrianized section of Queen Street between Cannon Street and Upper Thames Street, a cluster of buildings from the late 1980s/early 1990s display a range of postmodern design tricks. No. 36 Queen Street **080** was Terry Farrell's first completed project in the City (1982–86), and was praised by Simon Bradley for its intelligent composition and panache. At the time it was something of a pioneer, easily overlooked when 'much of its Secessionist-derived detail has become over-familiar by imitation elsewhere' (*The Buildings of England*, p. 582). Sadly it is now lost to Rolfe Judd's remodelling and recladding of 2012, ticking all the environmental boxes and adding extra valuable floor space. No. 33 **081** by EPR Architects for the London Chamber of Commerce (1990), with its big, symmetrical entrance and pink and brown granite – not as good as Farrell – survives next door, for the moment. Opposite, at 62–64 Queen Street **082**, Rolfe

↓ The arched entrance, projecting bays and columns of Pellipar House, 9 Cloak Lane 079, are intricately detailed with historic references.

Judd chose a safe architectural language of brick pastiche with a smart stone centrepiece (2008). By contrast, 50 Cannon Street **083**, on the corner with Queen Street, is refreshingly crisp and petite; the original design by Alec J. Shickle in 1978 was revitalized and reclad in glass by John Robertson Architects in 1996.

The closure of Queen Street as a through route for vehicles in 1993 as part of the 'ring of steel' security measures (see p. 22) has provided the opportunity for extensive landscaping, making it a pleasant route for pedestrians and cyclists. The latest piece of the jigsaw in the City Corporation's Queen Street project is the exquisite garden on the site of the church of St Pancras (burnt in the Great Fire) in Pancras Lane **084**. This tiny space, in a niche at the back of 80 Cheapside and facing the glass rear wall of 60 Queen Victoria Street, was transformed in 2012 by Studio Weave, and features a dense array of intricately carved wooden benches, like pews. It is full of ecclesiastic and heraldic references, and deserves an interpretation board. It adds greatly to the visual delight of the City, as does Alma Boyes's gentle statue of a cordwainer near by in Watling Street, unveiled in 2002.

East of Cannon Place, the Bank of China's office at 90–96 Cannon Street **085** is another large but routine facade of polished granite with a large central window, by GMW Architects (1991), while 108 Cannon Street **086** to the east is a less successful composition of 1990 from R. Seifert & Partners, with very flat stone cladding and alternately wide and narrow windows. More interestingly, a niche on the corner with Laurence Pountney Lane contains a curious sculpture called *Break the Wall of Distrust* (1990), commissioned by the property company Speyhawk from Zurab Tsereteli, the People's Artist of the USSR. The awkwardly set-back mini-tower of 110 Cannon Street **087**, a late 1970s precinct by EPR Architects (then Elsom Pack Roberts), underwent a makeover in 2012 by MoreySmith, with a fresh external skin and a new interior. During construction the hoardings proclaimed the 'refined, exciting, bright, stylish, striking, bespoke, boutique' development of 6500 square metres – hyperbole, perhaps, but an indication of the marketing for retrofit. The result is perfectly good. Metal mesh screens flank the new entrance foyer, which is predictably furnished with designer chairs and inoffensive modern art.

Much of nearby King William Street is affected by the colossal proposals, mainly below ground, for enlarging Bank station. This is what Transport for London describes as a 'capacity project', to alleviate the severe overcrowding caused by narrow corridors and platforms (currently only 2 metres wide). A new entrance and ticket hall with lifts and escalators will be constructed at 10 King William Street (one of the City's better 1970s buildings), following the excavation of a 30-metre-deep hole, but there will also be new access from Walbrook Square **073**. Work is due to start in 2015 and finish in 2021. The removal of spoil from the tunnelling will be a serious challenge, as will sticking to the current budget of £500 million.

→ The minimalist glass box of 50 Cannon Street **083**, at the junction with Queen Street, contrasts with the Georgian terrace to the left.

↓ St Pancras Garden **084**, Pancras Lane, is an attractive public space at the rear of 80 Cheapside **070**.

The Bank of China, 90–96 Cannon Street **085**, with 80 Cannon Street and Cannon Place **078** beyond.

The sculpture *Break the Wall of Distrust* occupies a niche on the corner of 108 Cannon Street **086** and Laurence Pountney Lane.

The area to the south of Cornhill and north of Lombard Street retains a remarkable warren of narrow lanes and alleyways, and a wealth of historic fabric. This context has been respected by new development, such as 21 Lombard Street **088** by John Seifert (2000) and 20 Birchin Lane **089** by his father, Richard, in 1989 (the latter in red brick, the former in stone). The medieval George Yard, however, has been greatly widened. The north side is occupied unassumingly by the tall red brick and shallow bow windows of St Michael's House, 1 George Yard **090**, by GMW Architects in 1995.

The real shock, particularly if one emerges from the intimate confines of the George & Vulture pub and St Michael's Alley, is the monumental bulk of Barclays Bank, 2 George Yard **091**, also known as 20 Gracechurch Street. Built between 1986 and 1994, and also designed by GMW Architects, it forms a complete contrast with St Michael's House, showing the other side of the coin of this firm's output. The four-storey stone plinth to Lombard Street and Gracechurch Street is a considerable improvement, thanks to ORMS's facelift in 2009, but soaring above are three enormous round-topped towers, the tallest 87 metres high in the middle, massive and domineering in the townscape. At best, it can be described as a skyline signature building, reminiscent of the Art Deco Chrysler Building in New York but without the spire or the finesse. The City Corporation claims that it is on the fringe of the 'eastern cluster', where tall buildings are preferred, and the boundaries of the Bank Conservation Area carefully skirt the site. In reality, it is isolated and over-dominant, the central tower visible along virtually the whole length of Cheapside. It should surely now be regarded as something of a dinosaur, an unfortunate mistake, a result perhaps of those desperate days when Canary Wharf was feared by the City fathers as competition, and when the promise of investment in the City by Barclays Bank was welcomed with open arms. George Yard itself is cluttered with a group of obtrusive ventilation shafts, like a family of Martian spaceships. There is certainly scope for improvement.

Barclays Bank  towers over George Yard.

4

THE CLUSTER
OF TOWERS

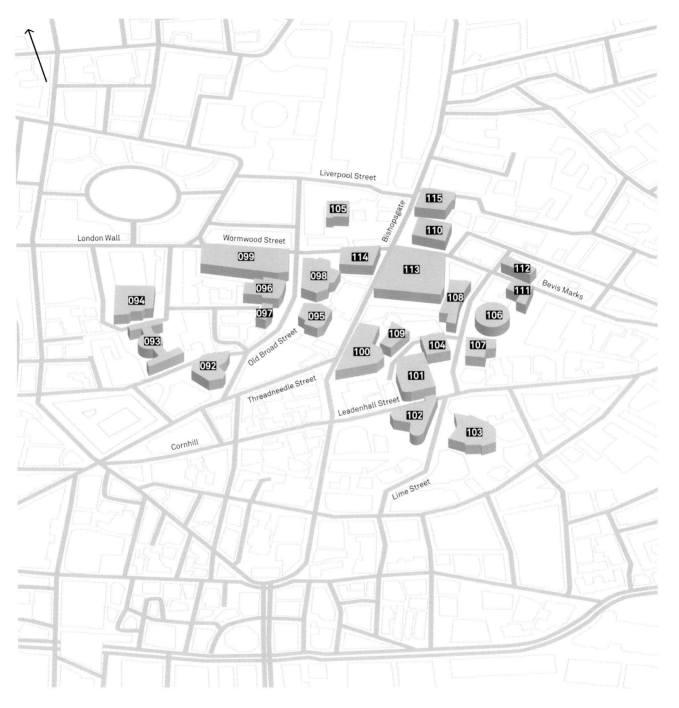

092 125 Old Broad Street 093 1 Angel Court 094 Drapers Gardens 095 Tower 42, 42 Old Broad Street 096 Pinners Hall, 105–108 Old Broad Street 097 111 Old Broad Street 098 33 Old Broad Street 099 Winchester House 100 Bishopsgate Tower, 22–24 Bishopsgate 101 Leadenhall Building 102 Lloyd's, 1 Lime Street 103 Willis Building 104 Aviva Tower, 1 Undershaft 105 Dashwood House, 69 Old Broad Street 106 30 St Mary Axe 107 Fitzwilliam House, 10 St Mary Axe 108 Exchequer Court, 33 St Mary Axe 109 1 Great St Helen's 110 Heron Tower, 110 Bishopsgate 111 6 Bevis Marks 112 60–70 St Mary Axe 113 100 Bishopsgate 114 99 Bishopsgate 115 Heron Plaza

Both London-wide and City Corporation planning policies have long favoured the idea of a cluster of towers concentrated in the north-east segment of the City, as opposed to a random scattering across the Square Mile. This has been largely based on the desirability of preserving views of the dome and western towers of St Paul's Cathedral, as a national and local symbol, and protection has been enshrined in strict planning codes since the 1930s. The St Paul's Heights controls may have been breached a few times before and after the Second World War, but many of those transgressions have since been undone and put right. The opportunities for tall buildings in the western half of the City are now extremely limited.

This chapter includes many of the most iconic new buildings in the City, and several of the most talked-about projects currently under construction. It is worth remembering that three IRA bombs were detonated in the City in the 1990s, all in this area: the first in the Stock Exchange in 1990, the second outside the Baltic Exchange in 1992 and the third in Bishopsgate in 1993. While these were catastrophic, killing and injuring innocent people and causing billions of pounds of damage to property and disruption to businesses, the destruction did enable several redevelopment schemes that might not otherwise have happened.

There is much to see in a small area. At the time of writing, development is well under way on a group of super-tall buildings that will add to the cluster. Of all the sub-areas in this book, this is the one that will change most dramatically in the next few years. It is very much a case of watching this or that space, as these new giants take shape. The high cost of these projects also means that nowhere else will be a better indicator of economic confidence.

The policy decision positively to encourage a concentration of high buildings in the eastern sector of the City, most recently enshrined in the Corporation's *City of London Tall Buildings Evidence Paper* (2010), was the result of various 1960s projects, approved in something of a planning vacuum. The Stock Exchange tower, designed by Llewelyn-Davies Weeks (now Llewelyn Davies Yeang) and executed by Fitzroy Robinson, was completed in 1969, replacing the wonderful but unlisted Exchange by Thomas Allason (1853) with a 97-metre-high, seven-sided Brutalist slab. The building lost its *raison d'être* when face-to-face trading ended in 1986, and its future looked uncertain, but it was eventually given a dramatic transformation by Grimshaw in 2008, and rechristened 125 Old Broad Street **092**. Gone are the unloved silver mullions, and instead new glazed facades extend upwards to hide the rooftop services. It looks like a fresh building.

Near by, between Throgmorton Street and Copthall Avenue, Fitzroy Robinson had also built 1 Angel Court **093** in 1979, a twenty-storey tower of chamfered, polished purple marble with an incoherent podium base. As at the Stock Exchange, a much-needed scheme by Fletcher Priest Architects, to reclad and build new low-level blocks with better public realm and pedestrian routes, has been

The emerging cluster of towers: looking west (right) from the restaurant of 30 St Mary Axe **106**, with Tower 42 **095** on the left, the Heron Tower **110** on the right and, in the foreground, the cleared site of 100 Bishopsgate **113**; and seen from the north (below) with the core of 20 Fenchurch Street **132** partially blocking the Shard in the distance. The Leadenhall Building **101**, which will fill this gap, will be almost as tall as the Heron Tower.

↓ Drapers Gardens **094**, Copthall Avenue, is a carefully sculpted essay in glass and steel.

↘ No. 125 Old Broad Street **092**, previously the Stock Exchange, has been reclad. On the left is part of the low-rise 60 Threadneedle Street **064**.

approved. On the opposite side of Copthall Avenue, Richard Seifert's thirty-storey Drapers Gardens tower (1967) was demolished in 2007, regretted by some who felt it was more elegant than his more celebrated Centre Point. The boxy glass replacement **094** by Foggo Associates, completed in 2009, lacks drama, but even with only half the number of floors achieves more lettable space in both quantity and quality, as well as three roof terraces and a pocket park. The development was sold to the investment bank Evans Randall in 2010 for £242 million. The planners were happy, too, as the reduction in height helps to separate the dome of St Paul's from the defined cluster of towers when viewed from Waterloo Bridge.

Seifert's magnum opus, however, does survive. The NatWest tower, near by at 42 Old Broad Street **095**, was completed in 1981 and rebranded in 1998 as Tower 42. Until the completion of Cesar Pelli's One Canada Square at Canary Wharf in 1991, Tower 42 was London's tallest building: 183 metres high, exactly 600 feet as Seifert planned it. GMW Architects had supervised extensive repairs after the Bishopsgate bomb, but in 1998 Fletcher Priest Architects designed a new lightweight glass entrance and remodelled the public realm; in 2000 the practice added the detached restaurant building (currently Wagamama) to the south side. This provided welcome relief, shielding the worst of the downdraughts from the soaring tower above and improving the streetscape.

Most of the other buildings on this section of the street are low-rise, notably Pinners Hall at 105–108 Old Broad Street **096**, a piece of pastiche classicism by Fitzroy Robinson (1993), and the well-mannered no. 111 **097** by Foggo Associates (1997), surprisingly subdued compared to the practice's 60 Queen Victoria Street (**072**; see chapter 3). To the north, in the shadow of Tower 42, EPR Architects' 33 Old Broad Street **098** is a late piece of chunky postmodernism (1996) that feels wearily outdated when compared to Winchester House opposite **099**, by Swanke Hayden Connell Architects, completed just three years later. Pre-let to Deutsche

Bank, the latter is elegantly modern in design, with curved corners and a gentle concave bow to the long frontage on London Wall. Clad in a honey-coloured French limestone, it would not look out of place in post-war Bath. This groundscraper, in an area of skyscrapers, fills a whole street block and more, spanning Great Winchester Street. The previous Winchester House was a group of nasty slabs built in 1968; their demolition in 1997, like that of Drapers Gardens, improved backdrop views of St Paul's. Winchester House won a City Trust Award in 2000.

It is worth taking the pedestrian route past Wagamama not only to appreciate the mass of Tower 42 but also to emerge on Bishopsgate opposite the construction site of the Pinnacle, 22–24 Bishopsgate **100**, more properly known as the Bishopsgate Tower, less properly as the Helter-skelter. If and when it is completed, it will be the highest building in the City, a new totem pole in the middle of the cluster, providing 88,000 square metres of offices and London's second-highest public viewing platform. The real-estate firm Union Investment and its architect, KPF, originally proposed a height of 307 metres, to rival the Shard south of the river, but this was scaled down to 288 metres to satisfy the Civil Aviation Authority, since the building is on the flight path to London City Airport. Planning consent was obtained in 2006, the site was sold to Arab Investments and construction began in 2008 with the sinking of the deepest piles ever in the United Kingdom, 65.5 metres below ground. The first cranes for the superstructure appeared in October 2009, but progress has stopped and started ever since. A £0.5-billion-pound shortfall was secured in June 2011, but in January 2012, having reached only the sixth storey of the core (out of sixty), work stopped again. It is presumably simply a matter of time and market circumstances. In June 2012 it was reported that Brookfield was trying to wrest control of the stalled development from Arab Investments, and had asked KPF to simplify its design in an attempt to reduce the construction cost by at least £50 million. One hopes

A pedestrian route past Tower 42 **095** links Old Broad Street and Bishopsgate. The tower has been given a new entrance and foyer.

Winchester House **099** has
a long, curving elevation to
London Wall and a shorter
frontage to Old Broad Street.

that the twisting, curling facades, clad in a snake-like skin of identical overlapping panes of glass, or the 2000 square metres of solar panels in the approved scheme are not reduced in order to save money.

The atmosphere of development fever is sustained by the colossal construction site of the Leadenhall Building **101**, round the corner in Leadenhall Street and behind the smoked-glass slabs of 4 and 6–8 Bishopsgate, the latter of which is now a seemingly inconsequential twenty-two-storey tower of 1981 by GMW Architects. Rogers Stirk Harbour + Partners' 225-metre tapering tower is destined to become another icon for London, and has been readily nicknamed the Cheesegrater in both the popular and the specialist press. This scheme, too, did not enjoy an easy birth. Adrian Penfold of developer British Land saw Graham Stirk's first sketches in 2001. Demolition of the previous building (also by GMW) was delayed first by a proposal for listing and then by the 2008 downturn, and eventually had to be done, bizarrely, from the bottom up, leaving the core until last. Proposed foundations had to be revised to reuse the existing. The massing of the new building – with forty-seven storeys and 57,000 square metres of offices, and four floors of shops and cafes – had to be reworked. Construction stalled in 2009, but at the time of writing was in full swing, following a joint-venture agreement between British Land and developer Oxford Properties Group, and a substantial pre-let to the insurance firm Aon. It is due to be completed in late 2014, and promises an extensive addition to the public realm of St Helen's Square.

For Richard Rogers, it has been a brilliant opportunity to complement his magnificent building for Lloyd's at 1 Lime Street **102**, directly opposite. Indeed, the new tower's slanting elevation to Leadenhall Street is as much in deference to his recently Grade I-listed masterpiece as to the protected view of St Paul's from Fleet Street. Designed in the 1970s and completed in 1986, Lloyd's was the first ostentatiously high-tech structure in the City, and the first to become 'world famous'. The most dynamic and controversial building in Britain at the time (humorists dubbed it 'the percolator', as successor to Lloyd's original coffee house), it almost single-handedly set the City on a course that it still follows today, breaking the shackles of conventional commercial architecture that had made the City a dull place arguably since the end of the exuberant Victorian and Edwardian era in 1914. Even today, Lloyd's seems cutting-edge and futuristic, more robotic machine than building. Fears that listing might fossilize or somehow restrict the building are surely unfounded. The innovative 'inside-out' concept, with the services on the outside (including Britain's first external wall-climbing lifts), has proved robust and flexible, allowing regular changes to be made inside (such as additional escalators), and easy maintenance and renewal of the external ducting. The uncluttered central atrium remains awe-inspiring, its glazed barrel roof a nod to that of the adjoining Victorian Leadenhall Market, and even to Joseph Paxton's Crystal Palace of 1851.

Lloyd's, 1 Lime Street **102**:
blue cranes for maintenance
and window cleaning sit
on the roof; service ducts,
pipes and emergency stairs
are located on the outside;
and inside there is a
spectacular central atrium.

Lloyd's **102** and the Willis Building **103** face each other across Lime Street, south of St Helen's Square. The proposed 'Scalpel' would replace the diminutive 52–54 Lime Street.

Norman Foster, Rogers's partner in the practice Team 4 in the 1960s, also showed great respect for the Lloyd's building when his firm was asked to design headquarters for the insurance firm Willis **103** on the north side of Lime Street. Foster's Willis Faber Building (1975) in Ipswich, one of his first triumphs, was listed Grade I in 1991, and it was fitting that Foster + Partners should be given the job for the company's gigantic new London office. The bulk (68,000 square metres) is broken into three massive curved steps, rising to twenty-nine storeys, limiting its impact on its neighbours while making best use of the site. At the corner of Fenchurch Avenue and Billiter Street a lower podium block, 25 Fenchurch Avenue, provides appropriate street scale, good public realm, shops and cafes. Four stone reliefs by the sculptor James Woodford were rescued from the previous building and relocated on the perimeter wall of the new. The whole scheme has a simple, unfussy elegance, and was a deserved winner of the New City Architecture Award in 2007. The perimeter wall and the whole setting of Lloyd's and the Willis Building are threatened by proposals for 52–54 Lime Street. In September 2012 a planning application was submitted on behalf of insurance firm W.R. Berkley for a forty-storey, 190-metre-high tower, designed by KPF as a colossal prism of glass and already dubbed 'the Scalpel'. If approved and pre-let, construction might start in 2013, and be completed in 2017.

North of Leadenhall Street, next to the Leadenhall Building, a sunken piazza provides a dramatic foreground to the Aviva Tower, 1 Undershaft **104**, formerly known as the Commercial Union building. This 1960s tower of twenty-eight storeys, designed by GMW Architects, is commonly regarded by architectural critics as the nearest approach of any office building in London to the purity of vision of Ludwig Mies van der Rohe's Seagram Building (1958) in New York. It was the first structure in the City to be taller than St Paul's. Shattered in the Baltic Exchange blast in 1992, it was reclad by RHWL Architects in 1993, with more

There is spacious public realm at the foot of the Willis Building **103** on Lime Street and Fenchurch Avenue.

careful restoration in 2003 to reinstate the bronze finish and achieve modern performance requirements. It remains one of the best of the dwindling number of truly modernist buildings in the City, and is surely another case for listing. The crisp refurbishment by Fletcher Priest Architects in 2008 of Dashwood House, 69 Old Broad Street **105** – originally a minimalist eighteen-storey box behind frontage buildings by Yorke Rosenberg Mardall (1976) – achieves a similar effect but without the grand setting of the Aviva Tower.

The eventual demolition, after much wringing of hands by conservationists, of the severely damaged Baltic Exchange in 1995 created a large development opportunity on the east side of St Mary Axe, running through to Bury Street. In 1996 Foster + Partners and landowner Trafalgar House proposed a super-skyscraper on the site, 386 metres and ninety-two storeys high, to be called the Millennium Tower. It would have been the highest building in Europe (far higher than Canary Wharf or indeed the eventual Shard in Southwark) and the sixth highest in the world, and at the time it was firmly rejected as a step too far. The height was finally reduced after objections from the Civil Aviation Authority over the flightpath to Heathrow Airport. The site, now known as 30 St Mary Axe **106**, was sold to the reinsurance firm Swiss Re, which retained Foster + Partners to design its headquarters. Foster's extraordinary architectural statement has become a visual symbol for the City, virtually on a par with the dome of St Paul's, and – with the London Eye, the Houses of Parliament and Tower Bridge – an emblem of London. That is no small achievement for a mere office block.

The design of the Swiss Re tower was supported by Jocelyn Stevens, then chairman of English Heritage, and approved without a public inquiry. When completed in 2003 it was the first new skyscraper (discounting the lump of Barclays Bank, described in chapter 3) in the City for more than twenty years. As an instantly popular landmark it paved the way for a new generation of towers,

The Aviva Tower, 1 Undershaft **104**, is seen from Lime Street with St Helen's Square in the foreground.

The 'Gherkin', 30 St Mary Axe **106**, soars above Fitzwilliam House **107** and the pinnacles of St Andrew Undershaft, with the edge of the Aviva Tower **104** on the left. It has a complex geometry.

even though it took some time to let. Quite why everyone calls it 'the Gherkin' is odd, since it is more like a Zeppelin airship balanced on end than a gherkin or any other vegetable in terms of form and colour. Its shape, with the bulging tower, is a clever way of creating more public realm at ground level (hard-landscaped with inscriptions of quirky poetry). The shaded spiral of lozenge-shaped panes has more of a fairground quality than the proposed Pinnacle, the 'Helter-skelter'. Claims for its low energy use and natural ventilation system have been queried. Its smooth profile, with no extrusions for services or equipment, is achieved by the provision of a separate building to house the plant, a six-storey glass box known as 20 Bury Street, with Soseki restaurant on the ground floor.

While 30 St Mary Axe takes all the plaudits, the drama is helped by its surprise factor and setting among smaller buildings. Spare a thought for Fitzwilliam House, 10 St Mary Axe **107**, designed in a Beaux Arts style by Hamilton Associates in 1991, or Exchequer Court at no. 33 **108**, a seven-storey banded-stone pastiche by Fitzroy Robinson (1995) directly opposite. Fitzroy Robinson's nearby scheme at Cunard Place (1997) is equally restrained. An even more conscious attempt to mend the disjuncture of the area and repair the erosion of intimate spaces and alleys was made by John Robertson Architects at 1 Great St Helen's **109** in 1998, an attractive convex green-glass curtain wall between sandstone uprights. It gives some dignity and enclosure to the adjacent church and its forecourt. The dreadful chasm of the 1970s vehicle ramp remains, however, slightly mitigated by Julian Opie's light feature *Three Men Walking* (2011) on St Mary Axe. This is a permanent spin-off from the Corporation's annual Great St Helen's Sculpture Project, which sees a changing display of temporary public art in the environs of the church.

The prominence of 30 St Mary Axe as a familiar landmark, including spectacular views from outside the City (at Whitechapel and Commercial Road,

↗ Michael Craig-Martin's *Hammer 2011*, part of the 2012 Great St Helen's Sculpture Project, on display at the foot of 30 St Mary Axe **106**, with Lloyd's **102** in the background.

→ The Beaux-Arts entrance of Fitzwilliam House, 10 St Mary Axe **107**, forms a perfect square to the street.

No. 1 Great St Helen's **109**, viewed from St Mary Axe, provides visual termination to the end of Undershaft. In the left foreground is the Aviva Tower **104**; to the right, in the background, is Tower 42 **095**.

for example), is soon to disappear. The completion of the Heron Tower, 110 Bishopsgate **110**, in March 2011 was the first visual challenge, and more are to come. At forty-six storeys and 230 metres (including the mast), the Heron Tower is currently the tallest in the City, built as speculative offices by developer Gerald Ronson and designed by KPF with Lee Polisano as lead architect. Ferociously opposed by English Heritage because of its height, it eventually won approval following a long public inquiry. The Mayor of London at the time, Ken Livingstone, was a strong supporter, liking the promise of public access to the top (not achieved at the Gherkin or Tower 42, and not yet provided, incidentally, at the Heron Tower). Ronson's idea was to encourage multi-letting by creating stacks of three-storey office 'villages', each of 3500 square metres with its own square atrium. The external skeleton expresses this model. All the services (including London's fastest lifts, at 7 metres per second) are on the south side, where the building rises sheer from the pavement of Camomile Street, thus allowing big free floor plates facing north, reducing solar gain and saving 60% on carbon emissions. Any views south over the City from the lifts are masked by thousands of small square photovoltaic cells, required by the current mayor, Boris Johnson, and the Greater London Authority. The foyer is adorned by an enormous fish tank, which is cleaned every three days by a team of divers. Despite such attractions, the space has proved hard to let; just twelve storeys had been taken by February 2012.

Closer to 30 St Mary Axe, and immediately overlooking its plaza, 6 Bevis Marks **111** is under construction, a sixteen-storey building with an all-weather roof terrace, designed by Fletcher Priest Architects. Just north of Bevis Marks, 60–70 St Mary Axe **112** will be bigger, 90 metres and twenty-four storeys high. A distinctive semi-elliptical design by Foggo Associates, nicknamed the 'Can of Ham', awaits the go-ahead and closure of existing leases, and would replace Elsworth Sykes Partnership's Eagle Star building (1988) at no. 60. Rather like a two-dimensional version of the Gherkin, its bulge is intended to reduce its apparent bulk on the street.

Even bigger, and due for completion in 2013/14, is 100 Bishopsgate **113**, a huge site where three new buildings will provide more than 80,000 square metres of Grade A offices for developers Brookfield and Great Portland Estates, plus shops, a livery hall and a new public library. The main element is a forty-storey, 165-metre-high tower, rather four-square compared to the other emerging towers despite a more complex base, and not the most exciting scheme to emerge from the drawing boards of either Allies and Morrison or Woods Bagot, which are collaborating on the design. Perhaps significantly, 100 Bishopsgate is one of the few proposed towers not to have been given a nickname. It promises to make 99 Bishopsgate **114** opposite – a twenty-six-storey slab and podium of 1976 by GMW Architects, stripped back to its frame and reclad in blue and white

A long view of the Heron Tower, 110 Bishopsgate **110**, from the Barbican's raised walkway, looks across the rooftops of Moorgate and Finsbury Circus.

Exchequer Court, 33 St Mary Axe **108**, occupies a long frontage on the west side of the street. Views of the Heron Tower **110** rising behind on Bishopsgate will disappear when 100 Bishopsgate **113** is built.

The podium block of
99 Bishopsgate **114**; its
tower is set back behind.

panels by the same firm in 1996 – seem interestingly slender. Leases on the previous buildings on the site of 100 Bishopsgate expired in 2011, and bulldozers moved in; one of the casualties was Kansallis House, 80 Bishopsgate, rebuilt only in 1995 by Fitzroy Robinson after the IRA bomb. The cleared construction site temporarily provided the tiny church of St Ethelburga with some breathing space, and tremendous oblique views of the Gherkin.

The current uninterrupted views of and from the Heron Tower to the north-east will also disappear. Following planning consent in January 2011, demolition and construction quickly commenced for the Heron Plaza **115**, a 135-metre tower immediately next door, set back from Bishopsgate to create the eponymous plaza, and with applied patinated copper specified as the cladding by PLP Architecture (Lee Polisano's offshoot of KPF). It will provide exclusive flats, restaurants and what the developer, Heron International, rather boastfully claims to be 'the first purpose-built luxury hotel in central London for thirty years'. Some may dispute that.

Before long this spate of new buildings will produce the effect intended by the cluster policy. Those 360-degree panoramas from roof terraces, sky rooms and viewing platforms will eventually all be looking at one another, if not actually shaking hands. From further away, the profiles of individual buildings will coalesce into a less distinct mass; but the City will have gained its group of towers to rival Canary Wharf.

The City at daybreak, looking south from the top of 30 St Mary Axe **106**. The Willis Building **103** and Lloyd's **102** are in the foreground, with the Shard across the river at London Bridge.

5

FENCHURCH STREET
AND MONUMENT

116 Landmark House, 99 Fenchurch Street/69 Leadenhall Street **117** Zurich Building, 90 Fenchurch Street **118** 76–86 Fenchurch Street **119** Lloyd's Register **120** Vitro Building, 60 Fenchurch Street **121** AIG Building, 58 Fenchurch Street **122** Fen Court **123** 120 Fenchurch Street **124** 8–13 Lime Street **125** New London House **126** 64–74 Mark Lane **127** Corn Exchange, 55 Mark Lane **128** 50 Mark Lane **129** Minster Court **130** Plantation Place **131** Plantation Lane **132** 20 Fenchurch Street **133** 10 Fenchurch Street **134** 168 Fenchurch Street/70 Gracechurch Street **135** Allianz House, 60 Gracechurch Street **136** Gracechurch House, 55–58 Gracechurch Street **137** 40 Gracechurch Street **138** Svenska House, 55 King William Street **139** 47–51 King William Street **140** Regis House, 39–45 King William Street **141** 24 King William Street **142** 6–8 Eastcheap **143** 10 Eastcheap **144** Pinnacle House, 23–26 St Dunstan's Hill **145** 24 Monument Street **146** Monument Yard

↓ The symmetrical elevation of the Zurich Building, 90 Fenchurch Street **117**, faces the junction with Leadenhall Street. To the left is 1 Aldgate **294**.

↘ Two acute corner buildings – Landmark House **116** on the left and 77 Leadenhall Street on the right – are viewed from Aldgate.

Fenchurch Street lies outside the City's preferred area for tall buildings, but is nevertheless an important part of the concentration of financial activities in the eastern half of the City. The streets around Fenchurch Street station and running north from Eastcheap have seen wholesale reconstruction since 1990. Fenchurch Street itself is now lined by an impressive variety of modern office buildings, which illustrate the changing requirements and fashions for the working environment.

At its northern end, occupying the acute corner, Landmark House, 99 Fenchurch Street and 69 Leadenhall Street **116**, is a typically chunky stone-clad design from the Terry Farrell Partnership (now Farrells), dating from 1987, when postmodernism was at its zenith. Indeed, following the recladding of 36 Queen Street (**080**; see chapter 3), it might be Farrell's most list-able work in the City. It is one of several near-contemporary buildings that form a small cluster displaying a wide range of the nuances and gimmickry of the time: Towergate, 77 Leadenhall Street, by GMW Architects, also from 1987; 78 Leadenhall Street by Ley, Colbeck & Partners (1991); 80–84 Leadenhall Street by Hamilton Associates (1990); and the Zurich Building at 90 Fenchurch Street **117** by EPR Architects (1990), which has a formulaic symmetry and heavy stone cladding. The setting of this group will change with the completion in 2014 of 76–86 Fenchurch Street **118**, a seventeen-storey block by Foster + Partners for the developer Shieldpoint with 32,000 square metres of offices above shops. The design of stone-framed glass is intended to appear monolithic and robust.

The real fun starts further south. When Richard Rogers Partnership (now Rogers Stirk Harbour + Partners) was commissioned in 1993 to provide new accommodation for Lloyd's Register **119**, the brief stipulated that T.E. Collcutt's substantial listed building (1901), which occupies the corner of Fenchurch Street and Lloyd's Avenue, be kept, extended and refurbished. Without a main street frontage, this limited the chance to repeat the architectural tour de force of

1 Lime Street (**102**; see chapter 4), but it offered other opportunities. The site, which is approached through an arch in 71 Fenchurch Street, occupies that of the former church of St Katherine Coleman (demolished in 1926). Best viewed close-up from the passageway of St Katherine's Row next to the East India Arms pub, the design solution has many similarities with the practice's 88 Wood Street (**035**; see chapter 2), which was built at the same time. Transparent glass protected by a sophisticated system of louvres, slim towers, external wall-climber lifts and the hallmark splashes of blue, red and yellow create a delicate and subtle composition. The landscape of slate shingle, monoliths and trees respects the historic graveyard, and – enhanced by the fountain – is an oasis of calm. Completed in 2000, the building won a Civic Trust Award and the World Architecture prize for the Best Commercial Building in 2002.

While Lloyd's Register is tucked away, apart from a very low-key frontage on Fenchurch Place, the Vitro Building at 60 Fenchurch Street **120** is extremely prominent, on the corner with Fenchurch Place and backing on to a public space. This twelve-storey, 8000-square-metre block by John McAslan + Partners is well proportioned, said by some critics to be inspired by the minimalist school of Ludwig Mies van der Rohe, but actually more complex than that. When finished in 2004 it provided a good contrast with the vertical ribs of the AIG Building next door at 58 Fenchurch Street **121**, designed by KPF and winner of the New City Architecture Award in 2003. The rear of no. 58, with its long frontage to Mark Lane, and the Vitro Building provide the enclosure to the public square and approach to Fenchurch Street station. This has been simply landscaped, and the new trees are still rather small for the scale of the buildings. It might be an opportunity, perhaps, for some public art.

On the north side of Fenchurch Street, Fen Court **122** was greatly improved by the City Corporation in 2008. This intimate space is the former churchyard of

↗ The setting of Lloyd's Register **119**, behind 71 Fenchurch Street, is enhanced by mature trees in the historic graveyard of St Katherine Coleman.

→ The Vitro Building, 60 Fenchurch Street **120**, is at the corner with Fenchurch Place.

The AIG Building **121** has its main frontage to Fenchurch Street (left). Windows to Mark Lane are carefully detailed (below).

St Gabriel Fenchurch, sensitively landscaped with a few chest tombs and flower beds protected by neat, low box hedges. To commemorate the abolition of transatlantic slavery in 1807, a moving artwork was commissioned in conjunction with Black British Heritage from Michael Visocchi, and opened in September 2008 by Archbishop Desmond Tutu. The composition is full of ambiguity. Seventeen sugar canes spring from the ground beside a preacher's pulpit or slave auctioneer's block, which is inscribed with words from Lemn Sissay's poem 'The Gilt of Cain', combining language from the Stock Exchange trading floor and the Old Testament. It depicts, perhaps, the guilt of cane.

It is to be hoped that this peaceful setting will not be spoiled by the imminent redevelopment of 120 Fenchurch Street **123**, where the low-rise smoked-glass block on the corner with Fen Court is to be replaced by a 58,000-square-metre office block designed by Eric Parry Architects. Optimistically described in the brochures as 'crystalline', the building (for developers Saxon Land and Greycoat CORE) has been scaled down from the original proposal for a thirty-nine-storey tower to seventeen storeys of offices above shops, but it could still overwhelm Fen Court. The set-back top floors are unlikely to be as invisible as the visualizations suggest. It is important, too, that the retail element is contained within the development itself and does not encroach on the tranquillity of Fen Court. A safer model might have been 8–13 Lime Street **124** of 2009, where Rolfe Judd's solid stone facade fits effortlessly into its context.

As with other mainline stations in the City, such as Liverpool Street and the now-defunct Holborn Viaduct, Fenchurch Street station was exploited for its 'air rights' (the valuable space above it). A rather lumpy scheme by Fitzroy Robinson over the platforms was completed in 1987, and is very much a child of its time. Next to the station, the smaller office tower of New London House **125**, with its inset corners, was given a new glass curtain wall and two-storey podium of

↗ The architect's visualization of the proposal for 120 Fenchurch Street **123** shows the set-back top floors blending with the sky.

→ Michael Visocchi's installation stands in the peaceful public gardens of Fen Court **122**.

warm brown stone in 1992 by Allies and Morrison, and was the practice's first scheme in the City. Occupying the rest of the south side of London Street, and indeed the whole street block through to Crutched Friars, is the construction site of 64–74 Mark Lane **126**, Bennetts Associates' latest office scheme in the City. This scheme for the developers Stanhope and Mitsui rises to sixteen storeys on London Street, matching the scale and materials of 58 and 60 Fenchurch Street, but steps dramatically down to Hart Street to respect the setting of the medieval church of St Olave. Spectacular winter gardens are planned under the sloping glass roof with southerly views to the river and beyond, with the high-level green walls of Bennetts Associates' new hotel in Pepys Street (**310**; see chapter 11) in the foreground.

South of Hart Street, most of the east side of Mark Lane is occupied by no. 55 **127**, Corn Exchange, an eight-storey range with six prominent projecting glazed bays, the rest clad in grey stone, designed by Fitzroy Robinson in 1996. No. 50 **128**, by Trehearne and Norman, Preston and Partners in 1990, is unusually narrow. Its single bay with strange horizontal pediment is seemingly squeezed between no. 55 and the bland hulk of Knollys House beyond, with its reflective glass and clutter of shops facing Byward Street and Great Tower Street.

The west side of Mark Lane is taken up for most of its length by the arcaded rear of Minster Court **129**, one of the most extraordinary buildings of its time (1987–91). It has been variously described as populist, phantasmagorical, hideous and wonderful. Its steep roofs and sharp gables soar into the sky like those of Dracula's castle or Gormenghast, and it was a worthy set for Cruella De Vil in the remake of *101 Dalmatians* (1996). Love it or loathe it, it is surely GMW Architects' most remarkable contribution to the City. The Wagnerian pomposity is best appreciated at its gated and forbidding main entrance on Mincing Lane, where Althea Wynne's sculpture *Three Horses*, installed above the steps in 1990 and inspired by the carved horses on the Doge's Palace in Venice, is pure theatrical kitsch. The scheme comprises three blocks, linked by glass roofs in the manner of an outsize conservatory, but there is no public way through to Mark Lane. The architect played the game to the end: even the little watchman's hut at the entrance to the underground car park on Mark Lane is clad in the same stone, with a pointed lead roof.

A totally different approach to redeveloping a complete street block was taken by Arup and British Land, its client, in 2004 for the Plantation Place complex **130**, west of Mincing Lane, extending from Fenchurch Street to Great Tower Street. The development is divided into two blocks. Facing Fenchurch Street, Plantation Place itself rises to fifteen storeys and 68 metres, and is simply detailed with the upper parts largely in glass. The best elevation is to Rood Lane, making a fine juxtaposition with the Wren tower of the guild church of St Margaret Pattens. Plantation Place South, or 60 Great Tower Street, is lower

Minster Court **129** rises dramatically above Mark Lane; the main entrance, on Mincing Lane, is even more theatrical.

Plantation Place **130**, as
seen in early 2012 from
the east end of Fenchurch
Street. No. 20 Fenchurch
Street **132** now rises
spectacularly above it.

and has finer details, using structural stone in a chequerboard pattern, with projecting blocks seemingly swung open like a giant Advent calendar to reveal the windows. Its clean white stone makes the brown chamfered shapes of Richard Seifert's 51 Eastcheap (1987) seem dated.

A generously wide, colourfully decorated internal public route runs north–south through the development. The atrium of Plantation Place is particularly impressive, even if the steps up and then down are rather inconsiderate. Separating the two blocks east–west is a new pathway, Plantation Lane **131**. The 1996 Turner Prize nominee Simon Patterson was commissioned to turn this twenty-first-century alley into an artwork, called *Time and Tide*. A light-box screen 6 metres high and 41 metres long portrays an image of the moon and is stunningly lit at night, but what catches the eye are the narrow granite paving slabs engraved with the names of ancient City streets and institutions interspersed with the chronology of historic events. As the lane bends, narrows and widens, so the parallel timelines and words disappear and re-emerge.

Amid such finesse it is tempting to be overwhelmed by the huge and controversial development immediately west. The 150-metre-high tower of the 'Walkie-Talkie', 20 Fenchurch Street **132**, is outside the City Corporation's preferred cluster, but was approved following a public inquiry in 2007. The design by the Uruguayan-born architect Rafael Viñoly was one point of controversy, looking more like an old-style mobile phone or an electric razor than the conventional 'slim' towers of the 'Pinnacle', 'Gherkin' or Heron (**100**, **106** and **110**; see chapter 4). Its location was another: it is closer than any other tall City building to the river, and threatens the setting and the World Heritage Site status of the Tower of London. Rights of lights problems also held up construction at first, but once these matters were resolved and suitably compensated the core rose at an impressive speed in 2012, and the tower is due to be completed in 2014. At its

← No. 20 Fenchurch Street **132**, known as the 'Walkie-Talkie' and shown here in visualization, makes a dramatic addition to the City skyline.

↓ Plantation Lane **131** runs from east to west between the two blocks of Plantation Place, framing the tower of St Margaret Pattens.

apex, on top of 64,000 square metres of offices, the three-storey observation deck or 'sky garden' promises to be fully and freely accessible to the public, but – as at the Heron Tower – it remains to be seen exactly what that will mean. Meanwhile Land Securities and Canary Wharf Group, the developers, are advertising their product as 'the curve that's ahead of its time', 'the building with more on top', 'sometimes the wrong way up is the right way up', and 'big thinkers need big floors'. Modifications to the floor plans have sought to improve efficiency, and the building should now accommodate 8000 workers rather than the original estimate of 6500. The insurance firm Markel was the first tenant to sign up, in June 2012, taking two upper floors at £65 per square foot for a twenty-year term. This was heralded as something of a coup in what had been a lacklustre lettings market. The tower has no podium; even though the base is substantially set back from the original street lines to provide wider pavements, arguably to the detriment of the tight grain of Rood and Philpot lanes, the City Corporation is planning to manage traffic so that the area can cope with a large influx of people. It remains to be seen whether the 'Walkie-Talkie' feels like one landmark too many.

Everything else near by feels modest, if not self-effacing. John Robertson Architects' refurbishment and extension in 2010 of 10 Fenchurch Street **133**, originally by Denys Lasdun in 1985, is severely plain with facades of planar glass. No. 168 Fenchurch Street **134**, also known as 70 Gracechurch Street, feels bulky despite being only eight storeys. First designed by John Simpson & Partners but taken over by BDP, it has horizontal fins that produce a strong, curved corner above the Marks and Spencer store on the ground floor. Completed in 2002, the development included the excavation to a depth of 20 metres of the Roman forum (more remains were found at 21 Lime Street, where Wilkinson Eyre Architects' scheme remains in abeyance). Allianz House, 60 Gracechurch Street **135**, of 1997, designed by the Halpern Partnership, occupies the southern corner with Fenchurch

↖ No. 168 Fenchurch Street and 70 Gracechurch Street **134** occupies a prominent position on the north-east corner of the junction.

← Allianz House, 60 Gracechurch Street **135**, provides a long street frontage south of the corner with Fenchurch Street.

Street with a gentler curve. The upper six storeys are supported on large double-height stone columns. Gracechurch House, 55–58 Gracechurch Street **136**, is a stone-faced classical pastiche by Sheppard Robson, built in 1992. Another low-key insertion is no. 40 opposite **137**, completed in 2011. Gibberd retained the facade of no. 37, dating from 1914, and added a new bookend to the north, with six storeys of stone and two storeys of glass set back on top, altogether providing 10,000 square metres of new offices. It is a graceful addition to a street still dominated by the unfortunate bulk of Barclays Bank (**091**; see chapter 3).

The desire to maintain Wren and Hooke's post-Fire of London Monument as a landmark has rightly restricted the scale of development in its vicinity, despite the obvious temptation for aggrandizement on the approach to London Bridge. In 1991 Sheppard Robson completed Svenska House, 55 King William Street **138**, in a similar style but reduced scale to the practice's Gracechurch House, with curved corners to the street junctions and a marble-clad entrance facing the beginning of Eastcheap. A plaque proudly states that it won the Copper Roofing Competition in 1991. Next door, 47–51 King William Street **139** was rebuilt by Jestico + Whiles in 1997, with seven storeys but modest and unfussy. Regis House, 39–45 King William Street **140**, a larger four-square block (also 1997) by GMW Architects, closely mimics the massing and faintly Egyptian style of the magnificent Adelaide House (John Burnett, 1925) by the bridge. Across the road, 24 King William Street **141** is similarly restrained. It was built by Ronald Ward and Partners in 1989, with stained glass by Goddard & Gibbs. Proposals to redevelop no. 33, on the west side, for developer Greycoat and investment company Topland are currently with John Robertson Architects. Planning permission was granted in June 2012 for a ten-storey all-glass replacement, no bigger than the existing (described as a 'carbuncle' by *Skyscraper News* in April 2012) but designed to fit the site, with a curved corner to Arthur Street.

↗ Gracechurch House, 55–58 Gracechurch Street **136**, is seen from the north.

→ No. 40 Gracechurch Street **137**, on the west side at the corner of Lombard Court, also incorporates the retained facade of no. 37.

↓ Looking down from the Monument to Monument Yard **146** and the pavilion roof, covered in mirrors.

↓↓ Nos 47–51 King William Street **139** makes an elegant junction with Monument Street.

The south side of Eastcheap is a modest ensemble of old and new. The flat-fronted nos 6–8 **142**, by Damond Lock Grabowski Partners (now DLG Architects) for Lloyd's Bank in 1990, is a multicoloured polished-stone block, which *The Buildings of England* (pp. 482–83) suggests 'rummages in Terry Farrell's box of tricks'. No. 10 **143** next door is more satisfactory, finished in honey-coloured stone, only six storeys and with a pretty corner turret to Botolph Lane; it was designed in 1986 by the Whinney Mackay-Lewis Partnership. Nos 30–40, built between St Mary at Hill and Idol Lane in 1992, are virtually a facsimile of the Victorian row that stood there previously.

The steep slopes of both St Mary at Hill and St Dunstan's Hill offer tremendous framed views of the Shard across the river at London Bridge, and back up the hill to Minster Court. Pinnacle House at 23–26 St Dunstan's Hill **144** is another example of small-scale contextual infill from the early 1990s, by the Elsworth Sykes Partnership. Using orange bricks and red metal window frames, this also has a corner turret, which defers to the gothic steeple of St Dunstan-in-the-East across the road. The exquisite garden among the ruins of the church is a frequent and deserving winner in the Small Public Gardens category of the London Garden Squares Competition, organized and judged by the London Gardens Society.

The most recent addition to the setting of the Monument is also the closest to it. No. 24 Monument Street **145**, previously occupied by the grim Centurion House (1984) and the timber footings of the original London Bridge, is being replaced by a new block designed by David Walker Architects, to be completed in 2013. It comprises 8000 square metres of speculative offices and an arcade of shops on the north, east and west sides, wrapping around Monument House and keeping the height well below the viewing gallery of the Monument and the church of St Magnus the Martyr opposite. Someone, surely, will grab the chance to open a bakery in Pudding Lane. There are ideas, too, for the redevelopment by John Robertson Architects of 11–19 Monument Street, on the north side; the proposed sweeping curves have been likened to the shape of a grand piano.

Improvements to the public realm of Monument Yard **146** were carried out in 2007 as part of the City Corporation's Street Scene Challenge initiative. Bere:Architects was commissioned to design a new sculptural pavilion for public toilets, and chose to treat the walls as a gabion, with stones encased in metal mesh. The roof is covered with fifty mirrors, which reflect the golden orb for those looking down from the viewing gallery of the Monument. Timber decking, bollards and seats provide people with somewhere to linger. The Monument itself, 61 metres high, was restored in 2009, since when it has received a 35% increase in visitors and the City Heritage Award in 2010. The panorama from the top is tremendous: well worth the 311 steps and the modest admission charge.

↓ Regis House, 39–45 King William Street **140**, defers to the architectural language and proportion of Adelaide House to the right. The Shard rises behind on the south side of London Bridge.

→ Pinnacle House, 23–26 St Dunstan's Hill **144**; Minster Court **129** forms a backdrop to this steeply sloping street.

← No. 10 Eastcheap **143** at the corner of Botolph Lane, with nos 6–8 **142** beyond and 24 King William Street **141** in the distance.

6

CHANCERY LANE
AND FLEET STREET

147 33 Holborn Circus **148** New Fetter Place, 8–10 Fetter Lane **149** 43 Fetter Lane **150** 1 New Fetter Lane **151** New Street Square **152** Athene Place, 66 Shoe Lane **153** St Andrew's House **154** Ray House, 6 St Andrew Street **155** 1 Gunpowder Square **156** 10–15 Fetter Lane **157** Rolls Building **158** John Wilkes statue **159** 122 Chancery Lane **160** Halsbury House, 35 Chancery Lane **161** 48 Chancery Lane **162** 40–45 Chancery Lane **163** 90 Fetter Lane **164** 3–5 Norwich Street **165** 40 Furnival Street **166** 20 Furnival Street **167** 34–35 Furnival Street **168** Finlaison House, 15–17 Furnival Street **169** 20 Cursitor Street **170** 131–141 Fleet Street **171** 120 Fleet Street **172** 10 St Bride Street **173** *Resolution* **174** 65 Fleet Street **175** Magpie Alley mural **176** 4 Bouverie Street **177** 21 Whitefriars Street **178** 8 Salisbury Square **179** St George and the Dragon sculpture **180** Northcliffe House, 26–28 Tudor Street **181** 21 Tudor Street **182** 1 Tudor Street **183** 60 Victoria Embankment **184** New Carmelite House **185** 100 Victoria Embankment

The western side of the City, beyond the valley of the Fleet River, was always outside the original Roman and medieval walls, and has developed and retained a particular character. For centuries the district was dominated by the two specialist trades of the law and the press. The foundation of the Inns of Court at the Temple, Lincoln's Inn and Gray's Inn in the seventeenth century and the Law Courts in the nineteenth encouraged a great concentration of lawyers and related service trades in their immediate vicinity. Newspapers traditionally located to this area because it was halfway between the two centres of power and news, Parliament and the financial hub.

Much has changed. Legal practices remain, ever merging and expanding, even though today – with large law firms located throughout the City and elsewhere – this district is no longer such an exclusive enclave. However, since the 1980s the journalists, newspaper offices and printing houses have almost completely gone. The fact that the national press is still known collectively as 'Fleet Street' is a real misnomer.

Some people in the property business regard this area, west of Farringdon Road and Farringdon Street, as part of the so-called 'Mid-Town', a slice of central London that runs westwards as far as Centre Point, and which embraces several new office developments in Holborn and St Giles lying within the London Borough of Camden. Some property 'experts' seem to forget that the wards of Castle Baynard and Farringdon Without are just as much part of the City of London as are Bishopsgate or Cornhill, while glibly claiming that developments in Finsbury Square, Spitalfields and even the Angel are in the City. In fact, this western section of the City remains protected from the West End by the large and exclusive enclaves of the Temple, the Law Courts, Lincoln's Inn and Gray's Inn, and the connections westwards are along the Embankment, Fleet Street and Holborn only.

It is not surprising that parts of this area have undergone enormous change since the late 1980s, and nowhere is that more evident than Fetter Lane and New Fetter Lane, running south from Holborn Circus to Fleet Street. Fetter Lane and Shoe Lane were very badly bombed in the Second World War and were largely rebuilt with dull 1950s and 1960s office slabs. One of the most prominent of these was the eleven-storey Daily Mirror Building (1960) on the corner of Holborn Circus and Fetter Lane, the last of the major newspaper offices to be rebuilt in the Fleet Street area. Its replacement at 33 Holborn Circus **147** in 2000 with Foster + Partners' new headquarters for Sainsbury's was a significant change in form and design. The elegant curved glass facade and reduced height – only eight storeys – set a new standard for Holborn Circus, improved the entrance into New Fetter Lane and enhanced views of St Paul's Cathedral from Primrose Hill. Although Foster had been working on other City schemes at the time, and had completed projects on the City fringe, 33 Holborn Circus was his first finished building actually inside the City. Sainsbury's was also a rather

The Sainsbury's
headquarters at 33 Holborn
Circus **147**. To the left the
sharp prow of New Street
Square **151** rises above
8–10 Fetter Lane **148**.

The curved entrance of
1 Plough Place **149** is part
of the development at
43 Fetter Lane, and faces
a small piazza.

unusual type of occupier for a prime City office location, gaining what it now describes as a 'Store Support Centre'.

Holborn Circus itself, previously an accident black spot where taxis and vans picked up too much speed on the unnecessarily wide carriageway, is undergoing a makeover by the City Corporation to improve safety and priority for pedestrians and cyclists, while also retaining (so the Victorian Society hopes) the central statue of Prince Albert *in situ*. That and the enhancements to the churchyard of St Andrew's by Bere:Architects could make the junction a destination rather than a place to avoid.

Immediately south of Sainsbury's, and due to be finished at the end of 2012, the ten-storey tower of 8–10 Fetter Lane **148** is being reconfigured by TateHindle as New Fetter Place, incorporating a new six-storey structure to respect and redefine the historic street pattern. Granite, zinc and glass rain-screens will provide textural variety. Next door is 43 Fetter Lane **149**, where 20,000 square metres of floor space have been provided by BFLS (2011). The new podium block, containing shops, and the narrowness of Fetter Lane, together with excellent new landscaping of the public realm to Plough Place, effectively reduce the impact of the twelve-storey tower. Opposite, 1 New Fetter Lane **150** is a strikingly elegant refit and extension of 2010 by SOM of a 1960s slab, with a new curved frontage picking up the street line.

All this is an appetizer for the most eye-catching development to have happened in this part of the City in recent years. New Street Square **151** and New Fetter Lane, developed at a cost of £200 million by Land Securities, is a comprehensive and imaginative piece of urban planning. For the architect, Bennetts Associates, the design brief was a real challenge and the eventual solution a source of considerable satisfaction, given the height constraints in this part of the City to protect views of St Paul's Cathedral from Waterloo Bridge

→ At 1 New Fetter Lane
150, a curved frontage has
been added to the 1960s
slab behind; to the right are
the jagged projections of
New Street Square **151**.

and Westminster. The scheme, completed in 2008, comprises five buildings, most striking of which is the twenty-storey prow at the north end, a dramatically sharp point at the curve in the street, and an acute angle that sets up the orthogonal geometry for the rest of the scheme.

The focus of the development, however, is a generous central square linked in all directions to the surrounding streets by pedestrian routes. Shops and cafes make it a destination in its own right; it is dramatically lit after dark and attractively landscaped with some mature trees. It remains a privately owned space, however: expect a tap on the shoulder from a security guard if you try to take photographs. The scale of the other buildings reduces to reflect the context of Gough Square and Dr Johnson's house to the south. The two-storey service building that accommodates Land Security's management offices provides a neat and ingenious enclosure to the south side of the square, and its east elevation is a delightfully luxuriant green wall planted with ferns and grasses. Sustainability and low energy consumption were key to the scheme; indeed, New Street Square was the first development in the City of London to achieve the top grade of BREEAM 'Excellent' (see p. 18).

Immediately to the east, either side of Little New Street, there is potential for more comprehensive redevelopment to extend the campus-like quality of New Street Square. Land Securities has commissioned Robin Partington Architects to prepare a masterplan to replace the forbidding and now largely empty post-war blocks, most of which were designed by Richard Seifert. These include the former International Press Centre, a grim eighteen-storey building on Shoe Lane. There is an opportunity to create something with a better urban-design vision than the individual developments that have occurred already in Shoe Lane and St Andrew Street, such as Athene Place, 66 Shoe Lane **152**, by EPR Architects in 2003 or St Andrew's House **153** by Covell Matthews Wheatley

↓ New Street Square **151** comprises a series of blocks and generous public spaces.

in 1989. Ray House at 6 St Andrew Street **154**, built by the developer Helical Bar in 1999 as a pre-let to the law firm Speechly Bircham, has a certain quirkiness of design and materials that already looks rather dated. Speechly Bircham has since moved into very smart offices in New Street Square. Also quirky, but worth seeking out, is 1 Gunpowder Square **155**, designed in 1990 by Simpson Gray Associates as a careful response to the proximity of Gough Square and its tight courts and alleyways. In 1997 *The Buildings of England* (p. 502) described it as 'rather top-heavy', but with its stone-dressed red brick and jetties, reminiscent of Norman Shaw, it is well put together with some thoughtful details. Near by, in Gough Square, Jon Bickley's *Hodge* (1997) is an amusing feline memorial to Samuel Johnson.

Back on Fetter Lane, the glassy extension and refurbishment of 10–15 Fetter Lane **156**, on the corner with West Harding Street, by TateHindle in 2005 is now rather overshadowed by the drama of New Street Square. On the west side of Fetter Lane, however, the newly completed Rolls Building **157** is in such a different architectural language that it stands by itself and makes its own strong statement. Designed by Woods Bagot and completed in 2010, it was a flagship commission from the Ministry of Justice, and houses for the first time under one roof the Chancery Division, the Admiralty and Commercial Court, and the Technology and Construction Court. It is now claimed to be the largest specialist centre for the resolution of financial, business and property litigation anywhere in the world. The architecture is on a dignified if bland scale, with a curved corner to Fetter Lane and a comfortable nine-storey height to this wide portion of the street. A naturalistic statue of the politician John Wilkes **158** by James Butler (1988; Butler's first commission for the City Corporation) sits happily in the foreground. The long south-facing frontage of the Rolls Building is quietly articulated by columns and panels of limestone with grey metal mullions for the

↓ No. 1 Gunpowder Square **155** is carefully detailed to respect the scale and intimacy of nearby Gough Square.

↘ The statue of John Wilkes **158** stands in front of the Rolls Building **157** on Fetter Lane.

glass. The footprint stretches west to provide a lower-scale frontage to 22 Chancery Lane. This is a carefully finished building, designed and budgeted to last for 100 years rather than the twenty-five of the average City office block. The redevelopment of St Dunstan's House, south of the Public Records Office on Fetter Lane, offers the prospect of a welcome residential insertion into the area. David Walker Architects' scheme for seventy-six flats was granted planning permission in December 2011. The new building will greatly improve the continuity of the street frontage along Fetter Lane, enhance the setting of Clifford's Inn Gardens and reinforce the traditional palette of materials in the area. The proportions of the windows and piers are informed by the Perpendicular style of the Public Records Office, although the proposed architectural language is modern.

Chancery Lane has seen much less change than Fetter Lane. Michael Squire's narrow infill of 1991 at no. 122 **159** and BDP's Halsbury House at no. 35 **160** from the same year are contextual. The grey granite cladding of the latter is enlivened only by the entrance artwork of stained glass in the form of a map. AROS Architects gave 48 Chancery Lane **161** a new glass curtain wall in 2008, for the fund manager Halifax Life and Invista Real Estate; the building is now occupied by the National Pro Bono Centre. Bennetts Associates' scheme for Derwent London to redevelop 40–45 Chancery Lane **162** with mixed offices and shops is now proceeding. The City Corporation itself and its consultant Burns + Nice have plans to improve the public realm all along Chancery Lane, which is at present too much of a rat-run for taxis and vans, and not as attractive for pedestrians and cyclists as it might be.

The network of side streets between Chancery Lane and Fetter Lane has seen considerable piecemeal redevelopment since the late 1980s, some worth noting. Green Lloyd Architects' redevelopment in 1992 of the old Mercers' School

↗ The massing of 10–15 Fetter Lane **156** is set back in an attempt to reduce its impact on the street, whereas New Street Square, on the left, rises more assertively.

→ No. 122 Chancery Lane **159** is squeezed between two older buildings on the west side of the street.

A variety of entrance treatments: Halsbury House, 35 Chancery Lane **160** (above); 48 Chancery Lane **161** (above, right); and 90 Fetter Lane **163** on the corner with Norwich Street (right).

site at 90 Fetter Lane **163**, on the corner with Norwich Street, is a solid affair of heavy brick and stone with semicircular oriels. Nos 3–5 Norwich Street **164** displays many of Terry Farrell's familiar architectural tricks from the late 1980s, even if the chunky stone cladding is arguably too monumental and muscular for this narrow street. The backwater of Furnival Street offers an interesting architectural medley. No. 40 **165**, designed by Architech in 1990, has a boldly bowed front of purple brick, and sits next to a curious neighbour, the entrance to a wartime underground bunker (1942). No. 20 **166**, by Covell Matthews Wheatley in 1989, is a pale banded brick slab with a crude triangular projection of green metal. By contrast, 34–35 **167**, by Goddard Manton Architects (1995), is described in *The Buildings of England* (p. 506) as 'like a late Victorian fancy warehouse', and Finlaison House at 15–17 **168** is an even safer and more recent Tudor pastiche (2003). By far the most stylish insert into these side streets is 20 Cursitor Street **169** by John Robertson Architects, completed in 2008. It is a modest building in a quiet, partly pedestrianized street, but its projecting bays have a satisfying rhythm and a human scale. It was a deserving finalist in the Office Agents Society's Office Development Awards in 2008.

Unrest and upheaval in the printing industry had begun before the financial Big Bang of 1986, but were a reaction to similar ideas of deregulation and anti-closed-shop legislation introduced by the Thatcher government. The startlingly swift departure of the newspapers from Fleet Street coincided with changes in the financial sector. The move of Rupert Murdoch's News International to Wapping in 1986 (including *The Times* from Gray's Inn Road) triggered a massive migration of the press out of the environs of Fleet Street. As a result, vast amounts of floor space and real estate became available for development.

The *Daily Telegraph* was one of the first Fleet Street giants to move to Docklands. In 1987 its huge site on the north side of Fleet Street, at nos 131–141

↗ The bowed frontage of 40 Furnival Street **165**, which stands next to a redundant wartime bunker.

→ The well-proportioned bays of 20 Cursitor Street **169** create a pleasing effect in this narrow street.

170, fell vacant and was acquired by the American investment bank Goldman Sachs. The American architect KPF kept the frontage buildings, but the old printing works to the rear were demolished and replaced by huge new dealing floors (1988–91). The same treatment was given ten years later to the *Daily Express* building, no. 120 **171**, immediately to the east, retaining Owen Williams's iconic Grade II*-listed 1930s frontage (according to Nikolaus Pevsner in *The Buildings of England*, p. 499, 'the first true curtain-walled building in London'). The client was again Goldman Sachs, doubling the size of its European headquarters with an additional 45,000 square metres, but now using John Robertson Architects. The opportunity was taken to complete the symmetry of the Art Deco frontage, upgrading the thermal and acoustic performance of the facade, and to restore the spectacular foyer. The functional new dealing floors to the rear, austerely clad in grey stone, create a monumental and sombre canyon along this quiet section of Shoe Lane, relieved only by the sloping lightweight glass bridges that connect the upper floors either side of the street. The huge bulk of the new building is effectively concealed from Fleet Street and Shoe Lane, but less so on St Bride Street and from across Ludgate Circus, where the set-back upper floors loom into view. On the opposite side of St Bride Street, no. 10 **172**, completed in 2010 by Rolfe Judd, presents a better scale to the street, as well as incorporating the facades of the triangular building at its apex. The public realm in Shoe Lane and St Bride Street, improved by Burns + Nice acting for the Corporation, using high-quality materials, provides an excellent setting for Antony Gormley's *Resolution* **173** of 2007. This life-size human form of rust-coloured cast-iron blocks is intended to look like a man from afar, but close up more like a mass of urban buildings.

On the south side of Fleet Street the departure of the *News of the World* and the *Daily Mail* provided an enormous site for a new headquarters for Freshfields (now Freshfields Bruckhaus Deringer), one of the City's largest legal firms. Here

↖ Glass bridges cross the pedestrian section of Shoe Lane, linking 120 and 131–141 Fleet Street **171** and **170**, both occupied by Goldman Sachs.

← Antony Gormley's sculpture *Resolution* **173** makes a deliberately ambiguous statement at the junction of Shoe Lane and St Bride Street.

↑ Behind the modest
frontage of 65 Fleet Street
174, the private courtyard
and rotunda make
an impressive main
entrance for Freshfields
Bruckhaus Deringer.

→ Magpie Alley, with
its tiled mural **175**, is
worth the search off
Bouverie Street.

there were few old buildings worth keeping. A comparatively modest frontage block at 65 Fleet Street **174**, with a postmodern classical arch and a sunken circular light well and obelisk in the private courtyard behind, cleverly disguises the megastructure to the rear. All were designed by Yorke Rosenberg Mardall in 1989. This vast eight-storey hulk, soberly clad in grey and black stone, forms a huge wedge with long and forbidding frontages to the narrow Bouverie and Whitefriars streets on either side. The only relief from this gloom is Magpie Alley, where a long mural **175** of black and white tiles lines the north wall of the passage, depicting a potted history of Fleet Street in photographs, illustrations and captions.

Bouverie Street, too, has been improved by Squire and Partners' stylish office development at no. 4 **176**, on the corner with Pleydell Street, winner of an Office Agents Society Office Development Award in 2000. Whitefriars Street has little to commend it, apart from Trehearne and Norman's office scheme of 1991 at no. 21 **177**; somewhat mannered, with its polychromatic brick, it has a symmetry that would be better appreciated in a wider street.

A more pleasant route south from Fleet Street is through Salisbury Court. Salisbury Square is a pleasant breathing space, despite the grim Fleetbank House on the west side. On the south side, 8 Salisbury Square **178** by EPR Architects in 1990, occupied by the accountancy firm KPMG, has more distinction with its chamfered brown stone and faceted facades. Dorset Rise runs south from the square down to Tudor Street, flanked on the left by the vast former headquarters of KPMG. These 1950s buildings were reclad in multicoloured granite panels in the 1980s by RHWL Architects, and when vacated did not project a desirable image for a modern office. Happily, in 2012 they were converted to a Premier Inn, which – with the Crown Plaza near by in Kingscote Street – forms a new hotel enclave in this south-west corner of the

↖ No. 4 Bouverie Street **176** makes an elegant corner with Pleydell Street.

↞ No. 8 Salisbury Square **178** benefits from its setting behind pleasantly landscaped gardens.

← A sculpture of St George and the Dragon **179** guards the Dorset Rise forecourt of the Premier Inn hotel.

City. Michael Sandle's magnificent sculpture of St George and the Dragon (1988) **179** stands proudly restored in the forecourt off Dorset Rise.

Tudor Street was once one of the City's livelier streets, boasting several taverns and bars frequented by hard-drinking, chain-smoking journalists, and reverberating to the sound of soaring sopranos and blaring trombones from the open windows of the Guildhall School of Music and Drama. Those are distant memories, although arguably the street has had some architectural enhancement. At the western end, Freshfields Bruckhaus Deringer has expanded into the former premises of the *Daily Mail*, Northcliffe House at nos 26–28 **180**. Rolfe Judd's scheme of 2001 combines the 1930s concrete structure with a new facade of curtain walling and a smart entrance on the junction with Bouverie Street. On the south side, at the corner with Carmelite Street, 21 Tudor Street **181** is an intricately detailed office scheme of 2003, designed by Harper Mackay Architects and occupied by the law firm Jones Day, following its merger with Gouldens. The current fashion for applied panels of slim orange terracotta is combined with Portland stone cladding, projecting bays, multi-paned metal windows and a transparent entrance to give a rich, varied and colourful elevation to both streets, although it achieved only a 'Good' BREEAM rating. The most recent addition to the street, no. 1 **182** at the eastern end, completed in 2011 by T.P. Bennett for the developer Stockland, is a complete contrast. This minimalist blue-tinted glass box sits on slender, white double-storey columns with a slightly awkwardly recessed entrance, and has been let to a different firm on each floor.

Most of Tudor Street, however, is dominated architecturally by the imposing elevations of the back of J.P. Morgan's headquarters, 60 Victoria Embankment **183**. This development by BDP in 1991 followed the relocation of the City of London Boys' School in 1986, retaining only the late Victorian French chateau-

A splayed glass entrance with an angled projection above has transformed the corner of Northcliffe House, 26–28 Tudor Street **180**, at the junction with Bouverie Street.

Three contrasting architectural styles in Tudor Street: the intricately detailed no. 21 **181** on the corner with Carmelite Street (above, left); the minimalist no. 1 **182** next to Kingscote Street (above); and the postmodernist fortification of 60 Victoria Embankment **183**, at the junction of Tudor Street and John Carpenter Street (left).

style 'palace' frontage to Victoria Embankment and replacing the rest with new groundscraper buildings either side of John Carpenter Street. According to Simon Bradley in *The Buildings of England* (p. 524), the scheme was symptomatic of the development of large unrestricted sites on the fringes of the City following financial deregulation. Architecturally the style is vaguely Chicago classical, with a double storey of granite blocks hard on to the pavement, banded and rusticated, and the street names engraved into the masonry. The impression to the passer-by is a mixture of the pompous and the fortress, almost reminiscent of old Newgate Prison. The tiny square openings protected by security grilles are neither for looking in nor for looking out. The overwhelming horizontality is barely relieved by the giant glazed opening higher up, and is increased by the huge projecting cornices that attempt to conceal the upper floors. It stands as a monument to its time, and one can but ponder on how architectural taste and client requirements have moved on since.

On Victoria Embankment, New Carmelite House **184** by Trehearne and Norman (1993) is from the same design stable as the firm's building in Whitefriars Street **177**. Unilever House, 100 Victoria Embankment **185**, is the outstanding architectural statement in the vicinity, with its giant stone pillars forming a quadrant on the corner with New Bridge Street, a major landmark from long views across the river. In 2007 the interior of this listed building was completely reworked by KPF, retaining the original facade of 1932. The rear section was rebuilt to a lower height in order to improve the views of St Paul's that Unilever House had infringed when it was first built. The scheme, which received English Heritage approval and won a City Corporation Heritage Award, reinstated the main entrance and refurbished the original foyer. Behind this a spectacular atrium provides a new core, bringing daylight and natural ventilation into the heart of the building. Pleasingly, and very much in the spirit of the age, this is a semi-public space, with a cafe, and although there are attendants on duty, the line of security into the wall-climber lifts and offices above is beyond the reception desk in the atrium. Splashes of lime green give the space vibrancy, while hanging in the middle of the space is a stunning artwork, *The Space Trumpet* (2007) by Conrad Shawcross. It is engineered so that the massive 'his master's voice' trumpets, located like pods on a space station, rotate over a sixty-day cycle to give those who work in the building a constantly changing image. Unilever is quite rightly immensely proud of what it has done here. Its brief to KPF was to re-equip the historic headquarters (now rebranded as 100VE) for a new century. The client and architect certainly succeeded, and also, happily, allowed the public a glimpse of how it was done.

The atrium of 100 Victoria Embankment **185** is enlivened by Conrad Shawcross's *Space Trumpet*.

7
SMITHFIELD
AND NEWGATE

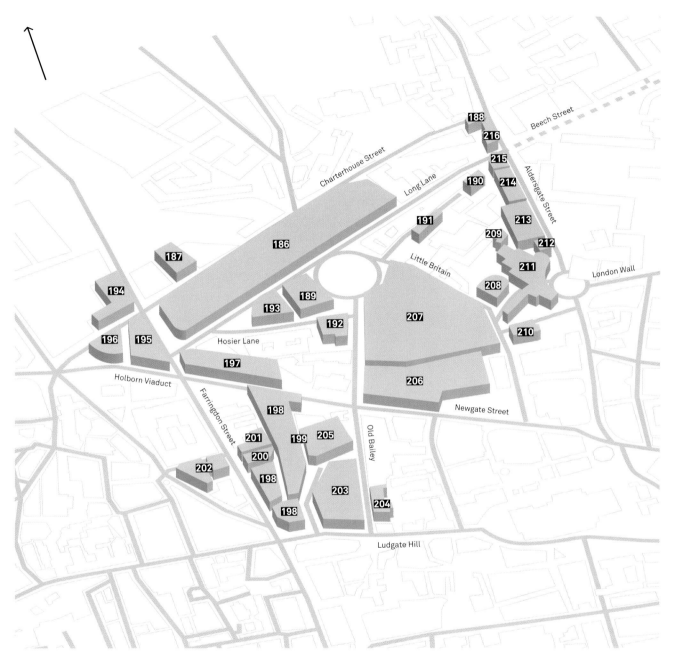

186 Smithfield Market **187** 47–53 Charterhouse Street **188** 12 Carthusian Street **189** Haberdashers' Hall **190** Farmers' and Fletchers' Hall **191** Founders' Hall **192** 1 Giltspur Street **193** 12 Smithfield Street **194** 17–19 Charterhouse Street **195** Atlantic House, 48 Farringdon Road/50 Holborn Viaduct **196** 40 Holborn Viaduct **197** Sixty London **198** Fleet Place **199** *Echo* **200** 20 Farringdon Street **201** Nexus Place, 23–25 Farringdon Street **202** Stonecutter Court, 77 Farringdon Street **203** 1 and 2 New Ludgate, 60 Ludgate Hill/30 Old Bailey **204** 7–10 Old Bailey **205** 20 Old Bailey **206** 100 Newgate Street **207** St Bartholomew's Hospital **208** Bartholomew Square **209** Spencer Heights, 28–29 Bartholomew Close **210** 75 Little Britain **211** 200 Aldersgate **212** London House, 172–176 Aldersgate Street **213** Mitre House, 160 Aldersgate Street **214** 150 Aldersgate Street **215** 140 Aldersgate Street **216** 137 Aldersgate Street

Given the pace of change and renewal in the City, the survival of a functioning Victorian meat market might seem anomalous, but it is to the City Corporation's credit as owner and operator that it is still there, cheek by jowl with several other venerable institutions, such as St Bartholomew's Hospital and the Charterhouse. Such 'living' history is why Smithfield is one of the most fascinating districts in all London, not just the City. The area also has many good examples of recent contextual architecture that show how conservation areas can be enhanced by good modern design. Since 1994 the line of Carthusian Street and Charterhouse Street has formed the border between the City and the London Borough of Islington (before then it followed meandering medieval parish boundaries); at times it is something of a political divide, but that is not apparent architecturally.

Smithfield Market **186** runs virtually the full length of Charterhouse Street and occupies a huge footprint, both above and below ground. Following intense debate about the future of the market during the 1970s and 1980s, the City Corporation finally opted to keep and renovate it, rather than to close or move it. Some said the decision was helped by the possibility that, under the original Royal Charter, ownership of the land might revert from the Corporation to the Crown should the market close. In order to meet new European hygiene requirements, HLM was commissioned to design new external canopies and pod-like loading docks on Horace Jones's building of 1868, and to carry out extensive internal upgrading and add office mezzanines either side of Central Avenue. Completed in 1995, all this was a significant improvement – particularly the removal of the ugly post-war canopies – although it is hard to believe that the jazzy repainting is faithful to the original colour scheme.

The Poultry Market (rebuilt after a fire in 1962) and the collection of later Victorian buildings to the west (partly rebuilt after bomb damage) were left largely unaltered by the upgrade work. As the meat trade shrank, so these buildings were progressively abandoned. In 2004 the Corporation resolved to concentrate the market in the listed and improved eastern blocks and to redevelop the rest in conjunction with a partner, the developer Thornfield Properties. Following a major public inquiry in 2007/2008, their scheme for new office blocks, designed by KPF, was rejected by the then Communities Secretary, Hazel Blears, a victory for English Heritage and the conservation lobby (although unfortunately not all the buildings were listed), and a rare setback for the City Corporation as both owner and planning authority. Thornfield went into administration in 2010, but its role as joint developer was taken on by Henderson Global Investors. KPF was replaced by John McAslan + Partners, which unveiled its ideas in October 2012. The proposals retain the original perimeter facades to the streets, with ground-floor shops and restaurants, but a six-storey office building inserted into the middle is hard to disguise and more contentious.

The south side of Smithfield Market **186** fronts West Smithfield. The modern canopies and loading bays both here and along the north side, on Charterhouse Street, provide protection against weather and pollution for the transfer of meat into and out of the market.

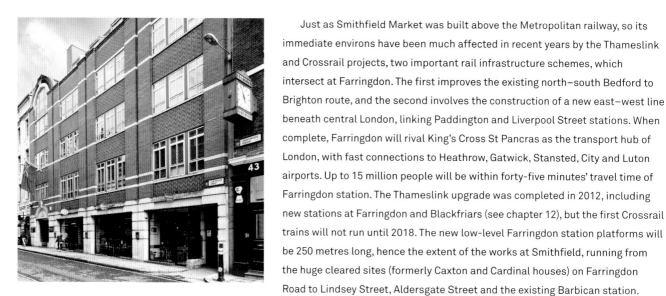

No. 12 Carthusian Street **188** blends well with the older warehouses next door. It backs on to the Metropolitan railway cutting and the workings for Crossrail.

↓↘ The walls and roof of the first-floor hall of the Haberdashers' Company **189**, West Smithfield, are clad in timber, while the cloister is built in traditional brick with a strongly expressed lead roof above the hall.

Just as Smithfield Market was built above the Metropolitan railway, so its immediate environs have been much affected in recent years by the Thameslink and Crossrail projects, two important rail infrastructure schemes, which intersect at Farringdon. The first improves the existing north–south Bedford to Brighton route, and the second involves the construction of a new east–west line beneath central London, linking Paddington and Liverpool Street stations. When complete, Farringdon will rival King's Cross St Pancras as the transport hub of London, with fast connections to Heathrow, Gatwick, Stansted, City and Luton airports. Up to 15 million people will be within forty-five minutes' travel time of Farringdon station. The Thameslink upgrade was completed in 2012, including new stations at Farringdon and Blackfriars (see chapter 12), but the first Crossrail trains will not run until 2018. The new low-level Farringdon station platforms will be 250 metres long, hence the extent of the works at Smithfield, running from the huge cleared sites (formerly Caxton and Cardinal houses) on Farringdon Road to Lindsey Street, Aldersgate Street and the existing Barbican station. The proposal for the new Farringdon East station entrance with five storeys of offices above, by PLP Architecture, looks too big and lumpy for the setting of Charterhouse Square, despite its promise of colourful terracotta framing.

It remains to be seen what will replace Cardinal and Caxton houses, but one hopes that it will be better than the demolished 1960s slabs. Next door, at 47–53 Charterhouse Street **187**, a former Port of London cold store was converted in 1992 by Citigen (part of E:ON) into a combined heat and power station, complete with a new chimney, to supply 31 megavolts of electricity and 25 megavolts of heat and cooling to the local area. Also unaffected by the railway works, 12 Carthusian Street **188** is a pleasant pastiche of the Victorian warehouse style by Ronald Ward and Partners, built in 1989, with herringbone brick detail and a round-topped gable over the main entrance. This mixed-use scheme of offices and flats was something of a novelty in the

City, and the idea was much promoted in the regeneration of the adjoining Clerkenwell by Islington Council.

South of the market, West Smithfield is one of the largest and most impressive open spaces in the City. Its paving and pedestrian environment have been much improved by the Corporation since 2002, constraining traffic movements, providing well for cyclists and generally making it easier to appreciate the splendid variety of buildings that front this spacious triangular precinct.

On the west side, easily missed through a small, dark entrance, is the wonderful premises of the Haberdashers' Company **189**, designed by Michael Hopkins and completed in 2002. Historically the Haberdashers were in Staining Lane, north of Gresham Street near the Guildhall. After bombing in 1940 they were the first livery company to rebuild (in 1954), and theirs was the first post-war hall to be demolished, when they decided to move in 1996. Michael Hopkins had recently completed his reconstruction of the Glyndebourne Opera House in East Sussex, and (nearer to hand) his intimate extension to the Charterhouse, behind Charterhouse Square. The sequestered and cloistered Haberdashers' Hall is in the same genre of load-bearing handmade red brick with powerful but beautifully executed cut brick arches, all held together with traditional lime mortar. The spectacular wooden ceiling and panelling in the hall are surmounted by high lead roofs and vents, almost in the manner of an oast house. It is only a shame that the gates from West Smithfield are kept locked, with visits only by appointment.

This is not the only livery hall in the area. The Butchers in Bartholomew Close are no surprise, nor perhaps is Farmers' and Fletchers' Hall **190** in Cloth Street, off Long Lane, an unassuming building of 1987 by Michael Twigg Brown & Partners. More surprisingly – certainly in visual terms – is Founders' Hall **191** in Cloth Fair, completed and extended in 1986 and 1990 respectively by Jeremy Sampson Lloyd. The fanciful concoction of jetties and gables pays homage to the survivor of the Great Fire on the north side of the street further west,

↗ The jetties and gables of Founders' Hall **191**, Cloth Fair, are a direct reference to the seventeenth-century houses that survive on the north side of the street, opposite the church.

→ No. 12 Smithfield Street **193** faces Smithfield General Market, and has a long side elevation to Hosier Lane.

although as a piece of neo-vernacular it lacks the finesse, perhaps, of the same architect's Pellipar House in Cloak Lane (**079**; see chapter 3).

Both new and old buildings in the Smithfield area display a range of vernacular materials, and there is more brick and render here than in the prestigious financial district with its Portland, York and exotic imported stone. The head office of City & Guilds at 1 Giltspur Street **192** provides strong red brick to the street, broken up with bands of stone. It was designed by GMW Architects in 1991. On the far corner with Cock Lane at first-floor level is the rescued, restored and re-erected Fat Boy of Pye Corner, a chubby golden cupid marking the furthest limit of the Great Fire in 1666. Hosier Lane, too, is lined with brick buildings from the late 1980s, as far as Smithfield Street. A dignified frontage on that corner, all in stone and glass, is 12 Smithfield Street **193** by CPMG in 2008, providing 15,000 square metres of offices over eight floors, including two basements. Terracotta panels appear on the side elevation to Hosier Lane.

The wide Farringdon Road is all that remains of the ironed-out valley of the Fleet River, which still runs in a culvert below the highway. To the west the land rises noticeably towards Holborn. On the north side of Charterhouse Street, nos 17–19 **194** is a block of 1992 by Livings Leslie Webber, with an odd mixture of shapes and materials: pink and white stone piers, segmental arches, bronze cladding and a curve to the corner. On the opposite side, Atlantic House **195**, also known as 48 Farringdon Road and 50 Holborn Viaduct (2010), is altogether more imposing. With 40 Holborn Viaduct **196** it forms a complete triangular street block, broken only by the tiny canyon of Shoe Lane. Both were designed by Rolfe Judd, and – although they were built for different clients and occupants – there is a strong family likeness.

No. 40 Holborn Viaduct, completed in 2008, provides a powerful focus to Holborn Circus; it is generously set back to create enough space for pedestrians and the planting of espaliered lime trees, linking with the larger public-realm improvements currently planned. The best view of its stone geometry and curving roof form is from the other side of this six-way roundabout, although the masons' skill is worth perusing close up. Beyond the main entrance to Atlantic House for the law firm Hogan Lovells, the development also included the construction in replica of the original north-west corner of the main Holborn Viaduct bridge, providing public stairs to Farringdon Road below. The missing north-east corner has been incorporated into the Sixty London development **197**, which is due to be completed in late 2013. KPF's replacement of the dull post-war blocks will provide 22,000 square metres for AXA Real Estate, and is one of the larger schemes currently under construction in the western part of the City, hence perhaps its rather pretentious name. At least an element of non-office is proposed with bars and shops spread over three floors, to be run by the bar group Drake & Morgan and called the Haberdashery.

← Atlantic House **195** forms the south-west side of the junction of Farringdon Road and Charterhouse Street. It also fronts Holborn Viaduct.

↙ Nos 17–19 Charterhouse Street **194** has a long frontage to Farringdon Road.

↓ No. 40 Holborn Viaduct **196** faces the broad, open space of Holborn Circus. To the right is Atlantic House **195**.

Fleet Place **198** contains generous and varied public spaces and pedestrian routes: beside and beneath no. 10 (left); a north–south route, adorned with Stephen Cox's *Echo* (below); and a concourse under the block fronting Holborn Viaduct (bottom).

More eye-catching architecture is on the opposite side of Holborn Viaduct. Bold white steel columns announce the entrance to Fleet Place **198**, a redevelopment of the old Holborn Viaduct station terminus made possible by the resurrection of the unused Snow Hill tunnel and the creation of the north–south Thameslink railway in 1989. The diversion and burying of the tracks, which slope steeply down from Blackfriars Bridge to pass under rather than over Ludgate Hill, provided a huge strip of land, stretching from Holborn Viaduct to Ludgate. Following a masterplan by RHWL Architects in 1987, the Fleet Place scheme was developed by the Heron Property Corporation (now Heron International) in conjunction with British Rail between 1992 and 2000. Fleet Place rode on the coat-tails of the Broadgate development (and Rosehaugh Stanhope Developments' resurrection after the recession). Although not quite as extensive, it has a similarly comprehensive feel, with the freedom from the constraints of an existing road pattern offered by redundant railway land and air-rights over existing tracks. As at Broadgate (see chapter 9), there is generous public space and pedestrian permeability through the scheme; it is ungated and open to all at all hours, a welcome characteristic in an increasingly security-conscious world.

The ground floor facing Holborn Viaduct is almost entirely open, although there is a feeling of having to duck under the offices of Fleet Place House, which are supported on splayed stilts. One circular base stone records the names of the architect, SOM, and the builder, Mowlem. The other four main blocks of the scheme – 1, 5 and 10 Fleet Place and 100 Ludgate Hill, all designed by SOM – have their own identity. No. 1 Fleet Place includes an entrance to City Thameslink station below; no. 5 retains the vestiges of Old Seacoal Lane, which snakes beneath; no. 10 has striking vertical fins in dark metal and polished stone; and 100 Ludgate Hill, now also called Santander House, shows more of the chunky American style seen at Broadgate. The public route that slopes

↗ The combination of dark polished stone with narrow vertical ribs of metal at 10 Fleet Place **198** is worth close inspection.

→ The zigzag bays at the rear of Nexus Place, 23–25 Farringdon Street **201**, are viewed from Fleet Place.

Projecting glass bays produce a strongly horizontal emphasis at 7–10 Old Bailey **204**, looking south towards Ludgate Hill.

↓ The artist's impression of 2 New Ludgate shows the use of colour to good effect.

↘ The setting of 20 Old Bailey **205**, opposite the Central Criminal Court, has been improved by the City Corporation's landscaping.

gently from north to south contains various sculptural balustrades and vent shafts faced in smooth black stone, and also Stephen Cox's *Echo* (1993) **199**, a facing pair of black humanoid figures commissioned by Broadgate Properties but sited at Fleet Place in 2000.

From the southern end of Fleet Place, a steep flight of steps leads down to the truncated Old Fleet Lane, where 20 Farringdon Street **200**, designed by T.P. Bennett in 1987, provides a bland wall with its grey cladding and tinted windows, relieved only by the pub on the corner. More interesting is Nexus Place, 23–25 Farringdon Street **201**, a flat-fronted nine-storey block of 1982 by Richard Seifert, originally known as Fleetway House, reclad and extended at the rear to thirteen storeys in 2009 by Sturgis Associates, with intricate zigzag bays. It is prominent from Fleet Place. Across this rather grim stretch of Farringdon Street, no. 77, Stonecutter Court **202**, described as 'strenuously articulated' in *The Buildings of England* (p. 485), seems positively jolly. It was completed in 1994 by RHWL Architects.

To the east of Fleet Place, the huge development of 30 Old Bailey and 60 Ludgate Hill **203** for Land Securities is taking shape, to be completed in late 2013. It comprises two nine-storey blocks: 1 New Ludgate, facing Ludgate Hill, designed by Fletcher Priest Architects; and 2 New Ludgate, fronting Old Bailey, by the Berlin firm Sauerbruch Hutton, which is renowned for its playful use of glass and colour. The scheme is a coordinated effort to provide 37,000 square metres of offices plus shops, restaurants and a new triangular public space, or 'piazzetta'. Roof gardens along Ludgate Hill are designed by Gustafson Porter.

The scheme will face 7–10 Old Bailey **204**, another architectural collaboration, between Avery Associates Architects and Sidell Gibson (2009). The flat wall of stone with its boxy glass projections both respects and contrasts with the neighbouring law courts, and received a commendation from the Civic

Trust in 2010. The 'ugly sister' is 20 Old Bailey **205**, which also imposes itself on Fleet Place at the rear, and is visible even from Farringdon Street. It was built in 1989 by RHWL Architects. The blockish rusticated granite base was presumably intended as a reference to the Central Criminal Courts, and possibly its predecessor, Newgate Prison, but today it appears crude and self-aggrandizing.

A far better example of imaginative contextualism was achieved on the north side of Newgate Street. Swanke Hayden Connell Architects' European headquarters for Bank of America Merrill Lynch (2001) at 100 Newgate Street **206** has an excellent scale, deferring to St Paul's Heights limitations, and cleverly incorporates historic fabric. The former Grade II*-listed Post Office provides a conference and exhibition space. Behind the retained gin palace and Victorian terrace on Newgate Street (saved from road widening), a new internal street links St Sepulchre's churchyard and the garden of Christchurch Newgate, with shops facing two ways and a foyer containing an art gallery with changing exhibitions. The arcaded buildings, only four storeys high but containing two of the largest trading floors in the world, create a fine setting for the ruined Christchurch by Christopher Wren, the original plan of which was re-created in the garden. Pergolas in the sumptuous herbaceous borders represent the columns of the nave, and the iron churchyard railings were immaculately restored and reinstated by Gibson Dennis Associates. The tower became a house (reputedly marketed for £4.5 million in 2009). Perhaps one day the full height and architectural detail of the east end of the nave will be re-erected, demolished as it was – outrageously and needlessly – by highway engineers in the 1970s.

To the north the precinct of St Bartholomew's Hospital **207** occupies almost as large a site as the meat market, and has just as long a history. It, too, has survived threats of closure and merger and the constant reorganization of the NHS, and it continues to provide a remarkable range and concentration of

↙ The headquarters of the Bank of America Merrill Lynch at 100 Newgate Street **206** overlooks the leafy garden of Christchurch Newgate.

↓ The first phase of the redevelopment at St Bartholomew's Hospital **207** provides an elegantly curved frontage to Little Britain and King Edward Street.

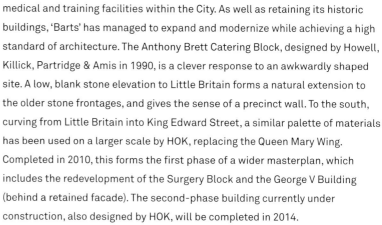

medical and training facilities within the City. As well as retaining its historic buildings, 'Barts' has managed to expand and modernize while achieving a high standard of architecture. The Anthony Brett Catering Block, designed by Howell, Killick, Partridge & Amis in 1990, is a clever response to an awkwardly shaped site. A low, blank stone elevation to Little Britain forms a natural extension to the older stone frontages, and gives the sense of a precinct wall. To the south, curving from Little Britain into King Edward Street, a similar palette of materials has been used on a larger scale by HOK, replacing the Queen Mary Wing. Completed in 2010, this forms the first phase of a wider masterplan, which includes the redevelopment of the Surgery Block and the George V Building (behind a retained facade). The second-phase building currently under construction, also designed by HOK, will be completed in 2014.

In 2011 Barts and the London NHS Trust sold most of its holdings east of Little Britain to the developer Helical Bar, which – with Sheppard Robson – in 2012 unveiled plans to create a 'new, vibrant quarter, adding to and enhancing the existing community'. Their Bartholomew Square proposal **208** consists of a new 21,000-square-metre office building on the corner of Little Britain (replacing the post-war nurses' accommodation of Gloucester House) and more than 250 new flats, with shops and restaurants. Much concern has been raised that the new offices and strident roof extensions above retained facades will overwhelm the intimate nature of Bartholomew Close. Phased development is hoped to start in 2014.

Little Britain has been much rebuilt since the decision (and a conservation battle lost) to complete the road connection between the London Wall dual carriageway and Newgate Street. This was part of the northern 'bypass' for the City, known as Route XI, which had been planned soon after the Second World War. Spencer Heights (28–29 Bartholomew Close) **209** and 75 Little Britain **210**, both designed by GMA Architecture in 1996/97, are residential blocks that seek to repair some of the damage. The former, in pallid cream brick, has feeble grey-brick soldier courses to the windows; the latter is in a richer red brick with rusticated render and ornate black grilles to the ground floor.

The environs are overshadowed by the forbidding bulk of 200 Aldersgate **211**, which straddles the new Montague Street and faces the roundabout. This office block, designed by Fitzroy Robinson and originally occupied in 1992 by the law firm Clifford Chance, rises in a series of steps to 91 metres. As well as erasing a network of ancient courts and alleys, it was far too tall and dark for its context, even though it steps down at the back to meet the red brick of 20 Little Britain. Following Clifford Chance's move to Canary Wharf, MoreySmith completed a major facelift in 2010, and the twenty-one storeys of accommodation are now being managed by Helical Bar as flexible multi-lettings. There is now easier access to the foyers, escalators up to a cafe and lounge on the first floor, and

← No. 75 Little Britain **210** is a residential block at the junction with King Edward Street, and backs on to Postman's Park. Dark metal grilles protect the lower-ground-floor windows.

↙ No. 200 Aldersgate **211** incorporates art at street level; One London Wall **030** is reflected in the glass.

→ No. 200 Aldersgate **211**, viewed from the raised rotunda of the Museum of London **218**. The new link block with upper-level cafe and lounge is on the left.

circular bull's-eye light installations by Rob and Nick Carter. Happily, the Corporation is talking of replacing the roundabout with a park and reducing the width of London Wall to one carriageway.

North of the roundabout, the west side of Aldersgate Street presents a continuous eight-storey wall of offices of limited distinction and uncoordinated materials. London House, nos 172–176 **212**, is of yellow brick and stone, while Mitre House at no. 160 **213** is clad in polished stone. This scheme by Seifert (1990) replaced a 1960s multi-storey car park with six levels of underground parking. At the rear, brown-brick flats with timber Juliet balconies face Bartholomew Close. John Gill Associates' 150 Aldersgate Street **214**, a similar fortress to Mitre House, was also built in 1990 and is depressingly unwelcoming. No. 140 **215**, completed in 2005 for Land Securities by Sidell Gibson, shows the extent to which fashions in office design changed over two decades. Natural stone forms a gentle curve to the corner, with a transparent glass ground floor, while at the rear orange terracotta makes an attractive contribution to Long Lane and to views out of Newbury and Middle streets.

On the north corner with Long Lane, 137 Aldersgate Street **216**, constructed in 1989 to designs by Rolfe Judd, incorporates the entrance to Barbican station and is worth a glance. The materials use a degree of colour, and the modest elevation is pleasingly broken into five projecting bays. Stairs lead to a footbridge across the wide road to the Barbican complex, as good a place as any to embark on the next chapter.

The west side of Aldersgate Street. London House **212** is on the left; the projecting bays belong to Mitre House **213**.

Seen from above, 140 Aldersgate  forms a curved corner with Long Lane. Orange terracotta makes a contrasting facade to the rear, on Cloth Street.

8

BARBICAN
AND MOORGATE

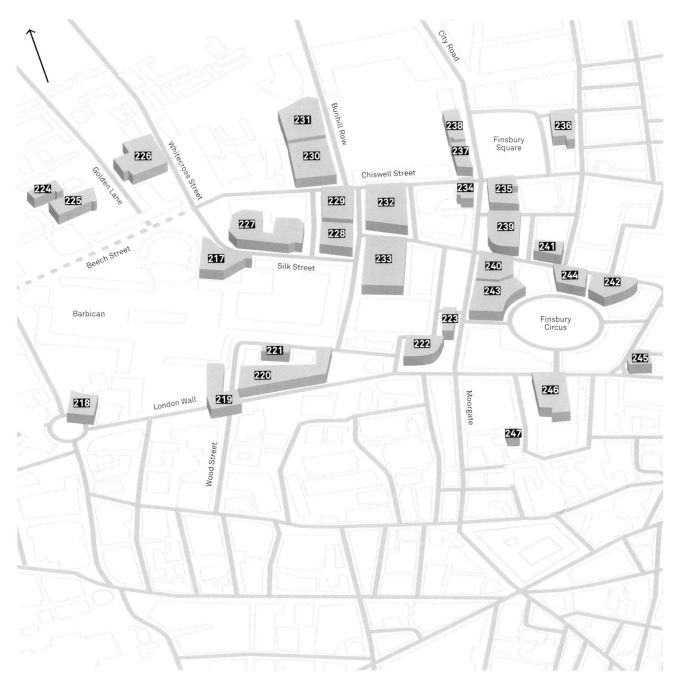

217 Barbican Arts Centre 218 Museum of London 219 Alban Gate 220 London Wall Place, 121 and 123 London Wall 221 72 Fore Street 222 Moor House 223 101 Moorgate 224 Tudor Rose Court, Fann Street 225 1 Golden Lane 226 Golden Lane Campus 227 Milton House/Shire House, 1 Silk Street 228 The Heron 229 Milton Gate 230 1 Bunhill Row 231 Cass Business School 232 Ropemaker Place 233 CityPoint 234 131 Finsbury Pavement 235 50 Finsbury Square 236 30 Finsbury Square 237 1-2 Finsbury Square 238 3–10 Finsbury Square 239 Helicon Building 240 120 Moorgate 241 South Place Hotel 242 Park House, 16–18 Finsbury Circus 243 1 Finsbury Circus and River Plate House, 7–11 Finsbury Circus 244 10 South Place 245 85 London Wall 246 60 London Wall 247 Apex London Wall Hotel, 7–9 Copthall Avenue

The Barbican is one of the most remarkable comprehensive post-war redevelopment schemes anywhere in Britain. It was made possible by the total devastation through bombing of a huge area north of Gresham Street, and a subsequent resolve and commitment to funding by the City Corporation, from the inception of the scheme in the 1950s until its eventual completion in the 1980s. This extraordinary megastructure, executed by one architectural firm – Chamberlin, Powell & Bon – covers 14 hectares. Its three angular residential towers are mighty landmarks and stand sentry-like, marking the northern edge of the City.

A crucial part of the Barbican scheme was the elevated walkway, intended to segregate pedestrians from traffic at the old street level. It was a concept so inspiring that the Corporation decided in 1959 that 'ped-ways' should be extended throughout the City. Had the vision been fulfilled, it would have left only a scattering of historic buildings, churches and livery halls, marooned at ground level. The idea was eventually abandoned in 1976, and the podium area of the Barbican is one of the best and most extensive surviving examples. The alternative ground-level pedestrian routes along the tunnel of Beech Street or beside the racing traffic of London Wall are grim indeed. The whole of the Barbican complex was listed in 2001, and the podium was added to the national register of historic parks and gardens. With its hard red-brick paving and rough concrete balustrades, it now appears rather tired and monotonous; it is sometimes windswept and can be daunting at night. Despite better signage it remains notoriously difficult to navigate, a result of the security and privacy requirements for the housing and the City of London School for Girls, and of the uncrossable lakes. The landscape architect Johanna Gibbons has been commissioned to make much-needed improvements, particularly to Cromwell and Ben Jonson highwalks, with the emphasis on improving the quality – including upgrading the lighting and seating – rather than changing the fundamental design. There is the potential for more conspicuous and joyous public art. At present Mendelssohn's Tree, unveiled by the composer Carl Davis in 1993, is easily missed on John Trundle Highway. It is an ancient stump from Burnham Beeches in Buckinghamshire (owned by the City Corporation), under which Felix Mendelssohn was believed to have sat. A stone-paved labyrinth by Patrick Dillon has been proposed for St Giles Terrace.

The Barbican Arts Centre **217** benefited from a revamp of its foyers in 2006. Allford Hall Monaghan Morris removed the accretion of ugly clutter and introduced a new, rational order to what had seemed a confusing layout. The entrance at the junction of Silk Street and Whitecross Street is also better, and conflict between pedestrians and servicing access has been reduced. The inevitable fact that most visitors to the Barbican Centre who arrive at Barbican station prefer to remain on the level, and do not choose to climb up to the

Highway and down again, means that the City Corporation has at last decided to improve the pedestrian environment in the grisly Beech Street tunnel. The neon lights at the entrance to the new cinema screens near the corner with Whitecross Street will provide further enticement.

To the south-west, filling the junction of London Wall and Aldersgate Street and oversailing the roundabout, the Museum of London **218** was not part of the Barbican, although its construction to the design of Powell & Moya was contemporary with that of the Arts Centre. The museum has also enjoyed a much-needed redesign, by Wilkinson Eyre Architects in 2010, and now has a more welcoming entrance, a shop and a cafe facing the London Wall ped-way. The forecourt is enhanced by two sculptures, Christopher Le Brun's *Union (Horse with Two Discs)* (1999–2000) and Martin Ludlow's *The Aldersgate Flame* (1981), a memorial to John Wesley's conversion. The proposed reduction of the traffic on London Wall and the roundabout will also help the setting (see p. 144).

The raised walkway along the north side of London Wall provides tremendous views of distant towers and some of the financial headquarters described in chapter 4. Once past the stylish new glazed entrance to 140 London Wall, one of the 1960s slabs on stilts, the unavoidable hulk ahead is Terry Farrell's Alban Gate **219** of 1992. This massive structure straddling the dual carriageway was the first project to abandon the simplicity and austerity of the post-war plan. *The Buildings of England* described it in 1997 as 'the cuckoo in the nest' (p. 544), and other critics have not been kind; Kenneth Allinson's 'bombastic and over-worked ... shoulder-padded "Gucci architecture"' (*London's Contemporary Architecture*, p. 45) is just one of many barbs. The offices, 125 London Wall, are approached from deck level, where a curious nude sculpture by Ivan Klapez sits in a glass niche overlooking Wood Street. The shop windows are held by springs to accommodate vibration from traffic below.

The main entrance (below, left) of the Barbican Arts Centre **217** on Silk Street has been greatly improved by better paving and new signage. Internally (below), the foyers and circulation areas now operate more successfully.

↓ The entrance to the Museum of London 218 is guarded by Christopher Le Brun's *Union (Horse with Two Discs)*.

↘ The naked dancers of Ivan Klapez's *Unity* perform at deck level in Alban Gate 219, above the northern arm of Wood Street.

↓↓ The Museum of London 218 spans the roundabout in the background of this view of Aldersgate Street from the Barbican's Lauderdale Tower.

↓ The entrance to the Museum of London 218 is guarded by Christopher Le Brun's *Union (Horse with Two Discs)*.

Bolted on to the western end, no. 130, also by Farrell and part of the overall scheme, contains flats, in red brick with stone dressings. It forms a bizarre contrast to the office monster. The cables to Bastion Highwalk give a quasi-drawbridge effect, while the balustraded gardens of Monkwell Square down the steps are faintly reminiscent of the garden designs of Gertrude Jekyll. Too many visual games have been played here, and there is little design coherence. By contrast, the re-landscaping (1995) of the Salters' Garden delightfully enhances the setting of a fine section of Roman wall and Basil Spence's bold Salters' Hall.

The area to the east is earmarked for redevelopment. London Wall Place, 121 and 123 London Wall 220, will replace St Alphage House and the forlorn, vacant shops with two new landmark buildings for the developer Hammerson, providing 46,450 square metres of speculative offices. Approved in June 2011, Make's design (described by the firm's founder, Ken Shuttleworth, as 'a series of railway carriages') retains the raised walkway and the established echelon geometry to London Wall. At sixteen storeys, it will be similar to Eric Parry's 5 Aldermanbury Square (036; see chapter 2), and it is due to be completed in 2015, depending on whether Hammerson continues with its plans or sells the site. Other low-rise 1960s slabs, including the former telephone exchange at 72 Fore Street 221, have been demolished to make way for a thirteen-storey development by HKR Architects. The adjacent 1960s Roman House has been converted into ninety flats, including two extra floors, for the developer Berkeley by Rolfe Judd, with interiors by the Manser Practice Architects + Designers.

The eastern section of the ped-way precinct is terminated emphatically by Moor House 222. Foster + Partners' glassy double-curve structure of 2005 rises to eighteen storeys over a two-storey base. With a roof profile that slopes down to Moorgate, it makes a dramatic transition in scale. For the pedestrian, an elegant glass public lift connects the raised walkway with terra firma and the

Alban Gate **219** straddles the dual carriageway of London Wall (above). Narrow sections of 5 Aldermanbury Square **036** and 88 Wood Street **035** appear on the right of the photograph. In the foreground is the red brick of Monkwell Square; its balustraded gardens (right) are perhaps more appropriate to an Edwardian country garden than a setting among office giants.

This view of Moor House **222** will disappear when the redevelopment of 101 Moorgate **223** and 21 Moorfields proceeds after the completion of Crossrail.

shops below. The building's sheer, uncompromising north wall will be partly hidden by the redevelopment of 101 Moorgate **223** (cleared of previous buildings in 2012), which will incorporate the western entrance to the new Moorgate/ Liverpool Street Crossrail station. Planning permission was granted in March 2012 for 10,000 square metres of shops and offices above the station, designed by John Robertson Architects using a mix of glazed and coloured terracotta cladding. Land Securities bought the adjacent site of 21 Moorfields in 2012 from Moises and Mendi Gertner, but no development can start until after Crossrail is finished in 2018.

While London Wall forms a clear southern edge to this area, Chiswell Street, Finsbury Square and adjacent streets encompass a more diffuse northern fringe to the City. Unless you look carefully at the street signs, it is hard to discern the borough boundary between the City and its neighbour, Islington. Most property developers, estate agents and indeed architectural writers have for many years regarded south Islington as part of the City, and it is true that this City fringe provides accommodation that is crucial to the function of the central business district. Not far north, the Old Street/City Road junction is now known as 'Silicon Roundabout', part of the emerging 'Tech City' area. Islington Council has been aware for as long as the City Corporation of the importance of innovative and good design, attractive public realm and lively ground-floor uses. In many ways, the City has been playing catch-up.

The Golden Lane Estate preceded the Barbican as a City Corporation residential commission, also from Chamberlin, Powell & Bon, and until boundary changes in 1994 lay mainly within Islington. Additional flats in the Cobalt Building, Bridgewater Square (a repetitively dull eight-storey block by Hunter & Partners, now Hunters) and the more homely thirty-six sheltered-housing flats in Tudor Rose Court, Fann Street **224**, by Avanti Architects, all built in 1997, help

The junction of Fann Street and Viscount Street, with Bridgewater Square on the corner and Tudor Rose Court **224** to the right.

↑ No. 1 Golden Lane **225** is a massive and overbearing extension to the original Cripplegate Institute on the right.

to link the two estates. On Golden Lane itself the former Cripplegate Institute and Free Library, no. 1 **225**, was retained, but in 1992 it was crudely heightened, distorting its original proportions, and grossly extended to the rear by the Ergon Design Group. The Golden Lane Campus **226** opposite, by Nicholas Hare Architects, was built for Islington Education Department in 2008 with funding assistance from the City Corporation, and provided a new primary school on the doorstep of the Barbican. Refreshingly colourful and inventive, it won the British Council for School Environments' Inspiring Design Award in 2009. The Corporation also contributed generously to the successful regeneration of Whitecross Street market, now a major attraction for local workers and residents at lunchtime.

The remains of the once-sprawling premises of the former Whitbread brewery on the corner of Milton and Chiswell streets are now hemmed in and overwhelmed by new buildings. At the southern end of Whitecross Street, 1 Silk Street **227**, known also as Milton House and Shire House, is an unremarkable amalgam of six-, twelve- and eighteen-storey slabs, originally in mirror glass but reclad in pastel shades in 1996 by Fitzroy Robinson for the law firm Linklaters.

The Heron **228** rises much higher. Due to be completed in 2013, this thirty-six-storey tower of 284 luxury flats by David Walker Architects is the first major housing development in the City since the Barbican, and will strengthen the Barbican residential enclave for those who can afford it. Prices start at £500,000, rising to £5 million for the penthouses. The developer, Heron Property Corporation, claimed that 80% were already sold before topping out in April 2012, mainly to foreign buyers. It is to be hoped that the flats will be more than just pieds-à-terre or 'crash pads', and that they will attract some genuine permanent residents. The justification, or excuse, for the lack of affordable housing in the scheme is that the six-storey podium contains new, much-needed facilities for the Guildhall School of Music and Drama, including

↗ No. 3 Bunhill Row provides a glassy frontage between the solid 1 Bunhill Row **230** and the Cass Business School **231** to the north.

↖ The Golden Lane Campus **226** offers contrasting facades: the frontage to Fortune Street Gardens is informal and the main entrance colourful.

→ The Chiswell Street frontage of Ropemaker Place **232** steps down to lessen the impact of the upper floors and maintain a human scale to the street.

a 625-seat concert hall, a training theatre and studios, fitted out by the arts team of RHWL Architects.

South of Silk Street, the wide section of Moor Lane running down to Fore Street is due to be transformed by the City Corporation into a linear park by removing most of the excessively wide roadway. This presents the chance to plant avenues of large trees, which over time will balance the huge scale of the surrounding buildings.

In the narrow northern section of Moor Lane, Denys Lasdun's Milton Gate **229**, once dubbed the 'green giant' because of its startling triple-skinned glass, now seems quite tame and elegant. When finished in 1991 it lay in Islington, but the post-1994 boundary puts it in the City. In 2008 Squire and Partners added a glazed entrance. On the north side of Chiswell Street, 1 Bunhill Row **230** replaced a dreary 1960s student-accommodation tower block with a more contextual scale in 2001. The developer Helical Bar and architect Sheppard Robson tailored the design to meet the wishes of the future occupant, the law firm Slaughter and May. According to Melvyn Hughes, a partner there at the time, the firm wanted its new office to be 'modern and timeless, and one in which its lawyers and their clients would feel comfortable'. The masonry cladding is safely reassuring, but the piece of 'old' stone wall inside the entrance is highly unconvincing. No. 3, to the north, by the same design team in 2007, is more adventurous; all in glass, it has a boldly expressed lift in the transparent entrance. The Cass Business School **231**, part of City University London, makes a solid bookend to the street block, using stack-bonded black engineering bricks for the walls. Designed by Bennetts Associates in 1999–2002 to provide Harvard-quality facilities, it has the feel of a City building, but on an education budget and with much lower energy consumption.

The architectural hotchpotch of 1980s buildings on Chiswell Street was ameliorated by the completion in 2010 of Ropemaker Place **232**. The redevelopment of this island block by British Land and Arup followed close on the heels of their partnership at Plantation Place (**130**; see chapter 5), and displays a similar knack for achieving generous floor space, in this case 83,600 square metres, without going super-high. A French colour consultant was engaged in an effort to prevent the glass finish appearing too grey, but the resultant mauve tint is still rather weak. On Chiswell Street the apparent scale reduces to six storeys, but the full mass is scarcely concealed on the sheer wall to Finsbury Street. It is claimed that Ropemaker Place is a highly sustainable development, with solar panels, brown roofs and greywater recycling. Worryingly, this is the third building on the site since the Second World War: Covell Matthews Wheatley's building of 1987 for Merrill Lynch was obsolete within fifteen years. One hopes that lessons are being learned.

The main architectural ambition of Ropemaker Place faces south and confronts the soaring scale of CityPoint **233** on the opposite side of Ropemaker

Street. Originally known as British Petroleum's Britannic Tower, by F. Milton Cashmore & Partners, and for a while after its completion in 1967 the tallest building in the City (120 metres), this was part of a small northern high-rise cluster that included the three blocks of the Barbican. An extravagant proposal by the Catalan architect Santiago Calatrava to extend it to 200 metres was rejected in 1996 and replaced in 2001 by a less ambitious, but nonetheless radical, reconstruction scheme by Sheppard Robson. This added a sculptural top and curved prows to each end, and created a wider footprint incorporating shops, enlarged office foyers and a spectacular new public route through the base.

The canyon of Chiswell Street is relieved by the wide expanse of Finsbury Square, Islington's most prestigious 'City' address, much rebuilt in recent years. The feeling of openness enjoyed by the bowling green (and for many months in 2011–12 by anti-capitalist campers) is largely thanks to the modest scale of the surrounding buildings, which have generally adhered to the planners' strict code of eight-storey Portland stone frontages. The design guidelines have nevertheless allowed individuality. Foggo Associates' 131 Finsbury Pavement **234** of 1998 is crisply articulated, and a rugged monolith by Stephen Cox on the corner with Chiswell Street is carved out of Indian stone. Foster + Partners' 50 Finsbury Square **235** on the other side of the road is more eye-catching, and was finished in 1999, before any of Foster's other projects in the City. The spacious double-height glazed entrance was also something of a novelty at the time, and that proved attractive for the new tenant, Bloomberg. No. 30 Finsbury Square **236** on the east side, by Eric Parry Architects and completed in 2002 for the investment company Scottish Widows, uses load-bearing limestone piers and horizontal pre-cast concrete – also considered to be innovative – and was arguably a more honest building, even if the ground floor lacks the generosity of no. 50. Shortlisted for the Stirling Prize in 2003, it remains one of Parry's

↖ Milton Gate **229**, seen here at the junction of Chiswell Street and Moor Lane, occupies a whole street block. The new entrance is on the right.

← On Finsbury Street the full height of Ropemaker Place **232** creates an extraordinary canyon.

CityPoint 233, south of Ropemaker Street, provides generous public realm, both under cover and in the open air.

No. 50 Finsbury Square **235**, seen here at the junction with Finsbury Pavement, complied with planners' requirements for eight storeys and Portland stone cladding.

No. 30 Finsbury Square **236** occupies half of the eastern side of the square.

signature buildings. Nos 1–2 **237**, by Horden Cherry Lee Architects in 2005, reverts to the Foster model of horizontal bands and vertical columns of clip-on stone panels, continued by the same practice in 2007 at 10 Chiswell Street, virtually a sister building. A similar solution has been adopted by Sheppard Robson for the remainder of the west side, nos 3–10 **238**, under construction in 2012. A ten-storey scheme for this long, thin building, backing on to the Honourable Artillery Company grounds, was rejected by a planning inspector as being too high. The pleasing scale of Finsbury Square looks set to be maintained, although it is hard to ignore some of the high towers to the south and east.

Sheppard Robson's most significant contribution to the area was made in 1997 with the Helicon Building **239** on the corner of Finsbury Pavement and South Place. This giant curve of glass protected by a silvery lattice, above a large Marks and Spencer, was considered by the *Architects' Journal* to be a 'breakthrough in two respects – firstly in its Neo-modernist style, breaking the hold of Postmodernism, and secondly for its inclusion of a large retail store on the ground floor and basement levels, prefiguring more recent City developments' (20 January 2011, p. 79). Describing it as 'an impressive gateway to the City from the north', the reviewer overlooked the fact that 1 South Place/70 Finsbury Pavement is actually not within the City, but instead forms a gateway to Islington from the south. A genuine entrance to the City is promised with the redevelopment of 120 Moorgate **240** on the opposite corner of South Place. Granted planning permission in 2011 and due to be completed in 2014, Lifschutz Davidson Sandilands' first City building will comprise a solid masonry frontage of seven storeys with a higher glass box behind.

The Helicon still looks good, well into its second decade. Allies and Morrison's mansarded and metallic replacement of Spencer and Coventry houses (which were sadly demolished in 2011) with the eighty-bed 'boutique' South Place Hotel **241** is restrained in comparison. Surely the old buildings could have been converted to provide something less anodyne.

Retro-fit has been successfully pursued near by in Finsbury Circus, a magnificent Edwardian set piece that has been respected and reinvigorated for the twenty-first century. Peter Inskip + Peter Jenkins Architects showed how it could be done back in 1989, when the interior of Edwin Lutyens's Britannic House was skilfully reordered, with a new atrium inserted into the former light wells. Park House, 16–18 Finsbury Circus **242**, was equally sensitively remodelled in 2008 by John Robertson Architects, with a new north facade to Eldon Street. No. 1 Finsbury Circus **243** was rebuilt as a successful pastiche in 1990 by Kenzie Lovell Partnership, and RIver Plate House next door at nos 7–11 is promised a complete overhaul by Wilkinson Eyre Architects. Finsbury Circus House of 1992 by GMW Architects provides the centrepiece of the north side, with its prominent pediment. Now renamed 10 South Place **244**, it was gutted in 2012 to create

The most impressive part
of the Helicon Building,
1 South Place and
70 Finsbury Pavement **239**,
is its curved corner, facing
the border with the City.

South Place Hotel **241**, at the junction with Dominion Street, has a flat and metallic finish, unlike anything else in the vicinity.

↓ In the northern segment of Finsbury Circus, Park House **242** contributes to a remarkable Edwardian architectural ensemble.

access from both north and south, with a new top floor designed by Fletcher Priest Architects. The completion of Crossrail will be a vast improvement, restoring the central public garden after the lengthy and disruptive construction works.

The contextual theme continues down to the section of London Wall east of Moorgate, where the highway engineers' ambitions to extend the motorway of Route XI (see p. 142) were fortunately abandoned. On the corner with Blomfield Street, 85 London Wall **245** by Casson Conder Partnership (1989) may seem overly mannered, with its bays, turrets and medley of stone, and so too 60 London Wall **246** on the south side, an attempt by Fitzroy Robinson in 1992 to make a long frontage appear as several different structures. Nevertheless these buildings, together with the surviving older fabric, provide an essential foil to the more dramatic statements near by, such as Moor House, or to the high towers further east. The Apex London Wall Hotel at 7–9 Copthall Avenue **247** is a more recent example (2009), where Ian Springford Architects has admirably married a cool stone frontage with warm red-brick warehouse-style elevations to Whalebone Court and Telegraph Street. The City needs new buildings like these: showing modesty as well as majesty.

Buildings on the south side of London Wall, either side of Copthall Street, have been designed to make long frontages appear as a group of smaller properties. No. 60 **246** is on the left.

9
BROADGATE

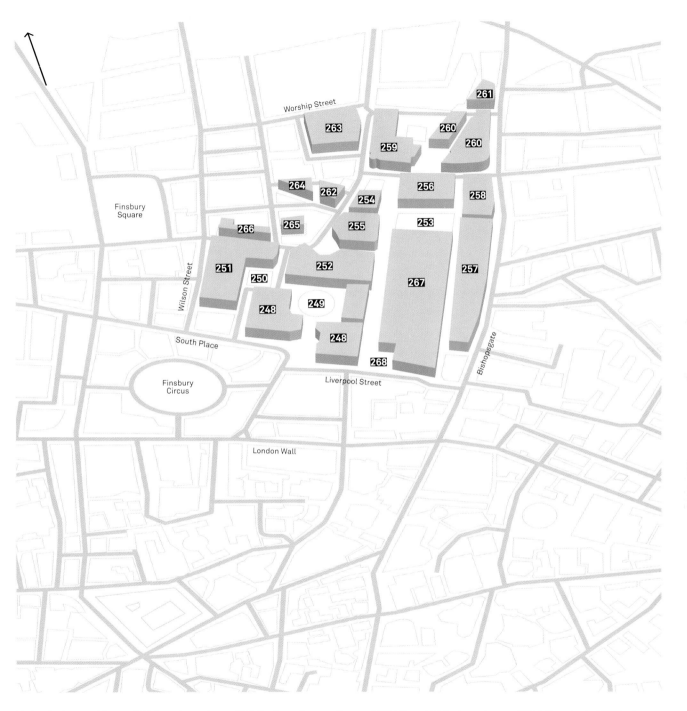

248 100 Liverpool Street **249** Broadgate Arena **250** Finsbury Avenue Square **251** 1,2 and 3 Finsbury Avenue **252** 5 Broadgate **253** Exchange Square **254** 10 Exchange Square **255** 1 Appold Street **256** Exchange House **257** Bishopsgate Exchange, 175 Bishopsgate **258** 199 Bishopsgate **259** Broadwalk House, 5 Appold Street **260** Broadgate Tower, 201 Bishopsgate **261** Principal Place **262** Bavaria House, 13–14 Appold Street **263** Broadgate West, 9 Appold Street **264** 30 Crown Place **265** 10 Crown Place **266** 1 Crown Place, 5–29 Sun Street **267** Liverpool Street station **268** Hope Square

Sculpture at Broadgate Arena **249**: Barry Flanagan's *Leaping Hare on Crescent and Bell*; and Richard Serra's *Fulcrum*.

If the Barbican is the City's most significant public-sector post-war development, then Broadgate is its largest and most ambitious privately led redevelopment project after the deregulation of 1986. It remains an impressive piece of urban planning, extending from Liverpool Street station for a half a kilometre north into the fringes of Shoreditch, beyond the City boundary. Rab Bennetts, who in 1986 was a young architect in Peter Foggo's Group 2 team at Arup, designing the first phase, describes Broadgate as radical in conception, staggeringly fast in execution and pivotal in the property and architectural world. Few could disagree.

The opportunity to create the Broadgate scheme was presented by the closure (and demolition in 1985) of Broad Street station, the original Victorian terminus of the North London line, and its extensive tracks, yards and sidings. Rail travel at that time did not seem to have a bright future. A joint-venture partnership of British Rail with Stuart Lipton and Godfrey Bradman's newly formed property company Rosehaugh Stanhope Developments (the successor to Greycoat) not only took in the vacant land but also developed over the sunken railway lines of the adjoining Liverpool Street station, covering more than 11 hectares in total. Broadgate, along with the development at Fenchurch Street station, was the first 'air rights' scheme in the City, and paved the way for others at Cannon Street and the old Holborn Viaduct stations.

In predicting and meeting a surge in demand for large-scale dealing floors, Lipton was keen to adopt fast construction methods that he had seen being pioneered in America. Arup was appointed as the architect following its commission by Greycoat in 1982 for an office building in Finsbury Avenue, facing Wilson Street. Lipton persuaded Arup to use steel framing rather than concrete throughout (including for floors), dry internal finishes and high-specification prefabricated cladding. It was expensive, but the speed of construction was extraordinary. Margaret Thatcher, who was invited to operate the crane with the first cladding panel in the summer of 1987, returned exactly twelve months later to open the first 60,000 square metres. By the end of 1989, a total of 200,000 square metres had been completed. Nothing like it had been done before in Britain. Broadgate, and Finsbury Avenue in particular, became the exemplar of steel construction in the United Kingdom, on the North American model.

Foggo's team at Arup was determined to plan a coherent and attractive layout for pedestrians, generous spaces in which Lipton and Bradman could indulge their passion for sculpture and art. They commissioned numerous new works from leading British and international artists, some to adorn the foyers, lobbies and atriums of their new buildings, but many also to stand outside, to be enjoyed by the public. The first phase, to the west of Liverpool Street station, was centred on two new fully pedestrianized public squares. Approached past the polished pink granite columns and lattice of 100 Liverpool Street **248**

Seasonal changes at Broadgate Arena **249**: looking north towards Broadgate Tower **260** in summer; and looking south across the ice rink towards 100 Liverpool Street **248** in winter.

George Segal's *Rush Hour* strides across Finsbury Avenue Square **250**, with 1 Finsbury Avenue **251** behind.

An octagonal canopy protects Whitecross Place, which separates 1 and 2 Finsbury Avenue **251** and provides a pedestrian route between Finsbury Avenue Square **250** and Wilson Street.

(considered at the time to be the smartest address in the development), with its humming cylindrical vent shafts in the pavement, the entrance to the Broadgate Arena or Circle **249** is narrow and dominated by the angular, rusting metal plates of Richard Serra's *Fulcrum*, commissioned in 1987. A sunken arcade of shops leads back to the station, but up the steps the amphitheatre of the arena makes a dramatic centrepiece. It hosts al fresco dining in the summer and ice skating in the winter, and it is worth climbing the stained concrete terraces for the view. On the east side, facing the entrance to the UBS offices, Barry Flanagan's *Leaping Hare on Crescent and Bell* (1988), in black steel, makes a playful and gravity-defying foreground for the solid pink Swedish granite that covers 8, 10 and 12 Broadgate. Lipton and the City planners had insisted on 'bankers' stone' to face the more prestigious buildings near Liverpool Street, but Foggo was equally insistent that its use merely as a screen should be clearly apparent. Plans being made by the developer British Land in 2012 to replace some of the ground-floor offices with shops will reinforce Broadgate Circle as a social hub.

The second public space, Finsbury Avenue Square **250**, is larger and more open, and enclosed to the west and north by the distinctive and austere geometry of Arup's 1, 2 and 3 Finsbury Avenue **251**, completed in 1988. Although less flamboyant than the pink polished stone and drum of the south side, the external dark-bronze framing and cross-bracing are elegant, sober in feel with their tinted glass, and exceedingly well proportioned. Finsbury Avenue ranks with Richard Rogers's flamboyant building for Lloyd's (**102**; see chapter 4) as a demonstration of low-key high-tech. It won the Royal Institute of British Architects' National Award (the precursor of the Stirling Prize) in 1991. George Segal's life-size sculpture *Rush Hour* (1987), of tight-lipped commuters dressed for wet weather, is a suitably understated adornment. In the north-west corner Whitecross Place runs beneath an octagonal glass canopy to Wilson Street, and the dull back elevations of offices that face Finsbury Square. To the south, Finsbury Avenue connects with Eldon Street, where Jacques Lipchitz's striking *Bellerophon Taming Pegasus* (1987) stands in front of a wall of rough honey-coloured stone. The landscaping of Finsbury Avenue Square was redesigned in 2009 to include a new lighting grid by Maurice Brill, with changing patterns and colours.

Amid such civility it is impossible to avoid the huge construction site to the north where Make's massive 5 Broadgate **252** is rising. The demolition in 2011 of the original 4 and 6 Broadgate provoked enormous controversy, and pitted conservation against economic growth in a way that exposed raw nerves not seen in the City, perhaps, since the Number One Poultry inquiry (**069**; see chapter 3). The overruling by the government minister Jeremy Hunt of English Heritage's recommendation to list these Arup-designed blocks was handled with decorum. Less dignified was the statement by Make's founder, Ken Shuttleworth, that Foggo (who died tragically young in 1993) had never liked his own design and would have wanted to see the buildings pulled down, an allegation strongly denied by Foggo's widow. When finished in 2015, Make's replacement will be the new headquarters for UBS in London, with 66,890 square metres of state-of-the-art trading facilities. Its thirteen storeys will certainly change the character of Broadgate Arena and Finsbury Avenue Square, not necessarily for the better, but by then it may have threatened the future of more of the original Broadgate blocks. It remains to be seen whether it will improve connections to the railway and bus stations along Sun Street Passage.

After 1988 Arup declined further commissions at Broadgate, and the second phase was given to the American firm SOM. Much of this was planned around a third public square, constructed immediately north of Liverpool Street station on a raft above the tracks. Exchange Square **253** is a larger but less unified architectural composition than the first two. The landscaping and public art are also less coherent: a line of trees, a patch of manicured croquet lawn and different levels of paving. Fernando Botero's *Broadgate Venus*, voluptuous or obese according to taste, on the east side contrasts with Xavier Corbero's severely malnourished *Broad Family* at the foot of the steps to Appold Street. No. 10 Exchange Square **254**, completed only in 2004, provides a new gateway into the square from the west, and headquarters for the law giant Herbert Smith (now merged with Freehills) and the global investment firm Western Asset. The huge eleven-storey curve of glass is grimly monolithic, but counterbalances the stolid pinkish-brown masonry of the chamfered cube of 1 Appold Street **255**. In the changing world of architectural fashion and lettability, and with 5 Broadgate rising immediately to the south, who knows if this will be the next piece of the Broadgate jigsaw to be removed.

The north side of Exchange Square is dominated by the monumental arch of Exchange House **256**, surely SOM's most spectacular contribution from the

↗ Xavier Corbero's *Broad Family* outside 10 Exchange Square **254**, with Bavaria House, 13–14 Appold Street **262** and the tall wedge of 30 Crown Place **264** beyond.

→ Jacques Lipchitz's *Bellerophon Taming Pegasus* in Finsbury Avenue.

↑← The north and east sides of Exchange Square **253** are enclosed by the colossal arch of Exchange House **256** and the solid mass of Bishopsgate Exchange **257**. The gable end of Liverpool Street station **267** is on the right. Fernando Botero's *Broadgate Venus* lies in front of Bishopsgate Exchange.

↗ No. 10 Exchange Square **254** is sandwiched between 1 Appold Street **255** to the left and Exchange House **256** on the right.

→→ The east-facing colonnade of Bishopsgate Exchange **257** is lined with shops and Beaux Arts-style lights.

→ The open ground floor of Exchange House **256** straddles the railway tracks.

1990s. With the railway below, there is no room for foundations, and the structure spans 78 metres either side of the tracks. The ground floor is entirely open except for the glass-box entrance hung from the offices above. There is no attempt to conceal this engineering tour de force: the massive girders are carried on mighty pedestals like colossal Meccano, and there are huge expansion joints in the pavement.

No such daring is visible along the east side of the square. Bishopsgate Exchange, 175 Bishopsgate **257**, forms a continuous strip, 250 metres long, of pseudo-American Beaux Arts pastiche, an extraordinary exercise in bronze panels, stone in various colours, coronet cupolas and gables, using every trick in the book. The eastern Bishopsgate elevation is relieved by a raised colonnade, adorned with 'period' lamps and balustrades, which catches the morning sun and provides a quieter apron for the shops, away from the traffic. Alongside such whimsy, 199 Bishopsgate **258** is inexplicably plain, refurbished in 2012 for British Land by John Robertson Architects to achieve BREEAM Excellence (see p. 18). Bruce McLean's metallic face *Eye-1* (1993) provides a welcome splash of colour on the pavement.

Until the boundary review in 1994, much of Broadgate was within the borough of Hackney. This caused considerable political tension, including concern that City offices were pushing too far north and threatening the character and traditions of Shoreditch, and that if they did then Hackney wanted a share of the profits. Broadwalk House, 5 Appold Street **259**, was a controversial incursion into Hackney north of Primrose Street when it was built in 1992, and was at the time the most northern phase of Broadgate. SOM used, uniquely for the Broadgate scheme, a concrete frame and cladding, fussily modelled and coloured orange to simulate terracotta. After two decades of exposure to pollution it was proving difficult to keep clean. Inside, the large-floor-plate

offices of the legal firm Ashurst and the bank Crédit Agricole were upgraded by Jaguar Building Services in 2009 to fulfil modern expectations, and much subdivided.

All this is now dwarfed by the soaring mass of Broadgate Tower, 201 Bishopsgate **260**, completed in 2008, and surely possible only because of the extension of the City boundary north to Worship Street. This angular landmark at the northern tip of the City – more of a glass slab than a spire, although it is 165 metres high – is well away from the cluster of towers further south on Bishopsgate. Some fear it will stimulate pressure for more high buildings on the large Bishopsgate Goodsyard site on the east side of Shoreditch High Street. Off Primrose Street, the piazza at the base of the tower is softened a little by a group of maple trees, but is nevertheless dominated by gigantic metal struts, which carry a sloping canopy of self-cleaning glass and seemingly (but not actually) brace the tower. A cafe on the western side provides a modicum of activity, but at present it feels like the end of the road. The piazza on Worship Street terminates awkwardly, with steps down to the pavement and a view over the vacant site of Principal Place **261**, where in 2012 a Foster + Partners proposal awaited the green light. The scheme for 55,000 square metres of medium-rise offices, a residential tower of 243 open-market flats, fifty-six affordable homes (at Hackney's insistence) and shops was on hold following the decision by the developer, Hammerson, to sell the site to Brookfield and the withdrawal of a substantial pre-let. For a while it seemed a fringe too far, but Berkeley Homes is now showing interest, boosted by the prospect of a high-rise Pringle Brandon Perkins + Will scheme on the adjacent site of the Shakespearian theatre on Curtain Road. In terms of the impact on the finer grain of Shoreditch, Avanti Architects' mixed-use scheme for 1 Shoreditch might be a better, if less profitable, model to follow.

The Broadgate Tower **260** presents a narrow southern face to Primrose Street and a colourful entrance off the piazza.

The long western flank of the Broadgate Tower 260 rises behind the simulated terracotta of Broadwalk House, 5 Appold Street 259.

No. 30 Crown Place  makes a bold statement in the pedestrianized section south of Clinton Street, and has a recessed entrance between the lower and taller sections of the development.

West of Appold Street and north of Sun Street remains firmly in Hackney. Here the influence of Broadgate has steadily taken a stronger grip. Bavaria House, 13–14 Appold Street **262**, designed by Covell Matthews Wheatley in 1989 and now home of the bank Bayern LB, is modest in scale, snugly curved at each corner, rather like a piece of metallic machinery. To the north, SOM's Broadgate West, 9 Appold Street **263**, of 1999 is a dull affair, looking like a blatant effort to cram as much as possible (45,000 square metres, in fact) on to the site. Glass boxes pile up to a height of thirteen storeys, making an uncompromising neighbour to Philip Webb's 1860s terrace on Worship Street and the small-scale printing and furniture workshops and domestic premises of historic Shoreditch beyond.

More care has been taken in the southern section of Clifton Street, now known as Crown Place. Horden Cherry Lee's no. 30 **264** for Greycoat is undoubtedly tall, too tall perhaps for nearby Finsbury Square, but as a landmark office it is worth looking at. The building, completed in 2009 and occupied by the law firm Pinsent Masons, forms a pale green glass prow facing west, with the roadway in front landscaped to create a forecourt. Its south side is a wall of glass on Earl Street ending in a fusion of geometries. With only eight storeys, 10 Crown Place **265** shows less ambition but commendable restraint. It was designed after a limited competition by local architect MacCormac Jamieson Prichard (now MJP Architects) in 1998. The grit-blasted white reconstituted-stone columns and beams form a convincing framework typical of MJP's modern contextual style, which can be seen also at Paternoster Square (**001**; see chapter 1).

Beside the Flying Horse public house on the corner of Wilson Street, the sadly neglected Georgian terrace in Sun Street is proposed for retention in the shadow of a glass office tower, part of the scheme for 1 Crown Place, 5–29 Sun Street **266**, designed by KPF and given planning permission by

Hackney Council in 2009. Further along Sun Street, the Stephen Cox abstract of *Ganapathi and Devi*, expressing the tension between opposing beliefs, has been temporarily – perhaps symbolically – removed while 5 Broadgate takes shape.

The most easily overlooked component in the development of Broadgate and its subsequent success was the enlargement of Liverpool Street station **267**, implemented between 1985 and 1991. The British Rail Architects' Department accepted the advice of Peter Foggo and Arup to extend the platforms and canopy northwards as an exact facsimile; it was so well done that the northern gable exposed to Exchange Square appears genuinely Victorian. British Rail employed Nick Darbishire and Alastair Lansley to redesign the passenger concourse and entrance, inserting lightweight galleries to improve the circulation and glass screens to ameliorate the climate. It showed, for the first time, that an old station did not have to be knocked down to be improved (as had happened so disastrously at London Euston), and by changing minds and attitudes paved the way for such projects as St Pancras and King's Cross. On the Liverpool Street forecourt, renamed Hope Square **268** in 2006, Frank Meisler and Arie Ovadia's touching memorial *Children of the Kindertransport* is a new attraction for tourists, and a good addition to an area that has the best concentration of public art in the City.

↙ The main entrance to 10 Crown Place **265** addresses the street in a conventional manner.

↓ Hope Square **268** and the memorial to the Kindertransport, on the south side of Liverpool Street station **267**.

10

SPITALFIELDS
AND HOUNDSDITCH

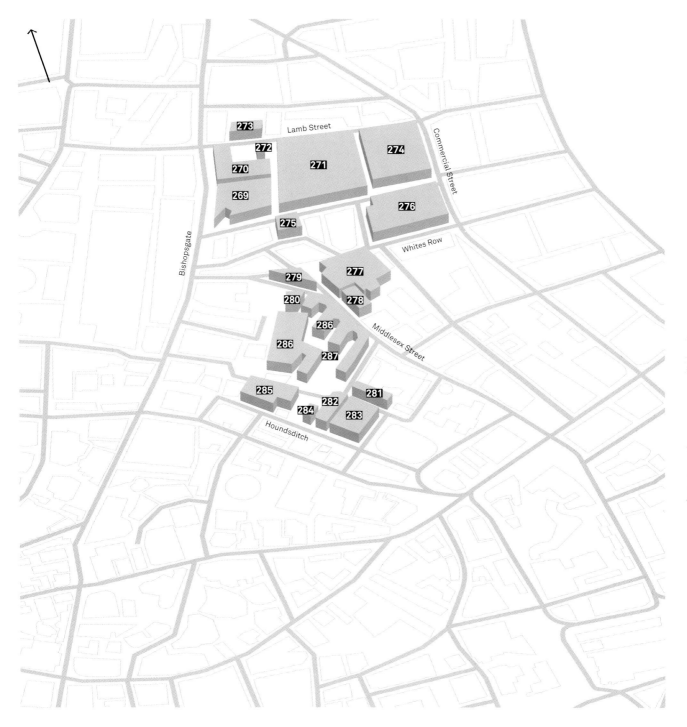

269 250 Bishopsgate 270 280 and 288 Bishopsgate 271 Bishops Square 272 20 Bishops Square 273 Eden House 274 Spitalfields Market 275 15–25 Artillery Lane 276 London Fruit and Wool Exchange 277 Nido Spitalfields, 100 Middlesex Street 278 102 Middlesex Street 279 110–114 Middlesex Street 280 East India House, 109–117 Middlesex Street 281 London Liverpool Street Hotel, 1 Harrow Place 282 Cutlers' Exchange, 123 Houndsditch 283 133 Houndsditch 284 117 Houndsditch 285 Premier Place 286 Devonshire Square 287 *Cnihtengild*

No. 250 Bishopsgate **269** forms an angular and strident corner with Brushfield Street to the right, and the main approach to Spitalfields Market from the west.

Just as Broadgate covers an area that originally straddled both the City of London and the London Borough of Hackney, so Spitalfields (or at least that part of it covered in this chapter: east of Bishopsgate and west of Commercial Street) is a district that falls largely outside the City, mainly within the borough of Tower Hamlets. After the boundary reform of 1994, the City actually lost territory to Tower Hamlets (a balancing act, perhaps, for gaining Broadgate), and that borough now administers everything north of Brushfield Street and east of Bishopsgate.

Spice is added by the fact that the City Corporation is a major landowner here. Beyond its boundaries the City cannot give itself planning permission, and so the transformation of Spitalfields is the culmination of a protracted planning saga, involving conflict between various political and developmental objectives and a vociferous local community.

The decision in 1987 to close the Spitalfields wholesale fruit and vegetable market (owned and run by the City Corporation), and its eventual relocation in 1991 to Temple Mills, Stratford, released a huge area of land for potential development and provoked a monumental planning battle. The Corporation as landowner saw it as a natural area for the expansion of City offices. The architecture critic Jonathan Glancey, writing in *The Guardian,* had likened the City to 'an overfed financier plumped up in a natty, pin-striped suit … fit to burst its boundaries' ('Office Politics', 17 December 2001) and desperate to spread east of Bishopsgate from the 'Brobdingnagian' Broadgate to the west. Tower Hamlets was interested in jobs for local people, rather than for bankers, as well as in housing and facilities that would benefit the impoverished local community. Conservationists wanted to preserve the Victorian market buildings and protect the setting of Hawksmoor's Christchurch and the early Georgian terraces to the east. Meanwhile, in a typically organic and entrepreneurial way, an alternative weekend retail market sprang up in the vacant buildings and, rather like that at Camden Lock, attracted huge crowds.

For a decade the City Corporation sparred with Tower Hamlets, and the Spitalfields Development Group tussled with the campaign group Spitalfields Market Under Threat (SMUT). Schemes and masterplans by Léon Krier, MJP Architects and EPR Architects were commissioned, debated and superseded. Three new office blocks facing Bishopsgate were approved in the late 1990s, helping to relieve some of the City's anxiety, but heightening the fears of the objectors. On the corner with Brushfield Street, 250 Bishopsgate **269** was designed by EPR and completed in 2000. With its corporate Royal Bank of Scotland totem pole on the pavement in front of its splayed corner entrance, it does little to lift the spirits. Nos 280 and 288 Bishopsgate **270**, both by Foggo Associates and completed a year later, are even simpler grey glass blocks, providing a further 33,000 square metres of offices. No. 280 rises to thirteen storeys to match the bulk of Broadgate opposite. No. 288 does at least step down to pay lip service to the scale of Spital Square, home of the Society for the Protection of Ancient Buildings.

In 2002 Tower Hamlets finally agreed a compromise scheme for Spitalfields Market, which secured the Victorian buildings on Commercial Street but allowed the 1920s western section to be demolished and replaced by 72,000 square metres of offices and 2 hectares of new public open space, financed by the developer Hammerson. Foster + Partners' Bishops Square **271**, finished in 2005, is self-effacing to the point of blandness, as discreet as three glass slabs and a twelve-storey headquarters for the law firm Allen & Overy could ever be. Thankfully, what still catches the attention when one enters Brushfield Street from Bishopsgate is Hawksmoor's magnificent spire at the far end. In the foreground a neat extension to the two-storey market frontage, now upmarket shops, is cleverly detailed.

↙ Kenny Hunter's *I Goat* stands on the north side of Brushfield Street, with Bishop's Court and the Heron Tower **110** behind.

↓ Nos 280 and 288 Bishopsgate **270**, together with no. 250 **269**, provide a continuous wall of corporate glass office blocks on the east side of the street. In the immediate left foreground is one of the elaborate Beaux Arts-style lamps of Bishopsgate Exchange **257**.

Offices in Bishops Square **271** are set in extensive public space. Ali Grant's *A Pear and a Fig* has now been moved to an entrance of the market arcade on Brushfield Street.

As if the planners were eager to outdo Broadgate, the public realm between the glassy office slabs is attractively landscaped and lavishly sprinkled with a frequently shifting mix of public art. Kenny Hunter's *I Goat*, near the west end of Brushfield Street, won the Bishops Square sculpture design competition in 2010 and is seemingly a permanent exhibit. It is an odd choice of subject standing on a pile of white packing cases, apparently representing the successive waves of immigrants into Spitalfields. Other artworks continue to come and go, or to be moved around. Ali Grant's *A Pear and a Fig* (2006) made a picturesque still-life beside the box hedges, trees, shrubs and lawns, but has been relocated to a market arcade entrance on Brushfield Street. Eleonora Aguiari's *Church* (2005) is an amusing bright red cut-out homage to Christchurch. Martynas Gaubas's *The Emigration* was a thought-provoking heart in a glass case in 2012, but was replaced until May 2013 by Martin Wild's *To Market, To Market*, one of a group of six metallic geometric shapes scattered around the concourse.

The demolition of the market sheds was the prelude to a major archaeological dig, one of the largest ever carried out in London, generously funded by the developer. The discovery of an elaborate coffin containing the body of a wealthy Roman woman made headlines in 1999. Hundreds of medieval and Roman bones were unearthed, together with the walls of the charnel house or chapel crypt of the priory and hospital of St Mary Spital. The masonry remains were preserved *in situ* and are imaginatively displayed and protected below a glass floor in the paving, with steps and a lift down for closer inspection and explanation. Paula Craft and John Pegg's nearby three-dimensional imaginary map of seventeenth-century London (with Civil War defences) makes a curious companion. Entitled *Lines of Communication* (2007), it now has a few tiny green weeds growing in the cracks, almost like miniature trees.

The rear elevations of 250 and 280 Bishopsgate **269** and **270** enclose the western side of Bishops Square. In this view looking south, 30 St Mary Axe **106** and the Heron Tower **110** can be seen in the distance.

The Broadgate Tower **260** is just visible behind 20 Bishops Square **272**. In the foreground, archaeological remains are displayed at basement level, beneath a glass floor.

At last, after the expanses of repetitive commercial glass, 20 Bishops Square **272** provides a delightful splash of colour. Matthew Lloyd Architects' residential block for the developer Native Land is a gem, and won an award from Grand Designs for Best Residential Development in 2009 and an award from the Royal Institute of British Architects (RIBA) in 2010. The RIBA judges' report describes the pleasingly multicoloured strips of orange, beige and brown terracotta that create the rain-screen as 'baguettes'. They do not look particularly edible, but the ground floor includes a cafe integrated into the neighbouring St Botolph's Hall, restored as part of the scheme. Eden House **273**, on the north side of Spital Square, was also completed in 2008 and also has five storeys, but reverts to grey glass and metal facing the street, albeit with a delicate sunshade of woven steel gauze. For the north and east elevations the architect, Scott Brownrigg, chose limestone and louvres to restrict light pollution and respect the privacy of residents in Folgate Street near by.

The north side of Bishops Square is its least appealing. Here, the grey orthogonal granite paving of what was Lamb Street feels oppressive, and the changing sculptures seem a rather forlorn attempt to bring life and interest. Wooden screens do their best to hide the ramp to the underground car parks.

The job of refurbishing and improving the surviving buildings of Spitalfields Market **274** was given in 2005 to two firms of architects, Jestico + Whiles and Julian Harrap Architects. It was done to a high standard, with such imaginative interventions as the five decorative metal gates. Crispin Place provides a north–south route between old and new, awash with places to eat under the cover of a chunky canopy connecting Bishops Square with the market. Only a short walk from the historic Sunday markets of Brick Lane and Petticoat Lane, it has become a weekend honeypot.

The south side of Brushfield Street is a mixed bag. The rear elevation of Bishop's Court does nobody any favours; it was quite rightly denounced in Tower Hamlets' Conservation Area guide in 2007 as 'not making a positive contribution'. Heery Architects & Engineers' 15–25 Artillery Lane **275** of 1988, on the corner with Fort Street, makes a better stab at enhancing the warren of alleys and narrow streets behind the Bishopsgate Institute. Further east, the former London Fruit and Wool Exchange **276** is also owned by the City Corporation, together with the ghastly multi-storey car park to the rear in Whites Row. In partnership with the developer Exemplar, and following extensive public consultation, Bennetts Associates designed a scheme to redevelop the entire block, including the car park. Tower Hamlets Council, the Spitalfields Historic Buildings Trust and the architectural historian Dan Cruickshank objected, preferring housing to offices and opposing the extinguishing of Duval Street (formerly the notorious Dorset Street of Jack the Ripper fame). They even commissioned an alternative scheme in 2012 from Johnston Architecture &

← Eden House, Spital Square **273**. The red tiled roofs of Folgate Street are to the right, and Broadgate Tower **260** soars behind on Bishopsgate.

The arcade on the south side of Spitalfields Market **274**, parallel to Brushfield Street, frames the spire of Christchurch.

The Nido Spitalfields tower **277** rises dramatically above its podium block on Frying Pan Alley (above) and the smaller buildings on Crispin Street (right). The western edges of the former London Fruit and Wool Exchange **276** and Whites Row car park are seen across Crispin Street. Seen from Bishopsgate (opposite), the tower looms above 110–114 Middlesex Street **279**.

Design, to keep more of the original fabric and rebuild Shepherd's Arch, which was destroyed in the Second World War. Bennetts' proposal retains only the frontage to Brushfield Street, dating from 1929; it reinstates the original pediment and removes the ugly 1960s extensions. A new symmetrical north–south axis would serve ground-floor shops, with 28,000 square metres of offices above. The Mayor of London, Boris Johnson, overruled local opposition and granted planning permission in October 2012. Assuming a pre-let, this final piece in the regeneration of Spitalfields might be completed by 2015.

Despite the gentrification of Spitalfields (including even the once shabby Brick Lane market), Petticoat Lane, or Middlesex and Wentworth streets, retains an edgy and shabby quality, being still full of rag-trade businesses, scruffy shopfronts, tawdry signs and semi-vacant upper floors. The Nido Spitalfields development at 100 Middlesex Street **277** was therefore seen by Tower Hamlets Council as very welcome new investment. Constructed in 2010, it is the tallest student-accommodation block in Britain, 112 metres and thirty-four floors high, providing 1200 beds for London Metropolitan University. With rents at £250 per week per person, it is presumably quite a money-spinner. The architect, T.P. Bennett, located the entrance in the narrow passage of Frying Pan Alley, where shops and cafes provide some life. Flush blue and grey panels work well on the five-storey podium, but their continuation on the tower becomes like a remorseless piece of marine camouflage. T.P. Bennett's scheme continues next door at 102 Middlesex Street **278**, in a simpler style but with the same ground-floor columns, providing offices and teaching space for the University of East Anglia. At least it is crisp and open in an otherwise dingy street.

Nos 110–114 Middlesex Street **279** is a disappointingly bland wedge-shaped block of 1989 by Yorke Rosenberg Mardall, four storeys of insipid brick, timid projecting bays and two set-back roof storeys. *The Buildings of England* of 1997 considered Harrison & West Architects' East India House, 109–117 Middlesex Street **280**, to be more pleasing, with its bands of yellow brick and pale stone (1991); the top of the southern turret is decorated with Judy Boyt's prancing horse. At street level it is almost as fortress-like as the smooth, polished granite of Richard Seifert's Cutlers' Gardens (see Devonshire Square, **286** below), which provides an impenetrable wall of ventilation grilles to the pavement. An attempt was made in 2004 by the City Corporation and its consultant Burns + Nice to improve the paving and lighting in Middlesex Street, but it has not fared well, and the raised planters become an impediment (and giant rubbish bins) when the Sunday market is in full swing.

Harrow Place connects Middlesex Street to Cutler Street. Between the curiously spelled Artizan Street and White Kennett Street, the London Liverpool Street Hotel, 1 Harrow Place **281**, is an off-the-peg design for Travelodge by Assael Architecture Studio and TTG Architects. It was completed in 2000, when

the City was still not regarded as a prime site for visitors. Times have changed, although the immediate environment of Harrow Place remains unpromising. Cutler Street itself is saddled with the rear elevations of a group of undistinguished postmodern offices: Cutlers' Exchange, 123 Houndsditch **282**, originally built in 1984 and extended in 1992 by RHWL Architects, all in smooth beige stone; and 133 Houndsditch **283** next door, by Carl Fisher & Partners in 1991. The latter is a formidably deep atrium block in various shades of grey, extremely unwelcoming but worth a detour to see the front entrance. The right-hand wall of the huge foyer has recently been lined with rough stone lit by downlighters, and the left-hand side in textured slate, in an effort to relieve the gloomy exterior.

Houndsditch may have improved its image since the Elizabethan chronicler John Stow attributed its name to the dead dogs that were regularly dumped there, but it has not been helped by the one-way traffic or by most of its architecture. 'An inert street of largely post-1960 vintage, its frontages featuring alternately blank tinted glass or witless postmodern detailing', was Kenneth Powell's description of it in the *Architects' Journal* of 28 March 2002. Povall Flood & Wilson's no. 117 **284** of 2000, a symmetrical composition clad in limestone, is an improvement.

It is perhaps not surprising that when the grim Houndsditch Telephone Exchange was closed, BT Property and its agent Simon Harris wanted a replacement that turned its back on Houndsditch and faced the more salubrious Devonshire Square. They and their successor, AXA Sun Life Properties, perhaps did not realize when Bennetts Associates was appointed as architect in 1996 that the result, Premier Place **285**, would be one of the City's more innovative new office buildings. In keeping with an early and passionate interest in American structural expressionism, and following the experience of working with Peter Foggo at Arup on Broadgate, Rab Bennetts was eager to offer an

↖ The Cutler Street frontage of Cutlers' Exchange, 123 Houndsditch **282**, viewed from Harrow Place.

← No. 133 Houndsditch **283** forms a long frontage to the north side of the street. Its bleakness might be ameliorated by some trees.

The main entrance of
Premier Place **285** is on
Devonshire Square **286**.
To the right, Barbon Alley
leads between Premier
Place and the neo-Georgian
electricity substation, to
Houndsditch.

alternative to the standard masonry-clad or glazed office facades so prevalent in the City. While there was nothing unusual about using a steel frame, as adopted at Broadgate and almost universally elsewhere in the City ever since because of its prefabrication and speedy construction on restricted sites, Bennetts's proposal was to express the structure externally, with a composition of posts, beams and window voids. This was a reversion to the honesty of Finsbury Avenue and a reaction against the 'stick-on' facades of Bishopsgate Exchange (**251** and **257**; see chapter 9).

Bennetts knew that 'architectural integrity is not a high priority in the City – our ideas had to be pragmatic and commercially viable' (quoted in Powell's article in the *Architects' Journal*, 2002). The initial proposal to use Cor-ten steel, which matures through oxidation, was dropped ('it made our clients nervous', Bennetts explained) in favour of a painted finish. He was able to convince his clients that the load-bearing steel facades were sufficiently engineered not to need cladding for fire protection, and that his design was no more expensive than a conventional one. Eventually completed in 2002, and occupied by the Royal Bank of Scotland, Premier Place remains a bold addition to the City's stock of new offices. Three corner service cores (an idea adopted by Foster + Partners at 10 Gresham Street, **059**; see chapter 2) not only make striking townscape features but also maximize uncluttered internal space. The design exploits the sloping site, with its entrance at first-floor level on Devonshire Square and servicing and basements beneath. The quality of the detailing and workmanship repays close inspection. It shows that even a blank elevation, such as that to Barbon Alley, can be beautifully done.

Improvements to the public realm in Devonshire Square **286** followed the completion of Premier Place, although not much could be done to disguise the neo-Georgian London Electricity Board substation, built in 1987 by Higgs and

Hill. The reinvention of Cutlers' Gardens by Rockpoint Group, its new owner, brought funding for further enhancement to the square, including espaliered limes and yew hedges, to specifications by Charles Funke Associates. Cutlers' Gardens was created by the redevelopment of the former East India Company premises by Stuart Lipton's development company, Greycoat, and Richard Seifert between 1978 and 1982, resulting in the loss of several magnificent eighteenth-century warehouses to dull replacements and an impenetrable fortress of monotonous offices. The building was rebranded in 2008 as Devonshire Square, with the aim of integrating with the urban environment outside, and residential and retail use has been introduced to encourage life outside working hours. Transparent office reception pods have been added by Fletcher Priest Architects, but most spectacular is the firm's roofing over of the western courtyard to provide evergreen trees, a water feature and shelter for outdoor seating. Perhaps it takes inspiration from Hay's Galleria on the South Bank, but it is done in a delightfully unostentatious manner.

   In the middle elevated arm of the central court, Denys Mitchell's striking *Cnihtengild* **287** of 1990, a mounted knight in armour, is a throwback to the pompous pre-recession days, and refers to ancient duels that took place in the area. The horse's coat is inlaid with blue glass. Devonshire Square is not yet as friendly nor as open to the public as one might like, certainly compared to Fleet Place, Broadgate or Spitalfields. Perhaps Blackstone, which bought the complex from Rockpoint in May 2012, will take heed. For now the square remains gated, closed at weekends, and patrolled by zealous security guards. Fletcher Priest's work may be an admirable example of retro-fit, but more could yet be done to improve connections with Middlesex Street and all points east.

Denys Mitchell's *Cnihtengild* **287**, elevated among neatly clipped box, occupies the central court of Devonshire Square.

11

ALDGATE
AND THE EAST

288 Aldgate House, 33 Aldgate High Street **289** Beaufort House, 15 St Botolph Street **290** Spitalfields Column **291** St Botolph's House, 138 Houndsditch **292** Mitre Square **293** Trinity EC3 **294** 1 Aldgate **295** 2–5 Minories **296** 150 Minories **297** Aldgate Tower **298** 55 Mansell Street **299** Insignia House, 83–85 Mansell Street **300** Goodman's Fields **301** Grange Tower Bridge Hotel, Prescot Street **302** 52 Minories **303** Tower Gateway station **304** 1 America Square **305** Jardine House, 6 Crutched Friars **306** Friary Court, 65 Crutched Friars **307** Grange City Hotel, 8–14 Cooper's Row **308** Novotel, 10 Pepys Street **309** Apex City of London Hotel, 1 Seething Lane **310** Double Tree by Hilton Hotel London – Tower of London, 7 Pepys Street **311** 10 Trinity Square

The City shares a long eastern border with the London Borough of Tower Hamlets, and it is at this boundary that the transition between wealth and poverty is most apparent and uncomfortable. For much of its length, heavy traffic on wide one-way streets makes it an unpleasant physical barrier to cross, in a way that is not so apparent on the City's western or northern boundaries. The gradient in land values moving eastwards must be one of the most extreme in London. It is also the case that many City workers do not choose to venture this way for refreshment, leisure or entertainment. Traditionally, the eastern part of the City has been dominated by the insurance sector. Investment managers, bankers and lawyers working in the west, centre or north of the City are rarely tempted eastwards.

The dreadful consequences of 1960s highway engineering still dominate the environment of Aldgate. Although one gyratory system was removed in 2010, returning Whitechapel High Street to two-way traffic and enabling the landscaping of Braham Street between Mansell and Leman streets, the huge roundabout fed by Duke's Place, Houndsditch, Middlesex Street, Mansell Street and Minories remains a maelstrom of buses, lorries, vans and intrepid cyclists. Pedestrians take second place amid acres of tarmac. Many buildings in the vicinity lack human scale or a pleasant ground-floor approach for visitors or passers-by. There are plans afoot, now agreed by Transport for London (which looks after London's trunk roads), to return three sides of the roundabout to two-way traffic, and to close the section of Duke's Place on the west side, thus linking Aldgate East station with Sir John Cass's Foundation Primary School. This might initially be done as an experiment, and the idea has been much promoted by the City Corporation, not surprisingly as the scheme improves the west side of Aldgate rather than the east. Meanwhile the traffic is a killer.

The Corporation's commitment to improving Aldgate was demonstrated by its commission of Studio Weave's Palace on Pillars, marking the start of High

The Palace on Pillars stands on a traffic island at the western end of Aldgate, a fanciful replica of the medieval gateway to the City of London and a reminder of the changing scale of buildings over the centuries.

Street 2012 and the route to the Olympic Games at Stratford. Erected on the site of the historic Aldgate, the skeletal, almost spectral timber gate was inspired by two dream poems, *The House of Fame* and *The Parliament of Fowls*, written by Geoffrey Chaucer when he resided in rooms above the arch.

Sharing the centre of the roundabout with St Botolph's Church and Aldgate East station, Aldgate House, 33 Aldgate High Street **288**, is colossal and lumpy. The recladding, spiced up with strips of blue, in 2008 by Sturgis Associates hides the 1970s pink granite. It is a definite improvement, but does not reduce the excessive bulk that dwarfs the charming group of seventeenth-century properties on the south side of Aldgate High Street. On the north side of the roundabout two even larger blocks balance the scale of Aldgate House. Beaufort House, 15 St Botolph Street **289**, designed in 1989 by RHWL Architects, rises to thirteen storeys and provides 37,000 square metres of large dealing floors and speculative offices. In date and in style, with its pompous pediments, variously coloured stone and heavy-handed detailing, it is remarkably similar to 20 Old Bailey (**205**; see chapter 7), by the same firm. The pedestrianization of the south end of White Kennett Street at least provides something of a forecourt, landscaped by Charles Funke Associates in 1990, and compensation for the harsh rear elevation on Middlesex Street. Richard Perry's Spitalfields Column **290** of 1995, now rather lost among bushes in the planter across the road, deserves a better setting.

St Botolph's House, 138 Houndsditch **291**, is also on an island site, west of White Kennett Street, and is the most pleasing addition to Aldgate in recent years. The developer Minerva commissioned Grimshaw to produce a building for flexible multi-letting, including the subdivision of individual floors, and it was opened in 2010. The ground level contains shops and a generous walk-through foyer from which everyone can admire the intriguing lift, with two cars in each

Beaufort House, 15 St Botolph Street **289**, faces the landscaping of White Kennett Street.

Aldgate House, 33 Aldgate High Street **288**. To the right the flank of Beaufort House **289** faces St Botolph Street, and to the left the Hoop and Grapes pub at 46 and 47 Aldgate High Street, with its clay-tiled roof, is a diminutive neighbour.

St Botolph's House,
138 Houndsditch **291**,
is carefully detailed at
street level (above), and
faces south towards the
church of St Botolph
without Aldgate (right).

shaft. Externally the building is a curvaceous oblong of horizontal blue bands, almost Art Deco in feel, extraordinarily different from Grimshaw's other City office in Gresham Street (**031**; see chapter 2); no production line is in evidence here, as with some architects. There is perhaps a slight family likeness with Minerva's other speculative office venture in the City, Foster's Walbrook (**076**; see chapter 3), which is also proving hard to let after completion. At St Botolph's House, however, the building itself is surely not the reason it has remained half empty.

The lack of interest from potential tenants has put several other speculative development schemes around Aldgate on hold. On the west side of Duke's Place, Helical Bar's Mitre Square scheme **292**, which was granted planning permission in June 2011, promises 27,000 square metres of prime office space, designed by Sheppard Robson, but needs a pre-let before the existing buildings will be demolished. The so-called Trinity EC3 scheme **293**, on the site of the Aldgate bus station and involving the demolition of its associated 1970s slabs, was approved in December 2007. Described somewhat pretentiously at the time by Foreign Office Architects (the oddly named husband-and-wife partnership of Farshid Moussavi and Alejandro Zaera-Polo) and its client, the developer Beetham, as a 'crystal cluster of multifaceted glass-walled towers', the three blocks of twelve, fifteen and twenty-three storeys could provide 100,000 square metres of offices, and a new bus station. The practice folded in 2011, and now there are fresh ideas from Zaha Hadid, adding potential new Peabody housing into the mix. Mackay and Partners' New Minories Hotel for Motel One, approved in the autumn of 2012, might become the first piece of the jigsaw, fronting 24–26 Minories and including 291 bedrooms in a sixteen-storey tower. It will not be difficult to improve on what is currently there.

More modest buildings have tried to present a brave face to the busy streets. Keith Dalton & Associates' 1 Aldgate **294** of 1990 is a substantial block of polished brown stone on the corner with Jewry Street, closer to the reassuring enclosure of Fenchurch Street. Near by, the same firm had designed the smaller green-clad 2–5 Minories **295** in 1988. No. 150 Minories **296** opposite is a sleek refit (2007) by Business Environment of an eight-storey 1970s block, providing small serviced offices (an important and sometimes neglected niche in the market). At no. 100, on the site of the former Sir John Cass School of Navigation, Buchanan Architects was in 2012 preparing a planning application for a 250-bed hotel.

South of the Aldgate roundabout, Mansell Street forms the boundary between the boroughs of the City and Tower Hamlets, and the route for northbound traffic skirting the City and avoiding the congestion-charge zone. At the Aldgate end neither side of the road has much to detain or delight the architectural enthusiast. Fitzroy Robinson's Sedgwick Centre of 1988, now renamed the Aldgate Tower **297** and occupied by the Royal Bank of Scotland,

Nos 2–5 Minories **295**, close to Aldgate, fits modestly and inconspicuously into the street scene. Its setting will change with the construction of the New Minories Hotel **293**, which promises a substantial increase in scale.

is a formidable hulk that does little to enhance the worthy landscaping of Braham Street. The addition of a heavy, solid awning to Mansell Street is no improvement. Standon House on the south side of Braham Street, also by Fitzroy Robinson, is scarcely better. EPR Architects' Mansell Court continues the late 1980s theme along that side of Mansell Street, with polished red stone and an impenetrable ground floor, despite the giant pediment. A second arch denotes the entrance around the corner at 1 Alie Street. The corner treatment of WorldPay's premises at no. 55 **298** with triple tubes of glass, designed in 1988 by Trehearne and Norman, Preston and Partners, is simply bizarre, like something out of a giant chemistry set. This firm had by then already produced the long deck-access residential slabs opposite, their perimeter walls producing a lifeless frontage along the west side of the street. This must surely be the least City-like part of the City.

One modern building stands out further south on the east side of Mansell Street. Nos 83–85, Insignia House **299**, is a wonderful antidote to the stolid monsters further north, and was nicely described in *The Buildings of England* (p. 553) as 'a draught of pure water after too many coloured sweets'. John Winter & Associates' transparent glass box, projecting boldly in front of the established building line and the white panels of the main elevation behind, is a defiant statement and a clever way of providing some environmental protection from a noisy and polluted street. In 1991, when it was completed, it was a stunning piece of minimalism, prescient of an architectural trend that emerged later in the decade in such buildings as the Helicon on Finsbury Pavement (**239**; see chapter 8). It is interesting that Insignia House and the Helicon are actually in neighbouring boroughs. The avant garde (the Lloyd's building excepted) was eschewed in the City at that time, or at least regarded with caution, only to be welcomed and encouraged in the late 1990s.

↖ The three circular lift shafts are a prominent feature of 55 Mansell Street **298** at its junction with Alie Street.

← Braham Street, seen here from Mansell Street, is now closed to traffic and has been landscaped.

Insignia House,
83–85 Mansell Street **299**,
opposite Portsoken Street,
catches the afternoon sun.

Student accommodation at 52 Minories **302** occupies the busy corner of Minories and Goodman's Yard. To the right, approached off Goodman's Yard, a new public garden has been created to provide some refuge from the traffic.

There is little sign of pressure for new office development on the Tower Hamlets side of Mansell Street, or beyond. From 2008, when building work stopped following the collapse of the Icelandic Landsbanki, until the spring of 2012 when construction resumed with new funders, the skeleton of 1 Commercial Street on the corner of Whitechapel High Street stood like a scarecrow. As completed, by Broadway Malyan for the developer Redrow, it has only six floors of offices, and more lucrative flats above. To the east on Leman Street (the one-way southbound counterbalance to Mansell Street) the development pressure is for residential buildings. Berkeley's phased development at Goodman's Fields **300** and 75 Leman Street is primarily for private flats. Liftschutz Davidson Sandilands' masterplan for the 2.8-hectare site is for 788 new homes, a hotel, student housing, offices, workshops and community space. Luxury living is the focus and selling point of the twenty-three-storey Altitude tower at 61–75 Alie Street for Barratt Homes. No doubt the Corporation is happy to see new housing that might appeal to City workers so close to its borders, allowing it to reserve its own sites for commercial development. It is also happy to see new hotels, including David Miller Architects' twenty-three-storey Leman Street Hotel for Pinehill Capital, granted planning permission in 2012. One hopes it will be more enchanting than the monolithic towers and brick panels of the Grange Tower Bridge Hotel in Prescot Street **301**, which was designed by Buchanan Architects and opened in 2011.

This eastern edge of the City certainly has a mixed-use feel. While the Corporation has been reluctant to encourage exclusively residential schemes, either converted or newly built, fearing that they fossilize and inhibit future change, it has allowed the redevelopment of 52 Minories **302**, ostensibly to provide 188 student rooms and flats. From £150 per week for the smallest room to £115 per night for the largest units, it is more likely to provide serviced apartments. Completed in the spring of 2012 and designed by BFLS for J.G. Land & Estates and Urbanest Student Accommodation, it lives up to its billing as a 'gateway' building, eleven storeys high on the curving corner, with green walls at the side and rear, and rated BREEAM 'Excellent' to boot (p. 18). It does its best to cheer up Goodman's Yard, which is arguably the least attractive street in the City (discounting the tunnel of Castle Baynard Street).

On the south side of Goodman's Yard, the conversion of Fitzroy Robinson's offices from 1983 into a Travelodge (2005) barely disguises its outward resemblance to a multi-storey car park. Lloyd's Chambers, on the north side – designed by the same architect in the same year but with its main entrance at the back on Portsoken Street – is scarcely better. Even in 1997 *The Buildings of England* struggled to find positive things to say about this corner of the City. It did note that Tower Gateway station **303** by Arup in 1987 was at that time the City's newest railway terminus, serving the Docklands Light Railway. For twelve years, until the Jubilee line extension opened in 1999, it was the fastest ride from the City to Canary Wharf, and it remains the most scenic. Perhaps the domed and barrel-vaulted canopies were exciting at the time, but they seem dated and grubby today.

To the west of Minories, Crosswall is a merciful escape from racetrack traffic and a return to the narrow streets and alleys that characterize the more pleasant parts of the City. At first sight 1 America Square **304** is quite a surprise, resembling something from 1930s New York, but less high. In this air-rights development of 1991 above and around the elevated tracks of the Fenchurch Street railway, RHWL Architects indulged in an Art Deco fantasy, as complete and extraordinary in its own way as GMW Architects' contemporary Gothic folly at Minster Court (**129**; see chapter 5). It is certainly more entertaining than RHWL's clunky and chunky Beaufort House (**289** above), particularly the jazzy chrome

The Art Deco detailing of 1 America Square **304** repays close inspection.

Michael Black's sculpture stands at the back of Friary Court, 65 Crutched Friars **306**, at the corner with Rangoon Street.

entrances decorated by Brian Clark's stained glass. Perhaps the architect drew inspiration from the 'moderne' faience style of nearby Ibex House (1937) in Minories, which was immaculately restored in 1995 by Rolfe Judd. The openness of America Square is a suitable setting for the bulk of no. 1. Unfortunately it did not inspire Burnet Tait & Partners in 1989 to produce anything of equivalent quality at no. 2, which is merely a 'wallpaper' facade of postmodern gimmickry. Other commentators have been even ruder.

At the west end of Crosswall, where the railway bridge spans the five-way junction, Jardine House, 6 Crutched Friars **305**, forms a flat-iron wedge at the acute corner, clad in pink granite but with lots of glass on the lower levels. It was designed in 1988 by Scott Brownrigg + Turner, and the interior was fitted out later by Michael Hopkins and Eva Jiricna, but is sadly not open to public view. On the opposite side, Friary Court, 65 Crutched Friars **306**, by Chapman Taylor (1985) is in similar pink stone. There is nothing startling or noteworthy about it until the rear corner with Rangoon Street, where Michael Black's jolly sculpture of two friars is cleverly hewn from the same granite as the building.

South of the railway bridge, a mini-district of hotels has developed since the turn of the century. It began, quite unassumingly, with the conversion and extension in 2002 of various small vacant buildings abutting the flank of America Square at 8–14 Cooper's Row into the Grange City Hotel **307**. Buchanan Architects reworked the slab of Richard Seifert's former Midland House to accommodate most of the 325 bedrooms, retaining the entrance and way through to the courtyard behind, which hides a surprise. Over the border by a metre or so into Tower Hamlets is the most spectacular surviving section of the wall to Roman Londinium, 11 metres high and 30 metres long. For once, the pallid architecture of the hotel is a good foil for this miraculous remnant of antiquity.

The Novotel, 10 Pepys Street **308**, was completed in 2002 on the corner of Cooper's Row, in undemonstrative pale-yellow stock brick, with rusticated artificial stone plinth and window dressings, and with quasi-shopfronts but without the shops. The architect, John Seifert (son of the illustrious Richard), specialized in hotels and offices, but his firm ceased trading in 2010. In common with the Grange City Hotel, the Apex City of London Hotel at 1 Seething Lane **309** (2006) was also a conversion and extension of former offices. With only 130 bedrooms, it more justifiably fits into the 'boutique' category that so many larger hotels claim. John Robertson Architects used brown terracotta to clad the extensions at the rear, which overlook the lovely churchyard of St Olave, and added a neat single-storey glazed frontage to Seething Lane.

A much more significant addition to hotel capacity in the area was the completion in 2010 of the Mint Hotel at 7 Pepys Street **310**, on a large site that runs through to Crutched Friars and was previously occupied by dull 1960s offices. With 583 bedrooms and suites, bars, restaurants and conference

The Grange City Hotel, 8–14 Cooper's Row 307, is an ensemble of several buildings. The Novotel, 10 Pepys Street 308, is to the right.

facilities spread over eleven floors, it is the largest hotel of its type in the City. For the architect, Bennetts Associates, it was an exciting new challenge, and one so successfully met that it has led to commissions for more hotels at home and abroad. The new building aims to reconnect with the tight urban grain of the narrow streets, in a way that the voids and setbacks of the previous blocks did not. This sense of enclosure is reinforced with public bars and cafes on the ground floor. Beyond the stunning porte cochère on Pepys Street, the spacious foyer is protected by a spectacular glass roof, with the central light well rising above. On the top floor, the Sky Lounge with its roof terraces offers skyline views in every direction, all accessible to the public. Bennetts and its client strove to make the Mint as 'green' as possible, literally through the covering of walls at high level with plants (as had been done at low level in New Street Square **151**; see chapter 6), but also with solar panels on the roof. It was disappointing when in 2011 the hotel chain City Inn sold out to the developer Blackstone, which changed the name to the jaw-breaking Double Tree by Hilton Hotel London – Tower of London. Proximity to the Tower and Tower Bridge is an obvious selling point for all these hotels, and is reflected prosaically in their names. Mint was short and sweet, and had a more subtle local connection.

Fuelled by the Olympics, a weak pound and an escalating flood of visitors to London, hotels remain a growth sector in an otherwise wobbly property market, and the City is now regarded as a good location for the luxury end of the scale. The announcement in 2011 of the acquisition by the Singapore-based developer KOP Group and the Chinese investment firm Reignwood of the enormous former headquarters of the Port of London Authority at 10 Trinity Square **311** was followed by proposals and planning permission in 2012 for a six-star 120-bed hotel with spa, members' club and forty-one exclusive private flats. The exterior of Edwin Cooper's iconic Grade II*-listed masterpiece of 1922 will remain, but the seven-storey 1970s infill is to be replaced. Woods Bagot and the interiors firm David Collins Studio aim to reinstate the original plan form and create a dynamic central courtyard under a new 'whirlpool' glass canopy. Due to open in 2014, it has been described by *GQ* magazine as 'uber-luxe' (22 September 2011), and aspires to set new standards for London. It remains to be seen whether the less affluent public will be able to make their own judgement.

The Mint Hotel is now called the Double Tree by Hilton Hotel London – Tower of London **310**. The porte cochère on narrow Pepys Street leads into a spectacular public foyer.

Looking south-east from the top of 30 St Mary Axe **106** towards Tower Bridge and the Tower of London. The green walls of the former Mint Hotel **310** appear above Lloyd's Register **119** with its oasis of trees off Fenchurch Street. Immediately left is the distinctive symmetry of 1 America Square **304**. Above the three steps of the Willis Building **103**, the Shard dominates the south side of the river.

12

THE RIVERSIDE

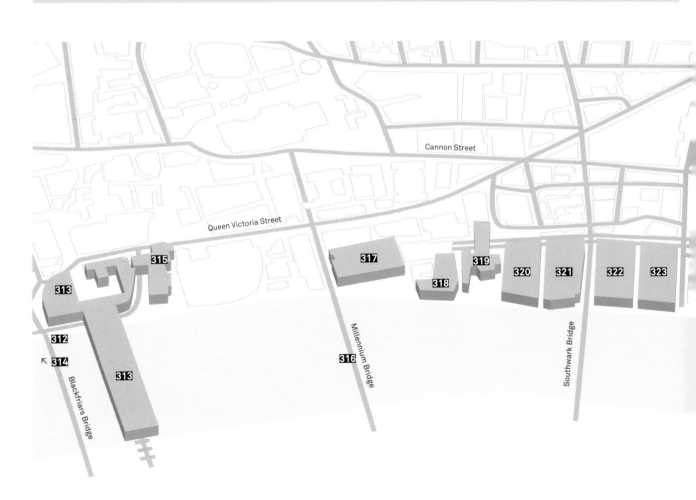

Cannon Street

Queen Victoria Street

315

313

312

314

313

Blackfriars Bridge

Millennium Bridge

316

317

318

319

320

321

322

323

Southwark Bridge

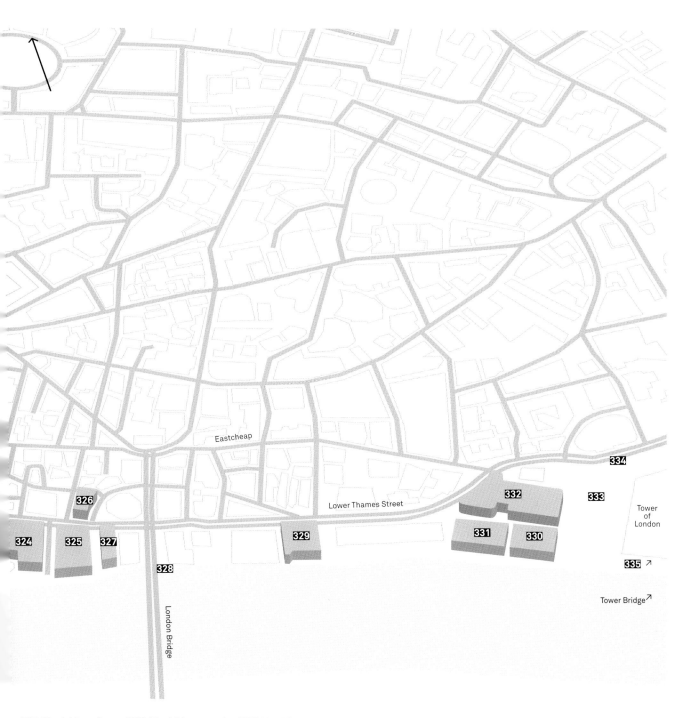

Eastcheap

Lower Thames Street

326

324 **325** **327**

328

London Bridge

329

332 **333** **334**

331 **330**

Tower of London

335 ↗

Tower Bridge ↗

312 Blackfriars Ramp **313** Blackfriars station **314** Blackfriars Bridge Foreshore **315** Puddle Dock **316** Millennium Bridge **317** Swiss Bank House **318** Sir John Lyon House **319** Queen Hithe Hotel **320** Thames Court, 1 Queenhithe **321** Vintners' Place **322** 10 Queen Street Place **323** Walbrook Wharf **324** Watermark Place, 1 Angel Lane **325** Riverbank House **326** 12 Arthur Street **327** Seal House, 1 Swan Lane **328** London Bridge Staircase **329** Old Billingsgate **330** Three Quays **331** Sugar Quay, 1 Water Lane **332** Tower Place **333** Tower Hill **334** *Building Worker* statue **335** Perkin Reveller

It is easy to forget that for centuries London was one of the largest ports in Europe. Navigability of the Thames and its lowest bridging point are the reason London is where it is. The decline of the docks and London's demise as a port after the Second World War meant that many of the City's riverside properties turned their backs on what had once been their lifeline. The post-war plan to construct a southern and northern motorway bypass to the City also had huge consequences for its riverside. The dual carriageway of Upper and Lower Thames streets effectively cut off the old wharves and river warehouses from the rest of the City, causing a far greater degree of severance than was ever the case with the more modest length of London Wall in the north. It continues to do so: pity the pedestrian who ends up in Castle Baynard Street.

However, the redundancy of the docks and quaysides sparked the idea of a riverside pedestrian route for the full length of the City of London. Before the Second World War, and indeed until the closure of such uses as Billingsgate Fish Market on Lower Thames Street (in the early 1980s), traditional riverside activity made such a plan unthinkable. Today that long-term vision, part also of a Thames path from source to mouth, has been almost completely realized, and gives a special and particular view of the City. The riverside walk also encompasses a series of small parks and plazas, making up 16,000 square metres of public space. The path connects with bridges that offer the opportunity to cross to the South Bank and enjoy the vistas across the water, and to approach the City on the newest and oldest crossings of the river. The idea for a temporary floating London River Park, moored along the north bank of the City to coincide with the Olympics in the summer of 2012, proved to be pie in the sky, or froth in the water. The worry, had it been built, was that there might have been commercial pressure to retain it indefinitely.

The river has been hailed as London's greatest asset, a strip of wildness that runs through the heart of the capital, powerful and dangerous, constantly ebbing

From London Bridge, the scale of Watermark Place **324** has been carefully controlled to preserve views of St Paul's Cathedral and the prominent towers of Cannon Street station. Riverbank House **325** makes a bolder river frontage.

and flowing. At the highest spring tides the water seems to rise perilously close to the top of the embankments and flood-protection walls, while at low tide beaches of sand, shingle, eroded bricks and oyster shells stretch towards the central channel. Whatever your take on the buildings, the riverside walk always has the water and its boats, beachcombers and wildlife to look at. Of all the chapters in this book, the riverside is most obviously a linear journey, and for want of a better reason than following the flow of fresh water to the sea with a prevailing wind on the back, it is here undertaken from west to east.

From the mature splendour of Victoria Embankment, the results of the City Corporation's Riverside Walk Enhancement Scheme of 2005 are soon in evidence. This began in 2002 with a report entitled *Upper and Lower Thames Streets and the Riverside Walk – Pedestrian Activity and Strategic Design Study*, commissioned from the consultant Space Syntax the previous year and paving the way for detailed improvements. The Blackfriars Ramp **312**, completed in 2009 and designed by the architectural firm The Facility, was one of the first of those. This once-dismal stretch beneath and between the road and railway bridges has been transformed by a roof of specially crafted curved mirrors, new paving and better lighting. A pedestrian link has been made to the Underground and rail stations. The extended Blackfriars Thameslink station **313**, which reopened in 2012, has platforms that occupy the full length of the railway bridge (built by John Wolfe-Barry and Henry Marc Brunel in 1880), shielded from the weather by canopies and screens designed by Tony Gee and Partners. On the roof, 4400 photovoltaic cells promise to provide half the station's power. The disappointment is that although waiting commuters can gaze through the glazed panels at the river flowing beneath, the structure itself impinges on the once magnificent panorama from the parallel road bridge. The spacious, vaulted northern station entrance and ticket office, by Jacobs Architecture, is more

The riverside walk near Puddle Dock, looking west towards Blackfriars station **313**, which spans the river, and the Blackfriars Ramp **312**.

uplifting. Blue strips on the curved glass frontage reflect the blue-coated vent and service shaft inside, which pops out of the top.

Glass minimalism on a smaller scale is also on show at Blackfriars Millennium Pier, funded by the City Corporation in 2000 as a pontoon for river craft. This modest structure and the whole shape of the riverbank on Victoria Embankment would be completely subsumed and altered by Thames Water's current proposals for a deep tunnel running for 32 kilometres beneath the river, to carry sewage and rainwater. The Thames Tunnel Scoping Report envisages a series of substantial build-outs into the river as part of the project. The Blackfriars Bridge Foreshore **314** is highly controversial, proposing to encroach into the river to provide permanent structures for both the construction and the operation of the new 'super sewer'. At Blackfriars the Fleet River Combined Sewage Overflow (the mixture of rainwater and sewage carried in the existing sewer flowing south) would drop via a new shaft into the deep tunnel below, rather than discharging into the river as it does now when flooded. The promotional material says that the wedge-shaped incursion will create new open space for London, but the consultation images show 'space for kiosks', a more likely scenario. The scheme remains highly contentious, in terms of both need and cost (£4 billion and rising); it is seen as either a vital necessity for London or a gravy train for consultants and contractors. If it is approved, work will start in 2016 and finish in 2022.

East of Blackfriars, Puddle Dock **315** remains for the moment an enclave of grey concrete 1970s development between the roaring highway and the lavender planters of the riverside walk. Although the whole site has been owned for several years by Blackfriars Investments Limited, much attention has been focused on the survival or otherwise of the Mermaid Theatre. Initial proposals to close and redevelop the theatre were opposed in 2003 by Ken Livingstone, the Greater London Authority and a host of thespians. As a result it was upgraded in 2004

↖ Visualization of the Puddle Dock Hotel (top), on the site of the Mermaid Conference and Events Centre.

↑← The entrance, ticket office and street frontage of Blackfriars station **313**.

into the Mermaid Conference and Events Centre, but the pressure did not go away. In September 2008 the City Corporation officially removed its theatre status (and thus any expensive obligation on a developer to incorporate a replacement in any new building). Despite continuing objections from the Theatres Trust, planning permission was granted in July 2010 for demolition and subsequent construction of the 251-bedroom Puddle Dock Hotel with conference facilities and restaurants. Constrained by the St Paul's Heights controls to seven storeys, with a double basement (flood-proof, it is to be hoped), Alsop Sparch's proposed design has been likened to the Media Centre by Future Systems at Lord's Cricket Ground, a similarly bold attempt to stand out from its context. If built, perhaps in 2014, it would be a startling addition to the riverside; as would the transformation of the White Lion Hill slip road into a 'green' ramp, free of vehicles, a way of taking pedestrians from the riverside path up to Queen Victoria Street.

The Puddle Dock Hotel might even take some attention away from the iconic Millennium Bridge **316**, which dominates this stretch of the river. The design by Foster + Partners and the sculptor Anthony Caro, engineered by Arup, has become such a symbol of 'modern London' that it is worth recalling that there was some anxiety at the planning stage about its acceptability. There were concerns that the structure, advertised as a 'blade of light', would block views of St Paul's from the river itself – for people on boats – and alternatives were explored that placed it to one side of the great vista of the dome. Good sense, and the then leading figure in the Corporation, Judith Mayhew, prevailed. The euphoric opening and early wobbles of the apparently flimsy bridge, together with its subsequent corrective stiffening, are now part of London's folklore. In fact the narrow and miraculously light steel fabric does not impede views: the supporting high-tension cables are kept low, alongside the deck, which is strong enough to

The Millennium Bridge **316** provides a direct pedestrian route between St Paul's Cathedral and the Tate Modern at Bankside. Stairs and ramps connect to the riverside walk with its polar sundial (right).

Swiss Bank House at
2 Lambeth Hill **317**, the
headquarters for Old
Mutual, faces the riverside
walk. The Millennium
Bridge **316** and the red
brick of the City of London
School are on the far left.

carry 5000 people at once over the 320-metre span. The Tate chimney to St Paul's dome has become London's latest processional route, carrying 5 million people a year, and the bridge itself is one of London's most thrilling vantage points.

Below the bridge, which is intelligently linked to the riverside path, is a polar sundial by Piers Nicholson, presented to the Corporation by the Worshipful Company of Tylers and Bricklayers and unveiled in December 1999. Either side of the bridge the buildings are low-key, the mid-1980s red brick of the City of London School to the west and a group of postmodern blocks to the east. Richard Seifert's Swiss Bank House of 1989 **317**, now offices for the investment firm Old Mutual, stretches deep inland, crossing over Upper Thames Street to Lambeth Hill, but makes little effort to enhance the river frontage. 'Crude decorative motifs in a child's building brick manner, altogether unworthy of its site' was *The Buildings of England*'s denunciation in 1997 (p. 618). In November 2012, renamed as Millennium Bridge House, a £35 million overhaul, including a simpler and lower facade, was unveiled by ORMS. Norfolk House next door, containing private flats, would also benefit from a redesign.

The redevelopment of Sir John Lyon House **318**, Upper Thames Street, by Sidell Gibson in 2009 provided an opportunity to create something livelier, which was happily achieved with flying colours. Modest in scale but striking in its use of different shades of beige and orange for a terracotta rain-screen to the retained frame of the previous office block, this development of sixty-five flats has won deserved praise as a positive contribution to the waterside. An arcaded ground floor and restaurant make provision for the continuation of the riverside path, but at present this ends disappointingly at the solid brick wall of Brook's Wharf, the last surviving riverside warehouse in the City. The pedestrian is diverted along the faceted red brick and sandstone of Broken Wharf House (refurbished by the developer Standford Properties in 2001) to brave the horrors of Upper

Seen from the Millennium Bridge **316**, Broken Wharf House and Sir John Lyon House **318** provide a colourful river frontage between Norfolk House **317** and the Victorian brick of Brook's Wharf. Tower 42 **095** and 30 St Mary Axe **106** rise behind.

Artist's impression of the proposed Queen Hithe Hotel **319**, where it would cross Upper Thames Street.

Thames Street and, across the traffic, the dreary back elevation of Senator House (**016**; see chapter 1). For a frustrating stretch the river is inaccessible. The cobbled Gardner's Lane leads only to rubbish bins; Stew Lane is also a dead end, but at least offers the Samuel Pepys pub and a glimpse of river. The riverside walk resumes at Queenhithe Dock.

Despite a new suspension-type pedestrian footbridge across Upper Thames Street, the massive hulk of Queensbridge House spanning the dual carriageway presents a huge challenge for anyone seeking improvements to the area. Proposals by Bennetts Associates and Resolution Properties for the Queen Hithe Hotel **319** would replace this and two other tired 1970s Hubbard Ford & Partners blocks with an elegant new series of buildings containing a 224-bedroom five-star hotel and private flats. Most importantly, it would complete the riverside walk (with cantilevers around Brook's Wharf) and, via its spacious and welcoming public foyers, could connect the historic Queenhithe Dock with Queen Victoria Street and St Paul's. It was granted planning permission in March 2012 and has much to offer, but demolition and construction above the incessant traffic of Upper Thames Street will be a logistical (and financial) headache.

Bennetts' scheme would make a good neighbour for Thames Court, 1 Queenhithe **320**, completed in 1998. Built speculatively, and now the European headquarters for the Dutch banking group Rabobank, this low-rise scheme makes the most of its corner position, fronting both the river and Queenhithe Dock, while also providing large floor plates and flexibility for the future. Inside, 27-metre trusses create column-free spaces. On the waterfront, the Alfred Plaque of 1986 records the 1100th anniversary of the resettlement of Roman London, rather than the start of the 'Big Bang' in the City. It is surprising that the main entrance is on the north-facing Upper Thames Street, where the architecture is less transparent, with yellow stone and dark grey metal. It makes

Thames Court, 1 Queenhithe **320**, faces Upper Thames Street with Queenhithe Dock beyond. In the foreground *The Barge Master and Swan Marker* stands across the road from Vintners' Place **321**.

an uncompromisingly honest contrast with Vintners' Place **321**, on both the Upper Thames Street and river frontages. Whinney Mackay-Lewis Partnership's quasi-classical edifice of 1993, described in *The Buildings of England* as a 'high point of naïve revivalism' (p. 617), is an extraordinary concoction of porticos and pediments, including a hollow echo of Fishmongers' Hall on the river, and a lavish if ill-considered mix of stone details, both inside and out. Commissioned by the Vintners' Company, it wraps around but signally fails to blend with the company's magnificent historic Hall. At least the Vintners installed Vivien Mallock's statue *The Barge Master and Swan Marker* on the other side of Upper Thames Street in 2007, as if to provide some light relief.

There are steep steps up to Southwark Bridge and a tunnel for the riverside path under its revetments. The bridge is the least used of all the river crossings, even less so after the closure of Queen Street to through traffic as part of the 'ring of steel'. Bicycles outnumber vehicles. From the middle there are magnificent views across the lowest part of the City, where St Paul's Heights restrictions have been most carefully managed. At least nine spires and steeples of Wren churches can be seen from here.

No. 10 Queen Street Place **322**, home of the law firm S.J. Berwin, occupies the river frontage east of the bridge, and extends right up to Upper Thames Street. Built in 1991 by Fitzroy Robinson as a dealing-floor groundscraper, it might have been doomed but for the excellent facelift it was given in 2006 by John Robertson Architects for the developer Blackstone. The new foyer is the best part, and it shows that without the risks and disruption of demolition and reconstruction, high value can be achieved. The building even won a British Council for Offices award. On the site of the ancient Dowgate, where the buried Walbrook stream flows into the Thames, the adjacent Walbrook Wharf **323** still has an important riverside function as the City Corporation's waste-transfer

↙ No. 10 Queen Street Place **322** runs from Upper Thames Street to Southwark Bridge.

↓ Vintners' Place **321** from Southwark Bridge. To the left is the glass facade of Thames Court **320**.

The riverside frontage (below) of the City Corporation's waste-transfer station at Walbrook Wharf **323** is sandwiched between 10 Queen Street Place **322** and Cannon Street station. Cannon Place **078** is behind, and the emerging core of 20 Fenchurch Street **132**. The Cleansing Department offices (below, right) face Upper Thames Street.

station. From here up to 400 tonnes of rubbish every day are loaded on to barges, which are then towed by tug to the appropriately named Mucking Marshes landfill site in Essex. At certain times the riverside path is closed for operational reasons, requiring a diversion via Upper Thames Street and back down Cousin Lane. Built by Cory Environmental in 1996, the site also houses the Corporation's Cleansing Department depot and offices, which present a smooth green glass wall to Upper Thames Street, reflecting the oddly disjointed architecture of Sidell Gibson's Dowgate Hill House opposite, also built in 1996.

Beyond the brick-vaulted undercroft of Cannon Street rail bridge, decorated with a snaking trail of blue floor lights, the riverside path emerges into Allhallows Lane and Hanseatic Walk, where it opens out into a generous and attractive public space surrounded by a stunning collection of recently completed buildings. Easily missed on a raised platform against the railway, a small plaque, unveiled in 2005 by the Duke of Kent, commemorates the German merchant community that thrived in this area from the thirteenth to the nineteenth centuries. Their premises, known as the Steelyard (derived from *Stalhof* or *Stilliarde*), were obliterated by the building of Cannon Street station. Maritime references are clearly on display in the new Watermark Place development **324**, which incorporates massive nautical timbers and metal hawsers on the riverside canopy. Known also as 1 Angel Lane – which helps to locate the main entrance of the occupier, the investment bank Nomura – the scheme by Fletcher Priest Architects comprises two blocks connected by a glazed atrium, and two more fluid riverside pavilions, which interweave with the open space. Completed in 2009, the building has rightly been highly praised, winning the Worshipful Company of Chartered Architects' New City Architecture award in 2010, as the best contribution to the City's streetscape and skyline. It is quite a contrast with its sinister 1970s predecessor, Mondial House, likened

Watermark Place, 1 Angel
Lane **324**, comprises
riverside pavilions with
larger offices behind. Metal
screens prevent direct
sunlight on the glass and
help to control temperature
and glare in the offices.

once by Prince Charles to a giant word processor. Nomura's foyer aims to impress; it is an enormous area to wander through, with elephant sculpture and Japanese art.

Less open to the public is Riverbank House **325** of 2010, between Angel Lane and Swan Lane. Although its height has been kept within planning constraints (just), the scale is prominent on the river compared to the pavilions of Watermark Place. David Walker Architects and executive architect EPR Architects have produced the optimum efficient space (45,000 square metres) for their client, the developer Pace Investments, in what seems a square but is in fact a trapezoidal block. The projecting balconies (terraces for smokers) at opposite corners help to rotate the geometry, and the splash of yellow to their undersides lifts the spirits. Triple glazing allows the use of clear glass and maximizes daylight to the deep floors. However, the main entrance on Upper Thames Street is disappointingly mean for an otherwise large and impressive building.

Directly opposite, 12 Arthur Street **326** is pleasing in a more conventional manner. On an awkward island site, bounded by Laurence Pountney and Martin lanes, HKR Architects' multi-let offices provide natural light to all 10,000 square metres of floor space, and a subtle curve in stone and bronze-framed windows to Arthur Street. Next to Riverbank House, the Sellar Property Group plans to redevelop Seal House, 1 Swan Lane **327**, with eleven-storey glass-clad offices when the current leases expire in 2014. David Chipperfield Architects' scheme employs a repetitive grid but is carefully shaped to encourage visual and physical links between Upper Thames Street and the riverside, and to provide a contemporary backdrop to Fishmongers' Hall.

It has long been an ambition of the City Corporation to improve the vertical connection between the riverside path and the east side of London Bridge. Bere:Architects was appointed in 2003 to design the London Bridge

↖ The riverside walk passes Watermark Place **324** and Riverbank House **325**, with its splashes of yellow.

← No. 12 Arthur Street **326** occupies an irregularly shaped site on the north side of Upper Thames Street.

Riverbank House, 2 Swan Lane **325**, forms a dramatic prow to the riverside walk.

Visualization of the proposed London Bridge Staircase **328**, with the car park of Adelaide House in the foreground and the redevelopment site of Seal House, 1 Swan Lane **327**, beyond London Bridge.

Staircase **328**, but owing to legal wrangles with neighbours, work on site started only in 2012. The Corporation's parking-meter revenue surplus and Bridge House Estates jointly funded the £225,000 cost, which is modest considering the improvement on offer. The design is daring, with the platform landings overhanging the river, protected by intricate, curved bowstring-truss metal screens. It will greatly help access to the attractive landscaping works, also designed by Bere:Architects, carried out below, outside Magnus House. A paving slab carved by apprentices from the Masons' Company records the Architectural Student Award of 2009 given to Priscilla Fernandes's *Flowerbench*, a curving stone bench engraved with plants. Many people come here to gawp at the Shard across the river, and Magnus House even has an elevated public viewing platform that connects behind to a fragment of the ped-way crossing Lower Thames Street. The occupiers of Adelaide House are presumably reluctant to give up part of their unsightly car park and bike shelters for a larger riverside garden.

Old Billingsgate **329**, closed in 1982 when the fish market moved to West India Dock, was converted in 1989 by Richard Rogers Partnership into a giant dealing floor with offices in the wings, despite unfounded fears that the whole structure might collapse when the frozen cellars thawed out. More recently it has become a venue for corporate hospitality and special events, available for hire, for which the riverside terrace is a fine ancillary asset. It is a happier solution than the Cubist office box in turquoise mirror glass, stepping up to fourteen storeys, that was built on the site of the former market car park at 10 Lower Thames Street by Covell Matthews Wheatley.

After the strange corridor of blue railings beside the Custom House, the riverside path stops temporarily at Water Lane, blocked by two large redevelopment schemes and diverted inland to Lower Thames Street. The site

The riverside from London Bridge (left to right): Magnus House, 10 Lower Thames Street and Old Billingsgate **329**.

lay unused for two decades, but construction is well under way at Three Quays **330**, where 3D Reid has designed a glassy nine-storey residential scheme to include ninety-seven serviced and sixty-four private flats (described as an 'aparthotel'), with interiors by Forme Design. The improved public space by the river will incorporate a sculpture by William Pye. Sugar Quay, 1 Water Lane **331**, received planning permission in 2010 for an office development with two abutting components, the smaller facing the river and relating to the scale of Custom House, the larger facing Lower Thames Street to match the larger buildings to the north. David Walker Architects claims to have been 'inspired by the clarity and solidarity of London's historic waterside'. Tate & Lyle still holds a lease on the site, which is owned by the Fishmongers' Company, but in April 2012 the appropriately named Candy brothers acquired an interest. Buoyed by the profits of housing the super-rich at 1 Hyde Park, their CPC Group has its eye on lucrative riverside flats at Sugar Quay, unlikely to be popular with the City planners. The Thames path diversion could last some time.

The Corporation would far prefer something to complement Foster + Partners' commercial Tower Place development **332** of 2002. This removed the unloved 1960s slabs of Vincula House, which had spoilt views of the Tower of London from the gallery of the Monument. Foster's replacement comprises two triangular office blocks with rounded corners, linked on the north side by a lofty canopy of glass supported on slim, tapering columns. At high level, glass walls keep out the worst of the weather, but an entirely open ground floor allows good natural ventilation. The generosity of scale is impressive, the glass held seemingly precariously (a clever trick), the trees watered automatically, and all immaculately maintained. It has greatly enhanced the setting of the church of All Hallows-by-the-Tower, the approach to the Tower of London and, on Great Tower Street, the memorial of 2005 to the Siege of Malta. With visitors in mind, the

New kiosks and paving have transformed the public realm at Tower Hill **333**. The offices of Tower Place **332** rise in the background.

Tower Place **332** provides sheltered public realm next to the church of All Hallows-by-the-Tower (left), and links directly to Tower Hill (below).

lower ground floor facing Petty Wales (no reference to Prince Charles) sensibly provides public toilets as well as the predictable fast-food outlets and souvenir shops, feeding and feeding off the tourists.

The Tower of London lies outside the City. For many years the setting of this World Heritage Site was nothing to be proud of, but a refurbishment in 2004 aimed to rectify matters. Stanton Williams was selected to produce a masterplan and detailed design. The result at Tower Hill **333** is a spacious new paved landscape large enough to handle the hordes of visitors, and three elegant, unfussy grey metal kiosks for ticket sales, bookshops and information. Historic Royal Palaces, the Pool of London Partnership and the Heritage Lottery Fund dipped into their pockets to pay for the works, but the main benefactor was the philanthropist Paul Getty, who was keen to make Tower Hill a place for public enjoyment rather than tribulation.

Having commenced this survey in chapter 1 at the topographical summit of the City in Panyer Alley, it is perhaps appropriate to finish on a more moralist high, albeit just outside the City. Further along Tower Hill, the statue of the *Building Worker* **334** was unveiled in October 2006 by Ken Livingstone and Alan Ritchie, general secretary of the Union of Construction, Allied Trades and Technicians, in recognition of 'the thousands of building workers who have lost their lives at work'. Not many architects, after all, actually die at their CAD screen (or town-planners and conservation officers, for that matter). Alan Wilson's powerful, larger-than-life figure looks purposefully across a section of the old Roman wall to the skyline of the City.

Having come this far it is worth continuing to Tower Bridge (outside the City but owned and maintained by the Corporation) with its ticket office, ingeniously designed by Bere:Architects in 2011 to maximize energy efficiency in both winter and summer. Below the parapet of Tower Bridge Road, sitting neatly beside the moat of the Tower and the abutment of the bridge, Tony Fretton Architects' Perkin Reveller restaurant **335** was completed in 2012, its flat roofs carpeted in gravel and the concrete walls sensitively coloured to match the adjacent stone. From the bridge there are fine views up and down the river, especially from the high-level walkway, from where the whole of the eastern City seems tightly clustered behind the Tower of London. To the west, the top of the dome of St Paul's rises above the new buildings on Cannon Street. As the river curves left towards Westminster, beyond the arches of Blackfriars Bridge, the trees of Temple Gardens indicate the western edge of the City. The whole river frontage of the Square Mile is encompassed in one sweeping panorama. It is a remarkable concentration of endeavour, energy, power, acumen and renewal.

Alan Wilson's *Building Worker* **334**, standing with his back to the Tower of London and facing the City, celebrates the contribution and sacrifice of a vast army employed in the construction industry.

FURTHER READING

Augar, P., *Chasing Alpha: How Reckless Growth and Unchecked Ambition Ruined the City's Golden Decade,* Bodley Head 2009

Barson, S., and Saint, A., *A Farewell to Fleet Street,* Historic Buildings and Monuments Commission for England/Allison & Busby 1988

Bradley, S., and Pevsner, N., *The Buildings of England: London 1: The City of London,* Penguin Books 1997

Bronk, R., *The Romantic Economist: Imagination in Economics,* Cambridge University Press 2009

Duffy, F., *Work and the City,* Black Dog 2008

——and Henney, A., *The Changing City,* Bulstrode Press 1989

Forshaw, A., *20th-Century Buildings in Islington,* Islington Society 2001

——and Bergström, T., *Smithfield Past and Present,* Robert Hale 1990

Kenyon, N. (ed.), *The City of London: Architectural Tradition and Innovation in the Square Mile*, Thames and Hudson 2011

Kynaston, D., *City of London: The History*, Chatto & Windus 2010

Powell, K., *21st-Century London: The New Architecture,* Merrell 2011

INDEX

Page numbers in *italic* refer to the illustrations

Abacus House 67
Adelaide House 111, *113*, 216, *216*
Aguiari, Eleonora 178
AIG Building 103, *104*, 106
Alban Gate 14, 56, 149–50, *151*
Alder Castle House *7*, 52
10 Aldermanbury 59
1 Aldermanbury Square 59
5 Aldermanbury Square 56–59, *58*, *61*, *62*, 150, *151*
200 Aldersgate 142–44, *143*
137 Aldersgate Street 144
140 Aldersgate Street 144, *145*
150 Aldersgate Street 144
Aldgate 14, 188–94
1 Aldgate *102*, 193
Aldgate House 191, *191*
Aldgate Tower 193–94
Allan, Walter Godfrey 30
Allason, Thomas 86
Allford Hall Monaghan Morris 148
Allianz House 110–11, *110*
Allies and Morrison 17, 32, 71, 74, 96, 106, 158
Alsop Sparch 207
Altitude Tower 196
1 America Square 14, 197–98, *197*, *201*
Amos Broome Associates 59
1 Angel Court 86–88
Angel Waterside 16
Apex City of London Hotel 198
Apex London Wall Hotel 161
1 Appold Street 167, *169*
Architech 123
AROS Architects 121
12 Arthur Street 214, *214*
15–25 Artillery Lane 181
Arup 13, 16, 24, 30, 38, 44, 52, 77, 106–108, 155, 164, 167, 173, 197, 207
Assael Architecture Studio 183
Atelier Foster Nouvel 74
Athene Place 119

Atlantic House 136, *137*
Aukett (Michael) Architects 46, 65, 70
Austral House 62
Avanti Architects 153, 170
Avery Associates Architects 140
Aviva Tower *75*, 92–93, *93*, *94*, 96

Baker, Herbert 6
Baltic Exchange 14, 86, 92, 93
Bank of America Merrill Lynch 141, *141*
2 Bank Buildings 64
Bank of China 64, 80, *81*
Bank Conservation Area 70, 82
Bank of England 8, 44, 70
Bank of New York Mellon Centre 36, *37*
Bank station 80
Banks (Elizabeth) Associates 42
Barbican 6, 12, 13, 16, 148
Barbican Arts Centre 148–49, *149*
Barclays Bank 14, 93, 111
Barclays Bank, 2 George Yard *25*, 82, *83*
Barratt Homes 196
Bartholomew Square 142
1 Basinghall Avenue 61–62, *61*, *62*
Bavaria House *167*, 172
BDP 110, 121, 127–29
Bear, Michael 24
Beaufort House 14, 191, *191*, 197
Beckett, Paul 10
Beetham 193
Bennett, Peter 10
Bennett, T.P. 16, 61, 62, 127, 140, 183
Bennetts, Rab 16, 164, 186
Bennetts Associates 16, 61, 106, 118, 121, 155, 181–83, 184–86, 200, 210
Bere:Architects 18, 112, 118, 214–16, 219
Berkeley 150, 170, 196
6 Bevis Marks 96

BFLS 118, 197
Bickley, Jon 120
20 Birchin Lane 82
Bishops Square 17, 177, *178*
20 Bishops Square *179*, 181
Bishopsgate 7, 86
6–8 Bishopsgate 90
99 Bishopsgate 96–99, *98*
100 Bishopsgate *87*, 96, *97*, 99
199 Bishopsgate 169
250 Bishopsgate *176*, 177, *177*, *179*
280 and 288 Bishopsgate 177, *177*, *179*
Bishopsgate Exchange *168*, 169, *169*, *177*, 186
Bishopsgate Tower (The Pinnacle) 16, 89–90, 108
Black, Michael 198, *198*
Blackfriars Bridge Foreshore 206
Blackfriars Investments Limited 206
Blackfriars Millennium Pier 206
Blackfriars Ramp 205, *205*
Blackfriars station *19*, 22, 134, 205–206, *205*, *206*
Blackstone 187, 200, 211
Blears, Hazel 132
Bloomberg 18, 26, 74, 156
Boleat, Mark 22
Boonham, Nigel 44
Botero, Fernando *167*, *168*
4 Bouverie Street 126, *126*
Bow Bells House 16, 45
Boyes, Alma 80
Boyt, Judy 183
Bracken House 13, 21, 41–42, *42*, *43*, 44
Bradley, Simon 38, 71, 78, 129
Bradman, Geoffrey 8, 164
Braham Street *194*
Brill, Maurice 166
Britannic House 158
Britannic Tower 14
British Land 13–14, 24, 62, 90, 106, 155, 166, 169
British Rail 139, 164, 173
Broadgate 7, 8, 13, 16, 24, 139, 164–73, 176

5 Broadgate 14, 166–67, 173
Broadgate Arena *164–65*, 166, 167
Broadgate Properties 140
Broadgate Tower *165*, 170, *170*, *171*, *179*, *180*
Broadgate West 172
Broadwalk House 169–70, *171*
Broadway Malyan 196
Broken Wharf House 208, *209*
Brookfield 89, 96, 170
Brown, Gordon 8
Brunel, Henry Marc 205
Buchanan Architects 36–38, 193, 196, 198
Building Environment 193
1 Bunhill Row 155, *155*
Burnet Tait & Partners 198
Burnett, John 111
Burns + Nice 59, 121, 124, 183
20 Bury Street 95
Butler, James 70, 120

Calatrava, Santiago 14, 156
Callister, Victor 22
Canary Wharf 10–12, 14, 26, 82, 88, 93, 99, 197
Canary Wharf Group 110
Cannon Place 77–78, *78*, *81*, *212*
20 Cannon Street *20*, 21, 42
25 Cannon Street *13*, *20*, *25*, 42–44, *43*
33 Cannon Street 44, *45*
50 Cannon Street 80, *81*
80 Cannon Street 77
90–96 Cannon Street 80, *81*
108 Cannon Street 80, *82*
110 Cannon Street 80
Cannon Street station 22, *78*, *78*, 164, *204*, 212, *212*
Caro, Anthony 207
Carter, Rob and Nick 144
69 Carter Lane 36
12 Carthusian Street 134–35
Cashmore (F. Milton) & Partners 156
Cass Business School 155, *155*
Cassidy, Michael 9, 16, 24
Casson Conder Partnership 161
Central St Giles 18
Centurion House 112
Chamberlin, Powell & Bon 148, 153
22 Chancery Lane 121
40–45 Chancery Lane 121
48 Chancery Lane 121, *122*
122 Chancery Lane 121, *121*
Chapman Taylor 38, 198

Charles, Prince of Wales 16, 21, 30, 44, 72, 214, 219
17–19 Charterhouse Street 136, *137*
47–53 Charterhouse Street 134, *134*
Cheapside 12–13, 22, 45, 46, 82
80 Cheapside 72, 80, *81*
100 Cheapside 65
107 Cheapside 64–65, *65*
150 Cheapside 46, *48*, 52
Cheesegrater *see* Leadenhall Building
Chipperfield (David) Architects 214
10 Chiswell Street 158
Citigen 134
City of London Corporation 9–10, 12–14, 18, 22–24, 27, 176–77
City of London Information Centre 38, *38*
City Place House 61, *61*
City Tower 61
CityPoint 14, *15*, 18, 155–56, *157*
Clark, Brian 35, *35*, 198
Cobalt Building 153–54
1 Coleman Street 16, 62, *62*, *63*
4 Coleman Street 62, *62*
Collcutt, T.E. 102
Collins (David) Studio 200
1 Commercial Street 196
Commercial Union 14, 92
Commerzbank 64
Cooper, Edwin 6, 200
Corbero, Xavier 167, *167*
Corn Exchange 106
14 Cornhill 70, *70*
62–64 Cornhill 71
Cory Environmental 212
Covell Matthews Wheatley 119–20, 123, 155, 172, 216
Cox, Stephen *138*, 140, 156, 173
CPC Group 217
CPMG 136
Craft, Paula 178
Craig-Martin, Michael *95*
Crossrail 12, 18, 26, 134, 153, 161
1 Crown Place 172–73
10 Crown Place 172, *173*
30 Crown Place 167, 172, *172*
Cunard Place 95
20 Cursitor Street 123, *123*
Cutlers' Exchange 184, *184*
Cutlers' Gardens 187

Daily Express building 124
Daily Mirror Building 116

Daily Telegraph building 123–24
Dalton (Keith) & Associates 193
Damond Lock Grabowski Partners 112
Darbishire, Nick 173
Dashwood House 93
Davies, Howard 8
Davies (D.Y.) Associates 59
Denton Corker Marshall 42
Derwent London 121
Deutsche Bank 17, 24, 88–89
Devonshire Square 183, *185–87*, 186–87
Dillon, Patrick 148
DLG Architects 70
Docklands 10–12
Docklands Light Railway 197
Donne, John 44
Dorset Rise 126, *126*
Double Tree Hotel 14, 198–200, *200*, *201*
Dowgate Hill House 212
Drapers Gardens 14, 88, *88*, 89
Dresdner Bank House 67
Duffy, Frank 26

Eagle Star building 96
East India House 183
6–8 Eastcheap 112
10 Eastcheap 112, *113*
51 Eastcheap 108
Eden House *180*, 181
Elsworth Sykes Partnership 96, 112
English Heritage 13, 93, 96, 129, 132, 166
EPR Architects 78, 80, 88, 102, 119, 126, 177, 194, 214
Ergon Design Group 154
Evans, Alan 59
Everett, Philip 10
Exchange House 13, 167–69, *168*, *169*
Exchange Square 167, *168*
10 Exchange Square 167, *167*, *169*
Exchequer Court 95, *97*
Exemplar 181

The Facility 205
Faraday House 30, 49
Farmers' and Fletchers' Hall 135–36
Farr, Martin 24
Farrell, Terry 14, 16, 30, 56, 78, 102, 112, 123, 149–50, *151*
Farringdon Road 136
Farringdon station 134

20 Farringdon Street 140
Fen Court 103–105, *105*
Fenchurch Street 102
10 Fenchurch Street 110
20 Fenchurch Street 9, 10, 11, 14, 17, *25*, *87*, 108–10, *108*, *109*, *212*
76–86 Fenchurch Street 102
120 Fenchurch Street 105, *105*
168 Fenchurch Street 110, *110*
Fenchurch Street station 105, 197
Fernandes, Priscilla 216
Festival Gardens 44, *46*
Fetter Lane 116
10–15 Fetter Lane 120, *121*
43 Fetter Lane 118
90 Fetter Lane *122*, 123
Finch, Paul 16
Finlaison House 123
Finsbury Avenue 13, 164
12 and 3 Finsbury Avenue 166, *166*
Finsbury Avenue Square 166, *166*
1 Finsbury Circus 158
131 Finsbury Pavement 156
Finsbury Square 14, 18, 22, 156–58
1–2 Finsbury Square 158
3–10 Finsbury Square 158
30 Finsbury Square 156–58, *158*
50 Finsbury Square 74, 156, *158*
Firefighters' War Memorial 38
Fisher (Carl) & Partners 184
Fitzroy Robinson 14, 16, 70, 71, 72, 74, 86–88, 95, 99, 105, 106, 142, 154, 161, 193–94, 197, 211
Fitzwilliam House 94, 95, *95*
Flanagan, Barry *164*, 166
Fleet Place 24, *138*, 139–40, *139*
Fleet Street 8, 14, 32, 116, 123, 124–26
65 Fleet Street *125*, 126
120 Fleet Street 124, *124*
131–141 Fleet Street 123–24, *124*
Fletcher Priest Architects 16, 17, 64, 65, 86–88, 93, 96, 140, 161, 187, 212
Foggo, Peter 164, 166–67, 173, 186
Foggo Associates 16, 72, 77, 88, 96, 156, 177
72 Fore Street 150
Foreign Office Architects 193
Forme Design 217

Foster + Partners 10, 14, 16, 17, 18, 52–55, 56, 67, 74, 77, 92, 93, 102, 116–18, 150–53, 156, 170, 177, 186, 193, 207–208, 217–19
Founders' Hall 135, *135*
Freshfields Bruckhaus Deringer 124, 127
Fretton (Tony) Architects 219
Friary Court 198, *198*
Frink, Elisabeth 46
Funke (Charles) Associates 41, 77, 187, 191
20 Furnival Street 123
34–35 Furnival Street 123
40 Furnival Street 123, *123*

Gaubas, Martynas 178
Gee (Tony) and Partners 205
Gensler 24, 52
Getty, Paul 219
The Gherkin *see* 30 St Mary Axe
Gibberd 64, 111
Gibberd (Frederick) Coombes & Partners 71
Gibbons, Johanna 148
Gibson Dennis Associates 141
Gifford, Roger 22
Gill (John) Associates 144
1 Giltspur Street 136
GMA Architecture 142
GMW Architects 14, 16, 35, 59, 61, 80, 82, 88, 90, 92, 96–99, 102, 106, 111, 136, 158, 197
Goddard & Gibbs 111
Goddard Manton Architects 123
Golden Lane 12, 13, 16
1 Golden Lane 154, *154*
Golden Lane Campus 154, *154*
Golden Lane Estate 153
Goldman Sachs 10, 14, 35, 124
Goodman's Fields 196
Gormley, Antony 24, 124, *124*
Gracechurch House 111, *111*
40 Gracechurch Street 111, *111*
Grange City Hotel 198, *199*
Grange St Paul's Hotel 36–38, *37*
Grange Tower Bridge Hotel 196
Grant, Ali 178, *178*
Great Portland Estates 96
1 Great St Helen's 95, *96*
Greathead, James 70, *70*
Green Lloyd Architects 121–23

Gresham Street 52
2 Gresham Street 52, *52*
10 Gresham Street 67, *67*, 186
20 Gresham Street 65, *66*
25 Gresham Street 55, *55*, 56,
    193
30 Gresham Street 64, *65*
31 Gresham Street 55, 59
51–57 Gresham Street 59
52 Gresham Street 64, *64*
54–60 Gresham Street 64, *64*
95 Gresham Street 64
97–99 Gresham Street 64
Greycoat 105, 111, 164, 172,
    187
Grimshaw 16, 55, 56, 86,
    191–93
Guildhall 52, 59–61, *60*
Guildhall Art Gallery 59–61, *60*
Guildhall School of Music and
    Drama 154–55
1 Gunpowder Square 120, *120*
Gustafson Porter 140
6 Gutter Lane 67, *67*

Haberdashers' Hall *134*, 135
Hackney 169–73
Hadid, Zaha 22, 193
Halpern Partnership 110–11
Halsbury House 121, *122*
Hamilton Associates 45–46,
    77, 95, 102
Hammerson 70, 150, 170, 177
Hampson, Annie 9–10, 21
Hare (Nicholas) Architects 154
Harper Mackay Architects 127
Harrap (Julian) Architects 181
Harrison & West Architects
    183
Hawksmoor, Nicholas 176, 177
Heal, Victor 44, 45, 64
Heatherwick, Thomas 24, 32,
    33
Heery Architects & Engineers
    181
Helical Bar 120, 142, 155, 193
Helicon Building 16, 158, *159*,
    194
Henderson Global Investors
    132
The Heron 154–55
Heron International 99
Heron Plaza 99
Heron Property Corporation
    139, 154
Heron Tower 14, 16, *25*, *63*, *87*,
    96, *97*, 99, 108, 110, *177*, *179*
Higgs and Hill 187
HKR Architects 150, 214
HLM 132
HOK 45, 142
33 Holborn Circus 116–18, *117*
40 Holborn Viaduct 136, *137*

Holford, William 30
Hooke, Robert 32, 111
Hope Square 173, *173*
Hopkins, Michael 16, 41–42,
    135, 198
Horden Cherry Lee Architects
    158, 172
Hosier Lane 136
117 Houndsditch 184
133 Houndsditch 184, *184*
Howell, Killick, Partridge &
    Amis 142
Hubbard Ford & Partners 210
Hunt, Jeremy 13–14, 166
Hunter, Kenny *171*, 178
Hunter & Partners 153

Ibex House, Minories 198
Insignia House 16, 194, *195*
Inskip (Peter) + Peter Jenkins
    Architects 158
International Press Centre 119
Invista Real Estate 121
Islington 153

Jacobs Architecture 205–206
Jaguar Building Services 170
Jardine House 198
Jestico + Whiles 181
Jiricna, Eva 198
Johnson, Boris 14, 96, 183
Johnson, Edward C. III 44
Johnson, Samuel 120
Johnston Architecture &
    Design 181–83
Jones, Horace 132

Kansallis House 99
Kenzie Lovell Partnership 158
Kindersley, Richard 49
24 King William Street 111,
    113
47–51 King William Street 111,
    112
Klapez, Ivan 149, *150*
Koolhaas, Rem 16–17, 74–77
KOP Group 200
KPF 16, 65, 89, 92, 96, 103,
    124, 129, 132, 136, 172
Krier, Léon 177

Land Securities 10, 45, 110,
    118–19, 140, 144, 153
Landmark House 102, *102*
Lansley, Alastair 173
Lasdun, Denys 110, 155
Le Brun, Christopher 149, *150*
Leadenhall Building 9, 11, 14,
    87, 90
77 Leadenhall Street 102, *102*
78 Leadenhall Street 102
80–84 Leadenhall Street 102
Leman Street Hotel 196

Ley, Colbeck & Partners 102
Lifschutz Davidson
    Sandilands 158, 196
8–13 Lime Street 105
52–54 Lime Street 92
Lipchitz, Jacques 166, *167*
Lipton, Stuart 8, 15, 164–66,
    187
Lister Drew & Associates 67
75 Little Britain 14, 142, *142*
100 Liverpool Street 164–66,
    165
Liverpool Street station 164,
    167, *168*, 173, *173*
Livings Leslie Webber 136
Livingstone, Ken 12, 14, 22, 96,
    206, 219
Llewelyn-Davies Weeks 86
Lloyd, Jeremy Sampson 78,
    135–36
Lloyd (Matthew) Architects 181
Lloyd's, 1 Lime Street 8, 13, 16,
    17, 90–92, *91*, *92*, *99*, 103,
    166
Lloyd's Chambers 197
Lloyd's Register 102–103, *103*,
    201
21 Lombard Street 82
54 Lombard Street 14
London Bridge 112, 214–16
London Bridge Staircase
    214–16, *216*
London Chamber of
    Commerce 78
London Fruit and Wool
    Exchange 181–83, *182*
London House 144, *144*
London Liverpool Street Hotel
    183–84
London Wall 6, 7, *7*, 24, 52, *63*,
    144, 148, 149, 153, 161, 204
60 London Wall 161, *161*
85 London Wall 161
London Wall Place 150
1 Love Lane 59, *59*
Lower Thames Street 6, 204
10 Lower Thames Street 216
100 Ludgate Hill 139
1–3 Ludgate Square 36
Ludlow, Martin 149
Lutyens, Edwin 6, 158

McAslan (John) + Partners 16,
    46, 103, 132
MacCormac Jamieson
    Prichard 172
    see also MJP Architects
Mackay and Partners 193
McLean, Bruce 169
Magnus House 216, *216*
Magpie Alley mural *125*, 126
Make 14, 17, 21, 38, 150,
    166–67

Mallock, Vivien 211
Mansell Court 194
55 Mansell Street 194, *194*
Manser Practice Architects +
    Designers 150
Mansion House 70, 71, 74
8–10 Mansion House Place 77
50 Mark Lane 106
64–74 Mark Lane 106
Mayhew, Judith 9, 21, 207
Meisler, Frank 173
Mendelssohn, Felix 148
Mermaid Theatre 206–207
Merrill Lynch 17, 18, 155
Metrovacesa 74
102 Middlesex Street 183
110–114 Middlesex Street
    183, *183*
Mies van der Rohe, Ludwig 71,
    92, 103
Millennium Bridge 9, 30, 38,
    207–208, *207*, *208*
Millennium Tower (proposed)
    93
Miller (David) Architects 196
Mills, John W. 38
Milton Gate 155, *156*
Milton House/Shire House 154
Minerva 77, 191–93
Ministry of Justice 120
2–5 Minories 193, *193*, 198
52 Minories 196–97, *196*
150 Minories 193
Minster Court 14, 106, *107*,
    112, 197
Mint (Double Tree) Hotel 14,
    198–200, *200*, *201*
Mitchell, Denys 187, *187*
Mitre House 144, *144*
Mitre Square 193
Mitsubishi Estate 32, 45
Mitsui 106
MJP Architects 32, 172, 177
Mondial House 212–14
Monkwell Square *151*
Monument 12, 32, 112, 217
11–19 Monument Street 112
24 Monument Street 112
Monument Yard 112, *112*
Moor House *63*, 150–53, *152*
21 Moorfields *152*
8–10 Moorgate 21, 71
12–18 Moorgate 71
101 Moorgate *152*, 163
120 Moorgate 158
MoreySmith 80, 142
Morgan, J.P. 14, 59, 127
Murray, Peter 24, 26
Museum of London 14, 55,
    149, *150*

100 New Bridge Street 35, *35*
New Carmelite House 129

New Court 17, *23*, 74–77, *74*, *75*
1 New Fetter Lane 118, *119*
New Fetter Place *117*, 118
New London House 105–106
1 and 2 New Ludgate 140
New Minories Hotel 193, *193*
New Street Square *15*, 16, *117*,
    118–19, *119*, 120, *121*, 200
Newgate 17, 18
100 Newgate Street 141, *141*
Nexus Place *139*, 140
Nicholson, Piers 208
Nido Spitalfields *182*, 183, *183*
Norfolk House 208, *209*
Northcliffe House 127, *127*
3–5 Norwich Street 123
Nouvel, Jean 16, 44–45, 74
Novotel, 10 Pepys Street 106,
    198, *199*
Number One Poultry 13, 16,
    71–72, *72*, 166

Obayashi 41
7–10 Old Bailey 140–41, *140*
20 Old Bailey *140*, 141, 191
Old Billingsgate 216, *216*
33 Old Broad Street 88
111 Old Broad Street 88
125 Old Broad Street 21, *71*,
    86, *88*
Old Change Court 41, *41*
Old Change House 41
1 Old Jewry 72, *73*
OMA 74
One Canada Square 10, 14, 88
One London Wall *7*, 52–55, *53*,
    56
One New Change 14, 16, *21*,
    22, *25*, *43*, 44–45, *47*, 74
Opie, Julian 24, 95
ORMS 61, 82, 208
Ovadia, Arie 173
Oxford Properties Group 90

Pageantmaster Court *34*
Palace on Pillars 190–91, *190*
Palumbo, Peter 71
Park House 158, *160*
Parry (Eric) Architects 16, 32,
    56–59, 64, 70–71, 105,
    156–58
Partington (Robin) Architects
    119
Paternoster Square 6, 14, 16,
    30–32, *31*, 46, 172
Patterson, Simon 108
Paxton, Joseph 90
Peach (Stanley) & Partners 64
Pegg, John 178
Pelli, Cesar 10, 88
Pellipar House 78, *79*, 136
Perkin Reveller restaurant 219
Perry, Richard 191

Pevsner, Nikolaus 38, 124
Piano, Renzo 18
10 Pilgrim Street 35
Pillar Property 61
The Pinnacle *see* Bishopsgate
 Tower
Pinnacle House 112, *113*
Pinners Hall 88
PKS Architects 36
Plantation Lane 108, *109*
Plantation Place 14, 18,
 106–108, *108, 109*, 155
Playhouse Yard 36
1 Plough Place 118, *118*
PLP Architecture 17, 99, 134
Polisano, Lee 17, 96, 99
Povall Flood & Wilson 184
Powell, Kenneth 32, 184, 186
Powell & Moya 149
Premier Place 184–86, *185*
Preston (Roger) & Partners 16
Principal Place 170
Pringle Brandon Perkins + Will
 72, 170
Procession House *34*, 35
Public Records Office 121
Puddle Dock 206–207
Puddle Dock Hotel *206*, 207
Pye, William 217

Quadrant Estates 65
Queen Hithe Hotel 210, *210*
33 Queen Street 78
36 Queen Street 78, 102
62–64 Queen Street 78–80
10 Queen Street Place 211,
 211, 212
60 Queen Victoria Street 72,
 73, 80, 88
71 Queen Victoria Street 41
95 Queen Victoria Street 38, *40*
98 Queen Victoria Street 38
101 Queen Victoria Street 38,
 39
160 Queen Victoria Street 36,
 36
Queensbridge House 210

Ray House 120
Redrow 196
Rees, Peter 9–10, 13, 15, 16,
 18, 21–22, 26
Regis House 111, *113*
Reignwood 200
Resolution Properties 210
RHWL Architects 14, 16, 35,
 44, 92, 126, 139, 140, 141,
 155, 184, 191, 197–98
Richardson, Albert 41, 42
River Plate House 158
Riverbank House 16, 17, 18,
 204, 214, *214, 215*
Riverside Walk 22

Robertson (John) Architects
 16, 24, 64–65, 80, 95, 110,
 111, 112, 123, 124, 153, 158,
 169, 198, 211
Rockpoint Group 187
Rogers (Richard) Partnership
 16, 18, 55–56, 90–92,
 102–103, 166, 216
Rogers Stirk Harbour +
 Partners 90
Rolfe Judd 41, 59, 64, 71,
 78–80, 105, 124, 127, 136,
 144, 150, 198
Rolls Building 120–21, *120*
Ronson, Gerald 96
Ropemaker Place 7, *15*, 155,
 155, 156
Rosehaugh Stanhope
 Developments 8, 139, 164
Rothschild bank *23*, 74–77
Route XI 142, 161
Royal Bank of Scotland 177,
 186, 193
Royal Exchange 70
Royal Institute of British
 Architects (RIBA) 59, 77,
 166, 181
Royex House 56

Sainsbury's 116–18, *117*
St Andrew's House 119–20
St Bartholomew's Hospital
 141–42, *141*
St Botolph's House *11*, 18,
 191–93, *192*
10 St Bride Street 124
St Dunstan's House 121
St Helen's Square 24
St Martin's 52
30 St Mary Axe (the Gherkin)
 9, *11*, 13, 16, 18, *75*, 93–96,
 94–95, 99, 108, *179*, *209*
60–70 St Mary Axe 96
St Michael's House 82
St Pancras Church garden 80,
 81
St Paul's Cathedral 12, *13*, 22,
 30–32, *39*, 46–49, *46*, 52, 88,
 89, 116, 118–19, 129, 207,
 219
St Paul's Cathedral Alignment
 Pavement 49
St Paul's Heights 14–15, 17,
 30, 86
St Swithin's Church garden 77,
 77
8 Salisbury Square 126, *126*
Salvation Army 38, *39*
Sandle, Michael 127
Sauerbruch Hutton 140
Saxon Land 105
'the Scalpel' *15*, 92
Scott, Richard Gilbert 59–60

Scott Brownrigg + Turner 181,
 198
Seal House 214, *216*
Segal, George 166, *166*
Seifert, John 82, 198
Seifert, Richard 14, 16, 67, 80,
 82, 88, 108, 119, 140, 144,
 183, 187, 198, 208
Sellar Property Group 214
Senator House 38, *40*, 41, 210
Serra, Richard *164*, 166
The Shard 11, 14, 26, *87*, 89,
 93, *99*, 112, *113*, *201*, 216
Shaw, Norman 120
Shawcross, Conrad 129, *129*
Shelley House 55
Sheppard Robson 16, 32, 38,
 55, 59, 72, 111, 142, 155,
 156, 158, 193
Shickle, Alec J. 80
Shoe Lane 116, 119, 124, *124*,
 136
Shuttleworth, Ken 17, 18, 21,
 150, 166–67
Sidell Gibson 17, 32, 45, 52, 62,
 64, 140, 144, 208, 212
'Silicon Roundabout' 26, 153
Simpson (John) & Partners
 30–32, 110
Simpson Gray Associates 120
Sir John Lyon House 208, *209*
Sixty London 136
Skinners' Company 78
Smithfield Market 131,
 132–34, *133*
12 Smithfield Street *135*, 136
SOM 16, 36, 55, 59, 62, 118,
 139, 167–69, 172
10 South Place 21, 158–61
South Place Hotel 158, *160*
Southwark Bridge 10, 211
Spence, Basil 150
Spencer Heights 142
Speyhawk 80
Spitalfields 14, 24, 174–83
Spitalfields Column 191
Spitalfields Market 176, 177,
 181, *181*
SPPARC Architecture 41
Springford (Ian) Architects 161
Squire, Michael 121
Squire and Partners 36, 126,
 155
Stancliffe, Martin 46–49
Standford Properties 208
Standon House 194
Stanhope 38, 45, 55, 106
Stanton Williams 219
Stevens, Jocelyn 93
Stirk, Graham 90
Stirling, James 71–72
Stock Exchange 8, 14, 32,
 86, 105

Stonecutter Court 140
Studio Weave 80, 190–91
Sturgis Associates 140, 191
Sugar Quay 217
Svenska House 111
Swanke Hayden Connell
 Architects 16, 17, 61, 88, 141
Swiss Bank House 208, *208*

TateHindle 118, 120
Temple Bar *31*, 32–35
Thames, River 204–19
Thames Court 210–11, *210*,
 211
Thames Water 206
Thameslink 18, 26, 35, 134,
 139, 205
Thatcher, Margaret 8, 10, 164
Thornfield Properties 132
1 Threadneedle Street 71
60 Threadneedle Street 70–71,
 71, 88
3D Reid 217
Three Quays 217
Thurley, Simon 13
Tower 42 14, 16, *25*, 71, *87*, 88,
 89, *89*, 96, *96*, *209*
Tower Bridge 219
Tower Gateway station 197
Tower Hamlets 176–77,
 181–83, 190
Tower Hill *217*, 219
Tower of London 12, 14, 108,
 217, 219
Tower Place 17, 217–19, *217*,
 218
Trehearne and Norman 16, 30,
 126, 129
Trehearne and Norman,
 Preston and Partners 106,
 194
Trinity EC3 193
10 Trinity Square 200
Tsereteli, Zurab 80, *82*
TTG Architects 183
TTSP 35
Tudor Rose Court 153–54, *153*
1 Tudor Street 127, *128*
21 Tudor Street 127, *128*
Twigg Brown (Michael) &
 Partners 135

Unilever House 129, *129*
Upper Thames Street 6, 24,
 204, 208–10

Victoria Embankment 205, 206
60 Victoria Embankment 14,
 127–29, *128*
Viñoly, Rafael 17, 108
Vintners' Place *210*, 211, *211*
Visocchi, Michael 105, *105*
Vitro Building 103, *103*, 106

The Walbrook *75*, *76*, 77, *77*,
 193
Walbrook Square 14, 18,
 72–74, *75*, 80
Walbrook Wharf 211–12, *212*
Walker (David) Architects 16,
 17, 45, 62, 112, 121, 154, 214,
 217
The 'Walkie-Talkie' 10, 108–10,
 109
Ward (Ronald) & Partners 111,
 134
Warwick Court 32, *33*
Watermark Place 17, *204*,
 212–14, *213*, *214*
Watling House 44, 45
Webb, Philip 172
West Smithfield 135
Wheeler, Charles 45
Whinney Mackay-Lewis
 Partnership 42, 112, 211
Whitecross Street market 154
21 Whitefriars Street 126, 129
Whitfield Partners 30–32, *31*
Wild, Martin 178
Wilford, Michael 72
Wilkes, John 120, *120*
Wilkinson Eyre Architects 110,
 149, 158
Williams, Owen 124
Willis Building 92, *92*, *99*, *201*
Wilson, Alan 219, *219*
Winchester House 17, 88–89,
 90
Winter (John) & Associates
 194
Wolfe-Barry, John 205
1 Wood Street 65, *66*
88 Wood Street 54, 55–56, *57*,
 103, *151*
100 Wood Street 54, 55, *56*
Woodford, James 92
Woods Bagot 16, 24, 71, 96,
 120, 200
Woolgate Exchange 62
Wootton, David 14–15
Wren, Christopher 6, 32, 52,
 74, 106, 111, 141, 211
Wynne, Althea 106

Yorke Rosenberg Mardall 93,
 126, 183

Zurich Building 102, *102*

The author and photographer are pleased to acknowledge the support of Fidelity Worldwide Investment in the publication of this book.

AUTHOR'S ACKNOWLEDGEMENTS
My thanks are due to Annie Hampson, Victor Callister, Peter Rees and Toni Bright of the City of London Corporation; David Walker of David Walker Architects; Graham Morrison and Romy Berlin of Allies and Morrison; Graham Stirk, Sarah Gaventa and Robert Fiehn of Rogers Stirk Harbour + Partners; Simon Davies of Threadneedle Asset Management; Katy Harris and Gayle Mault of Foster + Partners; Keith Priest and Lucy Priest, Fletcher Priest Architects; Rab Bennetts and Elizabeth Walker, Bennetts Associates; Justin Bere and Lucy Procter, Bere:Architects; Peter Murray of New London Architecture; Laureen Dillon of PLP Architecture; Laura Colapietro, Eric Parry Architects; Saxon Land BV; Greycoat CORE; Alsop Sparch; David Cole-Adams of the Worshipful Company of Chartered Architects; and Desmond Fitzpatrick of the City Heritage Association.

All references to *The Buildings of England* are to the edition of 1997; see Further Reading, page 220.

All maps are at a scale of approximately 1 cm to 33 m.

The following architectural firms are referred to by their initials throughout:
Gollins Melvin Ward (GMW) Architects
Kohn Pedersen Fox (KPF)
Renton Howard Wood Levin (RHWL)
Skidmore, Owings & Merrill (SOM)

First published in 2013 by Merrell Publishers, London and New York

Merrell Publishers Limited
81 Southwark Street
London SE1 0HX

merrellpublishers.com

Text copyright © 2013 Alec Forshaw
Photographs copyright © 2013 Alan Ainsworth, except page 112 top (© Bere:Architects/Peter Cook)
Renderings copyright © the architects and/or developers, as follows: page 105 top © Eric Parry Architects, Saxon Land and Greycoat CORE; page 109 left © Land Securities; page 140 bottom left © Fletcher Priest Architects; page 206 top © Alsop Sparch; page 210 top © Bennetts Associates; and page 216 top © Bere:Architects
Design and layout copyright © 2013 Merrell Publishers Limited

British Library Cataloguing in Publication Data:
A catalogue record for this book is available from the British Library.

ISBN 978-1-8589-4598-9

Produced by Merrell Publishers Limited
Designed by Alexandre Coco
Art Assistants: Tom Lobo Brennan and James Drayson
Project-managed by Rosanna Lewis
Indexed by Hilary Bird

Printed and bound in China

Jacket, front: Seen from Cannon Street, The Walbrook (on the right), completed by Foster + Partners in 2010, partially obscures the dome of St Paul's Cathedral.

9 781858 945989